MASSACRE
The Storming of Bolton

MASSACRE
The Storming of Bolton

DAVID CASSERLY

AMBERLEY

First published 2011

Amberley Publishing
The Hill, Stroud
Gloucestershire, GL5 4ER

www.amberleybooks.com

British Library Cataloguing in Publication Data.
A catalogue record for this book is available from the British Library.

ISBN 978-1-84868-976-3

Typeset in 10pt on 12pt Sabon.
Typesetting and Origination by Amberley Publishing.
Map illustrations by User Design.
Printed in the UK.

Contents

	A Note on Dates, Measurements and Spellings	7
Chapter 1	The Path to War	9
Chapter 2	Making of a Market Town: Bolton up to 1642	16
Chapter 3	Raising the Standard: The Coming of War, 1642	26
Chapter 4	Early Days: The First Civil War, 1642–1643	37
Chapter 5	The First Assault: 18 February 1643	55
Chapter 6	Struggle for Lancashire: Early 1643	66
Chapter 7	Stanley's Attack: 28 March 1643	70
Chapter 8	Brother Against Brother: 1643–1644	73
Chapter 9	'A better Souldier': The Siege of Lathom House	84
Chapter 10	The Gathering Storm: Rupert's March through Lancashire, May 1644	103
Chapter 11	Massacre: The Storming of Bolton, 28 May 1644	111
Chapter 12	Drive to Destruction: The First Civil War, 1644–1645	124
Chapter 13	Total War: The Second and Third Civil War, 1649–1651	135
Chapter 14	Judicial Murder: The Execution of James Stanley, 15 October 1651	154
Chapter 15	Aftermath: Consequences of Conflict	165
Appendix 1	Prisoners taken at Westhoughton Common: 15 December 1642	179
Appendix 2	Royalist Officers at Bolton: 28 March 1644	183
Appendix 3	List of those Killed in the Massacre: Bolton Parish Records, 28 March 1644	195
	Endnotes	197
	Select Bibliography	218

A Note on Dates, Measurements and Spellings

During the seventeenth century Britain still used the Julian calendar, not switching to the Gregorian calendar until 1752. Ignoring the Catholic Gregorian calendar during the 1640s, Protestant Britain used the Julian calendar where the New Year began on 25 March not 1 January. As a consequence events recorded at the time, such as the first attack on Bolton, would have been documented as being on 18 February 1642 as opposed to 18 February 1643 as the Gregorian calendar would record it. For clarity and ease of the reader all dates in this book have been modernised to the current Gregorian calendar.

The measurement and recording of distances in records of the time were also notoriously inexact and modern equivalents are given in most cases. Distance measurements were in leagues, made up of three miles, which were made up of eight furlongs, which were made up of 220 yards, with each yard being made up of three feet with each foot having 12 inches. The measurement of time was very much locally based, as the national standardisation of times across the country only came later with the coming of the railways and the timetables they brought with them. Wherever times are in quotation marks, they should be viewed in this context.

Spelling, for the most part, was phonetic as people wrote how they spoke, with even accents and dialects sometime discernable. Dictionaries were only just being published but they were more concerned with word definition than spelling. Wherever possible, original spellings have been retained in direct quotations but people and places outside direct quotations have been standardised and for the most part modernised.

Currency was in pounds sterling (£ derives from the letter L from the Latin *Librae*), which was divided into twenty shillings (s, from the Latin *solidi*), which in turn was divided into twelve pennies (d, from the Latin *denarii*). A penny could be divided into four farthings (from the Anglo-Saxon *feorthing*, a fourth part). An interesting and short-lived coin in circulation was the golden Unite. The Unite replaced the sovereign in 1604 to celebrate the unification of England and Scotland with the accession of James I and was valued at 20 shillings; it was discontinued in 1662.

Weights were in tons, which had twenty hundredweights, which were made up of eight stones (*st*), which itself could be divided into fourteen pounds (*lb*, a Germanic adaptation of the Latin phrase *libra pondo*, a pound weight) which were made up of sixteen ounces each. Just to complicate matters, the number of pounds in a stone varied by commodity; for example, for wool it could be 14, 15 or 24 pounds, while for beef it would be eight. Except in Hertfordshire, where it might be 12.

All imperial measurements have modern equivalents in the text, and Lancashire refers to the area that constituted the county before the 1974 boundary changes

CHAPTER 1

The Path to War

Lancashire in the seventeenth century was a predominantly rural county, with only 11 per cent of the 150,000 population living in towns of over 1,000 people. There were in fact only eleven of what we would call towns in 1642, which were the clothing mercantile towns of the south-east, Bolton, Bury, Rochdale, Blackburn, Salford and Manchester, the seaports of Liverpool and Lancaster and inland towns of Warrington, Wigan and Preston[1].

For administrative purposes the county was split into six 'Hundreds', a tenth-century parcelling of land which outlined an area of approximately one hundred 'hides' that had its own court and meeting place. Each Hundred was an administrative area important for running of local government and, more importantly in the coming war, for the recruitment and organising of the militia. Parochial in outlook, many Lancastrians at the time looked at their county being their country and probably thought little of what went on outside.

The Lancashire Hundreds were not standard in terms of area or character and varied greatly in size and makeup. The northern Londsdale Hundred was a large tract of highlands and moorland with smaller pockets of agricultural activity and pastoral land south of Morecambe Bay. Importantly for military considerations it had a number of medieval castles, in particular at Thurland and Hornby, and the major Norman fortification at Lancaster.

Amounderness Hundred consisted of the low-lying, boggy Fylde coast to the east, and the Pennines and the Forest of Bowland to the west. The most significant town in Amounderness was Preston, with its strategic position at a major crossing point of the River Ribble.

South of the River Ribble was Lancashire's smallest Hundred, Leyland. Considerably wealthier that its northern neighbours due to its fertile arable farmland, Leyland could be considered central Lancashire and had the strategic Houghton Tower, the fortified home of the Houghtons, within its boundaries. Inland from Leyland was the Blackburn Hundred, encompassing the eastern Pennines and part of the fertile Ribble Valley. The early medieval town of Blackburn gave the Hundred its name and was also one of the clothing mercantile towns that, due to the trade its merchants had throughout the country, was open and

Lancashire Hundreds. (Hundreds are shown here in bold text.)

amenable to new ideas. The Hundred also had the wild and bleak Forest of Pendle where the famous Pendle Witches trial occurred in 1612. Belief in witchcraft and the supernatural was still ingrained and widespread in the local psyche.

The Hundred of West Derby occupied the south-east corner of Lancashire and the Earls of Derby, from their residence at Lathom Hall, owned vast estates in the area. The port of Liverpool, with its harbour, its medieval castle and access to the Mersey river, was relatively small at the time with just twenty-four streets, one parish church and a chapel. However, compared to the surrounding area this was significant and one report described Liverpool as 'a market towne of great resort, a garrison towne and Cheefe port of these parts'[2]. Larger at the time was Wigan, with some 2,000 inhabitants, which produced copper, pewter and brass. The Wigan coalfields were being dug in earnest by the early 1600s, but due to the difficulty of moving any distance easily on boggy roads and the lack of the infrastructure to transport coal, economic development was slow.

The Salford Hundred in the south-east of the county bordered Yorkshire and Cheshire and, with the mercantile towns of Bolton, Rochdale and Manchester, was the most outward looking and receptive to new ideas of all the hundreds.

Manchester considered itself different, and the most important town in the county, the 'very London of these parts'[3]. With around 4,000 inhabitants, Manchester was the largest and probably most cosmopolitan town in the area and petitioned for the foundation of a university in 1641. Bolton, as with Manchester, owed its prosperity to the clothing trade, with merchants plying their trade as far as London, and with these trade routes came new ideas.

Although Lancashire had sixty parishes during the Civil War period, with sixty-three parish church's, the reformation had failed to convert many. Catholicism was strong, particularly outside the towns and in the west of the county. The majority of convicted recusants, those who refused to attend Anglican services and were presumably Catholics, in 1641–2 were in Lancashire. There would also be those who remained Catholic, but to avoid fines and legal ramifications reluctantly attended Anglican services. Lancashire was also a hotbed for the burgeoning radicals of Puritanism and Presbyterianism who believed in the literal word of scripture and were distrustful of what they might see as outside the literal word of God. Many of these Protestant nonconformists baulked at religious hierarchy and saw bishops as the trappings of 'Popery' and Catholicism. Some felt that no authority, be it a religious minister or the secular authority of the King, could come between them and their God. While nonconformists were never in a majority in Lancashire, there were considerable pockets in the south-east of the county where the trade of the market towns seems to have gone hand in hand with the new religion[4]. This was particularly true of Bolton, which due to its Puritanism gained the title the 'Geneva of the North'.

Outright violence between Catholics and Protestants was rare leading up to the Civil War, but did happen, as outlined in the dispute between Sir Ralph Assheton and William Blundell. It started in 1622, when Edward Rice of Little Crosby was bound over on a charge of recusancy. His failure to appear at Lancaster assizes led to a writ to seize goods and chattels and Sir Ralph Assheton, as Sheriff of Lancashire, sent bailiffs to take 'two oxen and a nagge' from Rice. The bailiffs were promptly set upon by a large armed crowd who took back what had been snatched, wounding one of the bailiffs in the process. It appears that William Blundell, a local Catholic gentleman, was accused of encouraging such actions and being an 'obstinate recusant', and Assheton sent the bailiffs after him in 1624. More violence followed with one of the bailiffs, Richard Hardman, being so badly hurt that he was 'in danger of Deathe.'

Despite the involvement of the Court of the Star Chamber in 1625, which appeared to resolve the matter, there was another attempt to seize the goods of William Blundell in August 1626 by a posse of twenty bailiffs who, after what was described as a riot, succeeded in taking goods to the value of £100. Hauled before the Star Chamber yet again, Blundell was heavily fined and dispossessed of Crosby Hall and only pardoned by the King in 1631.

A common, but incorrect, assumption is that in the Civil War the nobility and gentry were predominantly Royalist and the townsmen and peasantry were predominantly Parliamentarian. Admittedly the nobility in Lancashire were all Royalist; however, there were only three of them, James Stanley (then known as Lord Strange), Richard Molyneux (Second Viscount of Maryborough in Ireland), and Henry Parker (Thirteenth Baron Morley and Mounteagle). As regards the Lancashire gentry, with those who were baronets, knights, esquires or gentlemen it was a different story. There were 774 gentry families in Lancashire at the beginning of the Civil War and the allegiance of around two thirds, some 482, is not known. They may have been for one side or another, but in reality the vast majority would have been like the vast majority of the population: neutral and hoping to keep out of any conflict. Many more did not come out for either side until late in the war, such as Robert Mawdesley of Mawdesley who did not commit for Parliament until 1646[5].

Regarding the gentry families where their allegiance is known, 177 were Royalist and ninety-one were Parliamentarian and only in the Salford Hundred, which included Bolton, did Parliamentarian gentry families outnumber Royalist. Like many families in the coming conflict, some of the Lancashire gentry would be split, for example Sir Gilbert Houghton and his sons Roger, Gilbert and Henry would fight for the King while another son, Richard, would fight for Parliament[6].

Of the gentry families around Bolton, the Royalists were Anderton of Lostock, Janion of Blackrod and Norris of Blackrod. All were Catholic. The Parliamentarian families were Norris of Bolton, Bradshaw of Bradshaw, Bradshaw of Darcy Lever, Lever of Darcy Lever, Andrews of Little Lever, Worthington of Snydale and Barton of Smithills, with all bar the Bartons being Puritan. Only the Hultons of Over Hulton changed sides and the Cromptons of Darcy Lever, the Hultons of Hulton Park, Sir Thomas Barton at Smithills Hall and Laurence Bromilow at Hall 'ith Wood stayed neutral and played no part in the conflict[7].

The causes for the Civil War have been debated almost from the moment the last shot was fired. Essentially in Lancashire it can argued as having three main causes, firstly religion, although this was not strictly between Catholic and Protestant. It was also increasingly the Anglican establishment against the progressively more radical non-conformists. Secondly, power: the question of who actually had the power to govern the state, the King or Parliament, and, linked to that, money, i.e. who had the right to levy taxes and raise troops. The religious element would have particular relevance for Bolton in 1644 but as stated, the religious factor was not simply Catholic against Protestant, for the Royalists saw that the Protestant nonconformists' views undermined the King, indeed that they were rebels against the lawful monarch and his position as head of the established Church. The Parliamentarians saw Catholics as the enemy in their midst, and, that the King's advisors were betraying the rights of free born Englishmen and they would eventually betray the country to foreign papists. Some even classed King Charles as a secret Catholic, pointing to the fact that his wife, Henrietta Maria, was a French Catholic and could practice her religion discreetly but openly at court.

Lancashire was the most Catholic county in England, with many of the minor gentry believing in the 'old religion'. The recusancy laws were in force but not universally or rigorously applied, and this relaxed implementation meant that many families felt safe practicing Catholicism, albeit in private. Many nonconformist Protestants saw this as a wave of Catholicism that was, in their view, inextricably linked with the threat of foreign invasion, and it is clear that Lancashire had much anti-Catholic hysteria in the run up to the Civil War[8].

King Charles' attempt in 1637 to bring the Presbyterian Church of Scotland to heel with the imposition of bishops and Anglican worship led to open resistance in Scotland and the signing of the National Covenant of 1638. Determined to force his will, the King raised an ill-trained and poorly equipped English army, which marched on Scotland in 1639. It found a Scottish army on the border and as neither side wanted to force the issue, a settlement was reached in June. Fearing the Scots were negotiating with France, and not getting his way in the settlement, Charles recalled Parliament in 1640 after ruling the country alone for the previous eleven years. Known as the Short Parliament, instead of supporting the King it demanded redress for a number of grievances, including the abandonment of the unpopular ship money taxation and a change to the ecclesiastical system. Unwilling to agree to any challenge to his divine right to rule, the King promptly dissolved Parliament and then raised an army to once again attack Scotland. Instead, a Scottish Covenanter army under Alexander Leslie and James Graham, 1st Marquess of Montrose, crossed into England and scattered the King's unwilling forces. Forced into the humiliating defeat, he signed the Treaty of Ripon on 26 October 1640, which left Northumberland and County Durham ceded to the Scots as an interim measure, the town of Newcastle to be completely in Scottish hands and a pledge to pay the Scots' expenses – some £850 per day[9]. Humiliated, King Charles had to recall Parliament on 3 November 1640 so it could pass finance bills to pay for this disastrous Scottish adventure that would become known as the Bishops' War. Instead Parliament, known as the Long Parliament, began to enact reforms which were designed to deprive the King from ever ruling absolutely again, and it set both sides on a collision course.

In October 1641, events in Ireland may well have made civil war inevitable. In early 1641 some Parliamentarians and Scots Covenanters proposed invading Ireland to subdue organised Catholicism. On 18 August 1641, Parliament sent commissioners into Lancashire to disarm all convicted recusants. Frightened by this, a small group of Irish Catholic gentry planned to take over Dublin Castle and other towns in the name of the King to forestall any invasion and put pressure on what was seen, after the humiliation of the Bishops' War and the concessions made to the Long Parliament, as a weak king ready to accede to Catholic demands. The plan was to be carried out on 23 October 1641 but was betrayed, and some of the conspirators were arrested while others

King Charles I. (© National Portrait Gallery)

seized forts in the north of Ireland. What was planned as an almost bloodless coup spiralled out of control, with English troops conducting punitive actions in Wicklow and Cork, and in Ulster widespread attacks were conducted by the native population against English and Scottish settlers, which spread right across the country. Atrocity fed on atrocity and word spread quickly across the Irish Sea to Lancashire.

Refugees from the massacres began arriving in Lancashire, with Manchester identifying over a hundred[10]. With them came stories of atrocities carried out across the Irish Sea and the threat of invasion from Ireland was a real fear in the county. Parliament reluctantly agreed to the raising of an army for Ireland of some 6,000 Foot and 2,000 horse, and 'that a drum shall forthwith beaten for the calling in of volunteers'. The army would be under the command of Robert Sidney, Earl of Leicester, Lord Lieutenant of Ireland, but he remained in England and the field commander in Ireland was James Butler, Earl of Ormonde[11].

Among those Regiments raised for and in Ireland were those of Lord Byron, Lord Lisle, Henry Tillier, William Cromwell, Sir Michael Ernle and Sir Henry Tichbourne, all of whom, sometimes under different commanders, would eventually stand outside Bolton's walls on a rainy day in 1644.

In the midst of the crisis, after a stormy debate in the House of Commons on 22 November 1641, the Great Remonstrance was passed by 159 votes to 148. It was a long and wide-ranging document that listed all the grievances that Parliament had against the King. Blaming the King's advisors, including 'Jesuited papists', rather than the King himself, it portrayed Parliament as the true defender of the Protestant religion, the liberties of the people and, unsurprisingly, the privileges of Parliament. It called for Parliament to supervise the reform of the Church and to have approval and veto of all the King's ministers. The King rejected the Remonstrance on 23 December, but in reasoned and conciliatory terms that he hoped would appeal to the moderates and forestall conflict.

In this charged political atmosphere, the King heard news that convinced him that five members of the House of Commons – John Pym, John Hampden, Denzil Holles, Sir Arthur Haselrig and William Strode – had encouraged the Scots in the Bishops' War and were inciting the London Mob against him. The final straw came when he heard they were planning to impeach the Queen for alleged Catholic plots; he decided to act against them.

The King ordered the indictment for treason of the five members, and Lord Mandeville from the House of Lords, with a herald, was sent to the House of Commons on 3 January 1642, ordering that the five members be handed over. The House of Commons refused on the basis it was a breach of Parliamentary privilege, and so on Tuesday 4 January the King led troops into the House, intent on seizing the five. Marching into the chamber, he sat on the Speaker's Chair and, looking about, saw some conspicuous empty benches; the five had been warned by the Earl of Essex and had fled into hiding.

'I see the birds have flown,' said the King and left to angry shouts of 'Privilege! Privilege!' from some outraged MPs.

The attempted arrest and its disregard for the House of Commons led to uproar and rumours of civil war. The London Trained Bands mobilised in support of Parliament, and within days King Charles fled London. The King's personality and the intransigence of his divine right to rule was the spark for a tinderbox of religious, social and economic problems facing the country, and had brought his kingdom to the brink of civil war.

CHAPTER 2

Making of a Market Town: Bolton up to 1642

Bolton nestles in a natural valley on the West Pennine Moors on the banks of the River Croal, some 24 kilometres (15 miles) from Manchester and some 50 kilometres (30 miles) east of Liverpool. Close by is the stream known as Bradshaw Brook that runs into the Tonge River, which itself flows into the River Irwell south of the town. Little is known of the early inhabitants of the valley, but there is evidence of Bronze Age activity as a stone circle of eleven standing stones once stood at Chetham Close, near Egerton, some 6.4 kilometres (4 miles) to the north of Bolton. These standing stones were at one time up to 1.7 meters (65 inches) tall and 46 cm (18 inches) wide, the circle itself being 16 meters (51 feet 6 inches) in diameter. About 14 meters (46 feet) south west of the circle stood a solitary stone 48 cm (19 inches high) and 25cm (10 inches) wide, and another single stone some 31 meters (102 feet) south-south-east measuring 89 cm (35 inches) high and 43 cm (17 inches) wide. These stones, which had stood for thousands of years, have now disappeared, the result of a tenant farmer in 1871 taking a sledgehammer to them, leaving little more than flattened stumps[1]. More evidence of human activity was found in September 1825 when a barrow, a mound of earth and stones over a grave, also known as a tumulus, was found 400 meters (quarter of a mile) south-east of the parish church. Measuring about 9 meters (30 feet) in diameter, at the centre was found a skeleton and numerous grave goods, including bronze spearheads, while another barrow was found nearby in 1838, which also had a skeleton and grave goods, this time including a flint knife[2]. A cremation urn with the burnt bones of a small adult or child was found in a third barrow in November 1851, about 1.6 kilometres (1 mile) from the parish church, on the banks of the River Croal[3].

Clearly the valley had been a human settlement for some thousands of years; however, the beginning of the village that was to become Bolton is difficult to pinpoint. However, the church, the centre of any many early settlements, has occupied the elevated site overlooking the Croal river since at least Saxon times. The site, on a high bank by the river, and the circular graveyard boundary, suggests an early Christian site, perhaps as early as the

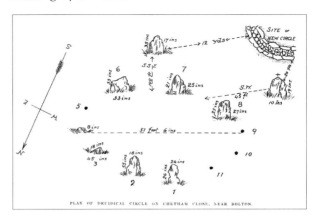

PLAN OF DRUIDICAL CIRCLE ON CHETHAM CLOSE, NEAR BOLTON.

Stone Circle – Egerton.

Anglo-Saxon/Christian conversion period[4]. When the old parish church of St Peter's was demolished in the late 1860s, a sixth-century Anglo-Saxon Cross was discovered along with a stone coffin dating from the eleventh century. The area had fresh water, as close to the church was a noted well, at Silverwell fields and Silverwell bottoms, backing onto the river, and a further well was at Spa Fields, further west alongside the Croal[5].

The village of Bolton remained an obscure backwater of Lancashire during the Norman conquest of 1066, but was included in the dividing up of England by William the Conqueror when he parcelled out the spoils to his supporters. One of his barons, Roger de Poicou, was granted 398 established Saxon manors stretching from the River Ribble and the River Mersey to the west of Manchester, a vast area covering Liverpool and most of Lancashire. Roger's family, the Montgomerys, were mentioned as owners of the Manor of Bolton in 1067 but the village, such as it was, was obviously still very small and poor. It may have featured in King William's review of the wealth of his new kingdom in 1086 known as the Domesday Book, but there is still debate as to the validity of this claim. The entry in question, for 'Bodleton', lists the names of Dubhan, Ealdraed, Earnwulf, Geoffrey, man of Thomas Archbishop of York, Gillemicel and Thorulf as living on and working the land.[6] But whether this relates to Bolton, or another village is not certain. What is known is that Roger de Poicou rebelled twice against King William, and after his defeat at Tewksbury in 1106 the family lost its estates. Those south of the River Ribble, including Bolton, were purchased to Ranulf de Briscasard, 3rd Earl of Chester, in 1228 and when he died childles,s his lands were eventually passed by marriage to William de Ferrers, the 4th Earl of Derby[7].

The first mention of the manor of Bolton was in 1212,[8] but in a time before standardised spellings the village was known under many spellings and pronunciations, including in the Pipe Rolls of 1185 as Boelton. There is mention of the 'mill of Bothelton' in 1202 and 1212[9]; the village is called Bowelton in the Royal Charter of 1251; Botelton in 1257; Boulton in 1266, when a 'Simon,

Bolton Parish Church during demolition in 1868.

Remains of the old parish church.

son of Micheal de Boulton' held land; and 'the eighth part of a certain mill' in the village of Boulton[10] before being known as the more familiar Bolton in 1307. The Feet of Fines mentions Bolton-on-the-Mores in 1331 and for most of its recorded history, including the seventeenth century, the village and soon to be town was known as Bolton-le-Moors. What Bolton, in its many spellings, actually means is still a subject of conjecture, one explanation being that Saxon Bothltun meant the village or farm, *tun,* with a special or important building, *bothl,* and another explanation is that it derives from the Saxon personal name of *Bothel,* meaning the original name meant Bothel's farm[11].

The sheep grazing on the windswept moors around Bolton provided fleeces that fed a burgeoning cottage industry producing woollen goods, and in 1251 William de Ferrers obtained from a Royal Charter King Henry III to hold a market in Bolton on Churchgate. In part, the charter granted in 'his aforesaid

Manor of Bowelton' permission to hold a market 'every seventh day; and also at the same place a fair once a year, extending over three days, that is to say on the eve and on the day and on the morrow of the feast of St Margaret the Virgin'. This market standardised and organised a trade that no doubt already existed and when William de Ferrers obtained, on 14 January 1253, another Royal Charter for Bolton, this time making it a free borough and granting permission for a market and fair, Bolton was no longer just a small village but on the way to being a market town with a prosperous future. At this time burgage plots, enclosed fields extending the confines of the town, were laid out on the thoroughfares of Churchgate and Deansgate.

William de Ferrers died the following year, on 28 March 1254, but his son, Robert, was only fifteen and although he inherited the title as the 6th Earl of Derby, and was knighted, he could not inherit the lands and power that went with it. He and his estates became a ward of Prince Edward, who promptly sold the wardship to Peter of Savoy for 6,000 marks, an act which may have had a bearing on Robert de Ferrer's actions later. In 1260 Robert inherited his vast estates, including Bolton, making the Ferrers one of the wealthiest families in the country. In 1263, when Simon de Montfort led the rebellion known as the Second Barons' War, Robert sided with the rebels, although this may have been for personal self interest and hatred of Prince Edward rather than the political aims of the barons. Simon de Montfort turned on Robert de Ferrers in January 1265, imprisoning him in the Tower of London, but support for de Montfort was soon draining away and he was defeated and killed in August 1265 at the battle of Evesham. King Henry III needed Robert de Ferrer's support, particularly in the North, so he was treated leniently, escaping with a pardon and a fine. Instead of accepting his good fortune, he joined in another rebellion the following year that also ended in defeat, this time at Chesterfield in May 1266. Robert was captured and this time his estates, including Bolton, were confiscated by the Crown and handed to Henry III's second son, Edmund, who held them for a time – although the de Ferrers family eventually regained them.

Untroubled by the changes in ownership, Bolton continued in steady growth as a market town specialising in woollen goods. In 1337 Flemish weavers had been attracted to the area to work in the burgeoning textile industry, and as well as their weaving skills they brought with them a fashion for wooden clogs, a fashion which took root throughout Lancashire. Coal was being dug in Bolton in 1374, and in 1385 a deed refers to the manor of Little Bolton, across the Croal River from Bolton, being the right by title of descendants of Roger de Bolton through his son's marriage to 'Ymayne daughter of Roger de Pilkington of Rovyngton', as by this time the manor of Bolton had passed by marriage from the Ferrers to the Pilkington family.

The Pilkingtons were an old Lancashire family that came from Pilkington, near Bury, and a fanciful tradition has it that Leonard de Pilkington stood with King Harold and his Saxon host on Senlac Hill at the battle of Hastings in 1066. From their manor house at Stand Hall near Pilkington, the family held large estates in Lancashire, including Bolton, by 1385.

The Pilkington crest of a mower, or man with a scythe, and its motto, 'And thus, And thus', is still seen in Bolton in its oldest pub in the form of the sign and name of Ye Olde Man and Scythe Public House on Churchgate. The pub has been standing in some form since before the time of William de Ferrers, as the oldest part of the existing building, the barrel vault cellar, has been dated to the twelfth century. One romantic story for the origin of the crest dates from the Battle of Bannockburn in 1314, when the defeated English lords, including one of the Pilkingtons, disguised themselves as peasant farmers to escape the wrath of the army of Robert the Bruce. A number of Lancashire families apparently claimed similar heritage for their own family crests, such as the Traffords, a man with a flail, the Mathers, a demi-mower, and the Ashtons, a mower[12]. A more prosaic, and likely, version is that the crest related to the Grim Reaper and that the other versions, such as the Traffords and Ashtons, were an indication that these families wanted to be closely associated to the powerful Pilkingtons[13].

In 1415, Sir John Pilkington, with a considerable retinue of three esquires, ten lances and forty-five archers, joined King Henry V at the battle of Agincourt. King Henry V was notoriously short of funds and, as security in lieu of wages for their service and their retinue, pledged to 'John Pilkington and William Bradshawe' a tablet of gold garnished with the arms of England and France and a gold chain wrought with letters and crowns. These royal jewels were not redeemed until December 1431[14].

The old Saxon/Norman church on Churchgate was replaced sometime between 1420–6 with one of the region's squat village churches with a nave, north and south aisles of five bays and a sturdy square tower at the west end in a style known as Perpendicular Gothic. The previous church may well have been dedicated to St Mary as the Chapel of the Virgin, as part of a statue, three feet in height, found during demolition in the tower wall was thought to have belonged to the early church[15]. In 1450, the parish church was 'improved with a chancel, the gift of Sir John Harrington, Knight', which was reached by three steps from the nave, but it had no chancel arch. The interior walls were wainscoted with oak while the walls, and the roof above, were ornamentally painted. The church may well have been built in a number of phases over many years, for an archway in the centre of the tower did not correspond to the width of the nave and the tower was not in line with the true centre of the church. There was a difference of 93 cm (3 feet) between the tower arch and the nave wall from one side to the other, indicating that they were built at different times with the tower thought to be an older structure. The tower had an additional layer of stone corresponding with the church, indicating some rebuilding or restoration had been carried out to ensure the stone of the tower and church matched. In 1536 the church was known as the Church of St Peter, Bolton-Le-Moors, and had three altars, the high one 'dedicated to the Most High', with the side chapels to 'St Peter and the Blessed Virgin'[16].

The Pilkington family held the manor of Bolton for over a century, until Sir Thomas Pilkington stood with Richard III at Bosworth Field in 1485, and although he survived the defeat, for his support of the Lancastrian King he lost much of his estates, including Bolton, which were handed to Sir Thomas Stanley, the new monarch's stepfather and soon to be Earl of Derby. However, the Pilkingtons did retain their holdings in nearby Rivington

In September 1513 Sir Edward Stanley led local forces, including a contingent of archers from Bolton, in the English army of Thomas Howard, the Earl of Surrey at the battle of Flodden Field, near the village of Branxton in Northumberland. In the last great medieval battle in the British Isles, the flower of Scottish nobility, including King James IV, were slain in a crushing defeat. It was also the swansong of the longbow, as artillery played a major part in the outcome of a battle for the first time. The Bolton archers were forever remembered in a few verses of a ballad that states

> For battle billmen both were bent;
> With Fellows fresh, and fierce in fights.
> Which Horton fields turned out in scores;
> With lusty lads – liver and Lights –
> From Blackburn and Bolton- i'th' – Moors

The Lusty Lads were also recalled in a stone inscription, long since lost, on the wall enclosing the parish churchyard that read:

> The bolt shot well I ween
> From arabalist of yew tree green,
> Many nobles prostrate lay
> At Glorious Flodden field[17]

An ancient yew tree stood on the south side of the parish churchyard and was said to have provided the wood for the bows and arrows of the Bolton Archers[18].

Bolton Parish Church.

The wool trade continued to flourish, as in 1535 it was noted that 'Bolton-upon-Moore Market stondeth most by cotton and coarse yerne. Divers villages in the Mores about Bolton do make cottons'[19]. The 'cottons' mentioned were actually woollen goods. A deputy Aulnager, an official to measure and stamp woollen goods, was ordered appointed at Bolton in 1566 in an obvious move to regulate the growing trade.

In the seventeenth century, the parish of Bolton covered a huge area of 33,000 acres consisting of eighteen townships and five chapels. The townships were Anglezarke, Blackrod, Great Bolton, Little Bolton, Bradshaw, Breightmet, Edgeworth, Entwistle, Harwood, Darcey Lever, Little Lever, Longworth, Lostock, Quarlton, Rivington, Sharples, Tonge and Turton. Close by was the equally large parish of Deane, which itself consisted of the townships of Farnworth, Halliwell, Heaton, Horwich, Kearsley, Little, Middle and Over Hulton, Runworth and Westhoughton[20].

A number of the closer townships played a part in Bolton's story during the Civil War. To the north of Bolton and immediately across the River Croal stands Little Bolton, a separate manor under a family that adopted de Bolton as their family name and had a manor house on the site, which became Little Bolton Town Hall much later. They too lost control when the Stanley family profited from Henry Tudor's largesse. The township of Halliwell lies to the north-west and the name derives from the Old English *halig wella*, a holy well, an ancient clear spring that supplied the area with water[21]. Within Halliwell is the fourteenth-century Smithills Hall, which William Radcliffe obtained in 1335, the family retaining the estate until 1485, when it passed to the Barton family who held it up until the Civil War. Heaton is to the west of Bolton and gained its name from the Old English *heah*, meaning high land, and *tun*, a settlement. The Heaton family, originally from Ulverston, settled there and Heaton Old Hall, which is now a farm, was the manor house and stands out on ground higher than the surrounding countryside[22].

Lostock Township is also west of Bolton and there are two differing explanations for the name. One is that it derives from Old English *blose* meaning pig or swine, and *stoc* meaning farm, while the other is from the Celtic *llostog* meaning beaver, indicating the village is on a stream where beavers were found. Lostock Hall was the home of the Anderton family.

The three Lever townships, Great, Little and Darcy Lever, seem to owe their name to the Old English word '*laefre*', meaning reeds. The land south of the River Croal became Great Lever, and that to the north Little Lever. When part of Little Lever passed to the Darcy family through marriage, it then became known as Darcy Lever. A family settled in the area and took the name de Lever, and were to play a prominent part in Bolton's history.

To the east is Brieghtmet, from the old English *breorht*, meaning bright, and *maed*, meaning meadow, hence bright meadow probably meant good pastureland. Bradshaw lies to the north-east of Bolton and comes from the

Old English word *sceaga*, meaning copse, and *brad*, meaning broad, hence the name means the broad copse. The Bradshaw family that took the name from the area also played a prominent part in the town's history, particularly during the Civil War.

The parish of Deane itself, also know as Deane Clough, is only 3.2 kilometres (2 miles) south-west of Bolton and the name comes from the Old English *denu* meaning valley, and *cloh* for ravine. The stream in the valley was known in Saxon times as Kirkbroke, meaning Church Brook, for the early chapel on the site which was first recorded in 1100.

The Protestant Reformation of the sixteenth century found many adherents in Bolton, due in part to the influx of new ideas to eastern Lancashire brought with the commerce of a busy market town. One such was George Marsh, who was born in the parish of Deane, near Bolton in 1515. Married at twenty-five Marsh spent most of his life on his farm raising a family, but with the death of his wife he placed his children in the care of their grandparents and left Lancashire to enter Cambridge University. Here he associated with others of the reformed faith, such as Laurence Sanders, and he eventually became curate to All Hallows Church in London, where his gift with words made him a popular preacher. For a time he was even employed by the King himself, but with Queen Mary's ascension to the throne he fell from favour and moved back north to preach in his birthplace of Deane, as well as around Lancashire. In 1555 Queen Mary's Catholic government's attitude to Protestant dissenters hardened and what became known as the Marian Persecutions began, an act for which she earned the epitaph 'Bloody Mary'. Justice Barton at Smithills Hall sent servants to arrest Marsh, but the tall preacher was not at home; however when he heard he duly gave himself up. During examination by Justice Barton in the withdrawing room at Smithills Hall, Marsh stamped his foot so hard re-affirming his faith that a footprint was said to be left in the stone floor[23]. He was found guilty of heresy and sentence was passed that he be burnt at the stake.

On a windy April day in 1555, George Marsh was taken to the traditional execution grounds at Broughton, a mile from Chester city centre. Being tied to the scaffold, he was given the chance to convert to Catholicism but he steadfastly refused, so the pyre was lit. After his death, his friends collected his ashes and buried them in the nearby cemetery of Saint Giles.

Despite this martyrdom, Bolton did not begin to develop a staunch Puritanism until 1598, when Ellis Sanderson was appointed as a Minister and was, in 1605, arraigned by the Bishop of Chester for a number of non-conformist offences. Another influence was James Gosnall, whose death in 1623 did much to promote Puritanism in Bolton as his will provided payment for a preacher in the town. The influence of Puritan ideas into Bolton and the neighbouring area of Deane was not resisted by the diocesan authorities to any degree, as Bishop Bridgeman of Chester appears to have turned somewhat of a blind eye to Puritan ministers. The clothiers of Bolton regularly travelled to London and Southampton on business, and these connections of trade between the urbanised areas of south-east Lancashire and the south-east of England assisted the development of Puritanism, as 'their constant converse and traffic with London doth promote civility and piety among tradesmen'. The influence spread to the minor gentry as six of the eleven in the immediate area, the Norrises' of Bolton, Bradshaws of Bradshaw, Bradshaws of Darcy Lever, Levers of Darcy Lever, Andrews of Little Lever, Worthingtons of Snydale in Westhoughton and the Bartons of Smithills, were Puritan. This Puritan island amid the sea of Catholic west Lancashire would have serious repercussions in the coming Civil War[24].

However, not all were swayed by the influence of Puritanism, least of all ministers such as James Pendlebury, Vicar of Deane from 1597 to 1637. Pendlebury was described as a 'lewd minister' and was charged with drunkenness, fornication and other offences. Nor were all Bolton's inhabitants sober, clean living Puritans, as in the years 1637–8 some thirty-eight ale houses were closed by magistrates in Bolton and Deane and no doubt many more remained open.

The moors around Bolton continued to produce predominantly woollen goods until the end of the sixteenth century. However, as the seventeenth century dawned two new products begin to make their appearance – 'cotton wool' and 'fustians'. Cotton wool was described in 1621 as 'a kind of Bombast or Downe, being a fruit of the earth growing upon little shrubs or bushes, brought into this Kingdome by the Turkie Merchants, from Smyrna, Cyprus, Acra and Sidon'[25]. Fustians were a combination of the new cotton wool and flax yarn, and one George Arnould was listed as a Fustian Weaver in Bolton in 1601.

By the 1620s, Bolton had its weekly market selling 'cottons' and fustians and one local, Richard Heywood of Little Lever, who traded in fustians in the 1620s and was described as very wealthy, as the manufacture of fustians 'was then a gainful calling[26].

This prosperity did not last, as bad weather and poor harvests, and a recession in the woollen trade which was vital to Bolton, caused widespread suffering and even famine by the 1630s. Prior to this, Bolton suffered from a disastrous outbreak of bubonic plague[27] in 1623, when 452 burials were recorded in the parish registers – perhaps a third of the population[28]. The Parish Registry makes chilling reading that winter:

A poor childe wich dyed att Gilbert Tayliers,	3 December
A pore man wich came oute of Sharples,	5 December
A pore childe	8 December
A pore woman	3 January
A pore wenche of Johns of Mary	10 January

A pore lade out of Bradshaw	11 January
A poore lade out of Broadhead	24 January
Towe poore ladies wich came out of Edgeworth	29 January
A poore fely out of Turton	1 February
A pore lade out of Quarlton	5 February
A pore wenche who dyed at Roger Cooke's	9 February[29]

The normal burial system could not cope and plague pits, like those identified in nearby Horwich and Rivington, had to be used. Baptisms did not start to rise substantially until 1625, when the virulence of the plague had begun to burn itself out.

Plague broke out again in Lancashire in 1630-2 but strict measures put in place to restrict the movement of travellers kept Bolton relatively safe as the infection was kept away. In 1635, a minor smallpox epidemic claimed forty-three victims who, it is recorded in the parish registers, succumbed to 'the pox'. However, as this was not reported elsewhere in Lancashire this seems an isolated outbreak. However, the decline in the woollen and textile industry had, by the late 1630s, become so bad that in September 1638 a Royal Commission had been established to examine 'the great decaye of the Trade of Clothes and Stuffs, and other like Manufactures of this Kingdome to the ympovershing of many thousands those livelihood and maintenance doth relye on the same'; one of the 'chiefe Townes' as reviewed by the commissioners was Bolton[30].

On the eve of the outbreak of the Civil War, in the spring and early summer of 1642, Bolton suffered from a fresh outbreak of 'the pox' where seventy-three died, all but seven being children. This appears to rule out smallpox as that would be expected, in a market town like Bolton, to spread slowly over a period of time and kill substantial numbers of adults. When the parish registrar describes a death due to 'the pox', he is talking about a death from a fever involving eruptive spots and this may mean that the epidemic was in fact measles and not smallpox. Whatever the cause of the outbreak, Bolton seems to have been a dangerously unhealthy place to live and with the end of this visitation of 'the pox', many would have thought the worst would have been over, but with the coming of war much worse was to come[31].

CHAPTER 3

Raising the Standard: The Coming of War, 1642

When King Charles left London on 10 January 1642, his authority was shattered and his regime in tatters after the failed attempt to arrest the five ringleaders in Parliament. As the county and country drifted to war, each side in Lancashire polarised and leaders emerged. The undisputed leader of the Royalist faction in Lancashire was James Stanley, then known as Lord Strange. Stanley was born on 31 January 1607 at Knowsley, the eldest of three sons of William Stanley, 6th Earl of Derby. Educated in Bolton, it is claimed he then studied at Oxford, but this is not proven, although it is known he had two domestic tutors, George Murray and Charles Earle. Murray later became Rector of Bury and Earle the Rector of Winwick, and both no doubt influenced the religious opinion of their charge as James Stanley became a devout Anglican. In 1625 he was elected MP for Liverpool, but the Stanley fortunes were not as they had been after years of litigation regarding William Stanley's estates. It was perhaps with this in mind that James travelled to Europe in search of a suitably wealthy and noble wife. The lady chosen was Charlotte de la Tremoille, daughter of the French nobleman Claude de la Tremoille. Charlotte was born in 1601 and her mother, Duchesse de la Tremoille, was the daughter of William 'the Silent' of Orange, and it was said she inherited some Dutch steel from her grandfather. They were married on 26 June 1626 in the Palace of Orange in The Hague, in the presence of the King and Queen of Bohemia and other European royalty and nobles.

In May 1628, James Stanley was summoned to take his seat in the House of Peers in what would be King Charles I's third Parliament. It was in this Parliament that a certain Oliver Cromwell, member for Huntingdon, first made his appearance on the Parliamentary stage.

After Charles dissolved that Parliament, James Stanley seems to have spent some time at court, but despite his unswerving loyalty to the Crown he does not appear to have been popular with the King and his entourage. He and his wife soon moved from court and spent more time in his estates in the north, particularly Lathom House and their homes in Knowsley and on the Isle of Man. On the death of James' mother, around 1637, his father William moved to a house on the River Dee near Chester and effectively retired, handing over to the running of the huge family estates to James. In February 1639, he attended a summons to meet the King at York as he was on his way to suppress the Scots in the Bishops' War, and he would attend the King again as war clouds gathered in 1642.

His path through the conflicting politics of the time can be seen as occupying the middle ground, which earned him distrust within some circles at court, and indeed he was actually seen as potential leader of the Parliamentary opposition in early 1642, but when decisions had to be made he came down firmly on the side of the King. By no means a soldier, as his future was to show clearly, he was initially to become the undisputed leader of the Lancashire Royalists.

Second only to the Stanley family in influence and power in Lancashire were the Catholic Molyneux family. The Molyneux family were particularly influential in south-west Lancashire, where many of the local gentry, such as Fazackerly of Fazackerly, Fazackerly of Kirkby, Hulme of Maghull, Mercer of West Derby and Standish of West Derby, had been in the Molyneux's service.

Richard, 2nd Viscount Molyneux was born in around 1623[1] and was the son of Sir Richard Molyneux of Sefton, who was created Viscount Molyneux of Maryborough in the Irish Peerage in December 1628[2]. In 1639 he was betrothed to Henrietta Maria, the eldest daughter of James Stanley, although the marriage had not taken place by the start of the Civil War and this possibly influenced the relationship between the two noblemen. There is no evidence he played any part with the Trained Bands or fought in Europe; in fact there is little evidence of what Richard Molyneux was doing from 1636 to 1642.

A very junior member of the Royalists at this early stage was Thomas Tyldesley of Myerscough Hall, near Garstang, who was born on 3 September 1612, the son of Edward Tyldesley of Moreleys. Brought up a Catholic, he fought in the Thirty Years' War before returning to England to marry Frances Standish in 1634[3]. As he was only twenty-two at the time, it is unlikely he held high command; however, whatever military experience he did have would have been invaluable, particularly as his being a Catholic meant he was debarred from service in the Trained Bands. His leadership and personal courage would soon raise him to prominence as the third most important Royalist in Lancashire, after Stanley and Molyneux.

In addition to these three was Sir John Girlington of Thurland, a Catholic, who was born on 19 July 1613 at Kirkby Malham in Yorkshire and was High Sheriff of Lancashire in 1642, while another leading Royalist was William Farrington of Worden, who had also been High Sheriff of Lancashire in 1636.

Sir Gilbert Houghton of Houghton was aged fifty-one in 1642 and lived at Houghton Tower, which was a large fortified house on a hilltop between Preston and Blackburn. King James I visited Houghton Tower in August 1617 and Sir Gilbert's father, Sir Richard Houghton, had the entire length of the half-mile avenue leading to the house laid with a red carpet. It is claimed that

An Impeachment of High Treason, Exhibited
in PARLIAMENT,
Against *IAMES*, L STRANGE, Sonne and Heire Apparant of WILLIAM Earle of *Derby*, by the COMMONS assembled in *Parliament*, in the Names of themselves, and all the Commons of ENGLAND.

With an
Order of the Lords *and* Commons in PARLIAMENT, for the apprehending of the said *LORD*, to be published in all Churches, Chappels, Markets, and Townes in the County of Lancaster and Chester.

16 *September*, 1642:
Ordered by the Lords in Parliament Assembled, that this Impeachment, with the Order, shall be forthwith printed and published,

Iohn Browne Cleric. Parliament.

Impeachment of James Stanley, issued for siding with the King.

it was on his visit that King James dubbed the loin of beef 'Sirloin' while in the Banqueting Hall. It is also believed that William Shakespeare was a tutor at Houghton Tower at one time. Three of Sir Gilbert's sons would follow him into the King's service, but his eldest surviving son, Richard, would fight for Parliament.

The Gerards, an old Lancashire family, would also provide many officers for the emerging Royalist forces, including Sir Gilbert Gerard, his twin brother Ratclyffe and, in particular, Sir Gilberts nephew Charles, who went on to raise his own Regiment.

Of those that emerged as leaders for Parliament in the county, foremost in fervour, if not in stature, was Alexander Rigby. He was born in 1594, the eldest son of Alexander Rigby and Alice, daughter of Leonard Ashawe of Shaw, probably at Middleton Hall, Goosnarch, about eight miles north of Preston. Educated at Wigan School, he was admitted to Gray's Inn on 1 November 1610, gained a BA from St John's College Cambridge in 1614 and an MA in 1615 and was called to the bar on 17 November 1617. He became Justice of the Peace for Lancashire in 1638 and then Deputy Lieutenant. While living at Rigby, near Kirkham, he became Member of Parliament for Wigan and in 1640 was involved in what would become known as the Short Parliament. He also bought a charter as Governor of Lygonia, a district in the province of Maine, North America – although he never travelled there. He appears to have had a particular enmity for James Stanley, Lord Strange, which seems to go beyond political and be personal; the origin of which is unclear.

Richard Shuttleworth of Gawthorpe Hall, which he inherited from his uncle, was born in 1587 and with his wife had eleven children, all of whom were born at Gawthorpe. He was responsible for committing the Pendle witches for trial in 1612 and served as High Sheriff of Lancashire in 1618 and 1638, and was elected MP for Preston in 1641. Shuttleworth has been portrayed as avaricious, his actions based purely on self interest, and in Royalist eyes he was seen as a cynical opportunist 'fattened ... upon the spoils of better houses than his own'[4]. But he was also a moderate man of Presbyterian views. Five of his sons, Richard the younger, Nicholas, Ughtred, Barton and William, would all take up arms with him for Parliament.

Ralph Assheton, son of Richard Assheton of Middleton, was born on 31 March 1606 and was a man of great energy and ability who would rise to command all the Parliamentary forces in Lancashire. He was educated at Sidney Sussex, Cambridge, which, as well as being a hotbed of Puritanism, was also Oliver Cromwell's college[5]. He took over his family estates on the death of his father in 1618 and little is known of his activities until 1631, when he refused the knighthood that went with his position, possibly the first act of defiance to the Stuart monarchy. In 1640, he was returned to the House of Commons as one of three MPs for Lancashire. John Bradshaw of Bradshaw Hall near Bolton, also a Puritan, would serve in Assheton's Regiment[6].

John Moore of Bank Hall near Liverpool was the leader of the Puritans in his locality. Returned as Member of Parliament for Liverpool, he was described as a bitter and unscrupulous man whose household was described as 'hell upon earth as was utterly intollerable' and containing a 'packe of arrant thieves' and 'profained bitter scoffers at piety' by Adam Martindale, who was Moore's clerk for a time[7].

While supporters of both sides took stock, the majority in the county took a neutral stance in these early months. Even at this stage it was not certain that fighting would actually take place, but it was becoming increasingly likely. An issue that both sides faced was that should hostilities begin, neither side had an army to fight with. Most towns and cities looked to defend themselves, even if they were not sure against what, and weapons of various sorts were being obtainied or refurbished, gunpowder stocks inspected, ordnance sought and the men that were available put into training as tension throughout the county mounted.

In the 1640s there was no standing army and should war come, it would not only be a civil war but in a very real sense a civilians war. Apart from a few Royal bodyguards, such as the Yeomen of the Guard, and gunners manning key fortifications and the Navy, an army would be only be recruited as and when it was needed. The system used to recruit was based on the counties and the hundreds, with the King's Lord Lieutenant having the authority to call out all able-bodied men aged sixteen to sixty for service. This ill-trained levy would be of little use in time of war or national emergency, therefore the solution was the 'Trained Bands'. These were a small number of those men available who were specially chosen to receive a higher level of individual and unit training, to be able to use the new weapons and tactics of the time. This militia was to be used in times of war or to maintain civil order in peacetime, and those recruited must be men 'able and active' and 'none of the meaner sort, nor servants; but only such as be of the Gentrie, Free-holders, and be good Farmers, or their sonnes'[8]. In 1626, experienced sergeants were brought from the continental wars to improve the training they received and to drill this militia[9], which was primarily made up of infantry companies in Lancashire.

The Trained Bands had to take an oath of allegiance as part of their induction, which precluded all Catholics joining apart from those who practiced in secret. In 1639, a 'Certificate of the Musters' had each hundred providing an infantry complement of 100 men made up of seventy musketeers, thirty pikes and a much smaller cavalry contingent. The officers were captains, men of local influence and prestige, and were named as Robert Charnock for the Leyland Hundred, Henry Byrom for Salford, Roger Nowell for Blackburn, William Farington for Amounderness and George Dudding for Lonsdale, with the Earl of Derby no doubt heading those of West Derby. Two troops of Horse are listed, with Richard Shuttleworth leading twenty-five Lances and John Atherton leading seventy-seven Horse. In addition, 7,400 untrained troops were listed and had considerable arms at their disposal. Arranged on the same lines as the Trained Bands, by the Hundred, some of their officers would find distinction in the coming war, such as the Royalists Sir William Gerrard, Edward Rawsthorne, William Farington and Gilbert Houghton and the Parliamentarians Alexander Rigby and John Starkie[10]. These officers and men would form the nucleus of the forces that would fight in Lancashire.

The armies that both sides would build were typical of the period and made up of Foot, Horse and Cannon: Foot being the Infantry, Horse the Cavalry and Cannon the artillery. The Foot were organised into Regiments, which were divided into companies, the most popular being ten companies to a Regiment. A typical company had a Company Commander, a Lieutenant, an Ensign, two Sergeants, three Corporals, two Drummers and about 100 men at full strength. The Regiments' commanders were, in order of seniority, the Colonel, after whom the Regiment gained its name, the Lieutenant Colonel, the Sergeant Major then a number of Captains with the three senior officers having the companies with the most men. Although each company should have 100 men, in practice there was no fixed system, particularly with Lancashire's local forces, with some companies having 200 men and others eighty or less with many permutations in between. Some Regiments had three companies while some had as many as thirteen. In most cases, the strength of a Regiment in the field was between 250 to 300 men in total.

Each Foot Regiment had both pikemen and musketeers. Pikemen were armed with a pike, normally about 16 feet long with a metal head and strips of metal extending about 2 feet down the side to prevent the top being cut off. For protection, the pikemen would often have a steel helmet of various designs and those well armed had back and breast plates with steel tassets (thigh protectors) hinged to the bottom of the breast plate. The majority would have to rely on just the protection of a leather buff coat or perhaps not even that. The main role of the pikemen was to ward off enemy cavalry and thus protect the other infantryman in the Regiment, the musketeer.

The musketeer was mostly armed with a smoothbore matchlock musket with a barrel length of around 42 to 48 inches. The muskets were heavy and early in the war forked rests were often used with the longer barrelled muskets while the shorter barrels issued wholesale after 1643 did not require one. Powder was in twelve wooden or tin containers, known as the twelve apostles, on a bandolier running from the left shoulder to the right hip. Each container held a measured charge that would be used to fire one lead ball and when the twelve were used the musketeer's would retire to the company 'budge barrel' to refill their charges.

The Drummers were mature and responsible soldiers who used the drum to transmit orders and the Drum Major was the Senior Non Commissioned Officer of the Regiment. Each company had its own ensign or colour, which was a flag made of silk or taffeta approximately 6 foot by 6 foot 6 inches, mounted on a short pole and used in the smoke and confusion of battle by soldiers to identify where their company was. Sometimes companies were even described as 'Colours'. The company's most junior officer, also known as the Ensign, carried the Colour into battle.

The Cavalry, known as the Horse, were organised into troops, usually sixty strong but often less, particularly in Lancashire. Each troop had a troop commander, a lieutenant, and a junior officer – known as a Cornet – while the remainder were NCOs and troopers. Five or six troops together would make up a Regiment and the troop commanders were, in order of seniority, the Colonel, after whom the Regiment gained its name, the Lieutenant Colonel, the Sergeant Major then a number of Captains with the three senior officers having troops with the most men.

Cavalry were of two main types: the 'great horse' and the Dragoons. The great horse were made up of horsemen who were known as 'harquebusiers' or 'carbineers' who were armed with swords, pistols and, in some cases, carbines and short pole axes. Their main tactic was the charge with sword and pistol. Protection was usually a back and breast plate, sometimes with a steel collar called a gorget, and with an open helmet called a lobster pot, due to its scaled armour, with a peak to which was attached either three connecting bars or a single sliding bar to protect the face. For added protection beneath the back and breast plate, the trooper would wear a buff leather coat of thick hide. Dragoons, classed as part of the Horse, were in fact mounted infantry who usually fought on foot. They probably derived the name from the Dragon, a short matchlock weapon of musket bore, which they originally carried. Mounted on inferior horses to those of the great horse, they were to give added firepower to the great horse and were organised in companies rather than troops.

Each troop of Horse or company of dragoons carried its own colour or cornet. Much smaller than the infantry colours, the cavalry colours were roughly two feet square and mostly fringed. They were unique to their troop and attached by tasselled strings to a lance. The Dragoon colours, called guidons or cornets, were the same size as cavalry colours but were elongated and had two rounded swallow tails. Two trumpeters were on the strength of each troop, and as well as sounding calls for orders they were the Colonel's messengers[11].

Most soldiers wore their own civilian clothes, although the tradition of uniformed coats had existed since Tudor times, with the colour of coat being decided on what was available or what their Colonel could afford[12]. The problem was that both armies were similarly equipped and dressed, either in civilian clothes or the same colour coats, causing what one Parliamentarian said was 'a great inconvenience upon service, we cannot know one another from the enemy'[13]. Both sides tried to avoid clashes between their own troops by adopting field signs such as white cloth in the headband, or around the arm, springs of green foliage or, in a sign that almost became universal for the

Horse Parliamentarians, wore an orange/tawny sash while the Royalists wore a red one. Each side would also have a field word or battle cry, but on occasion both sides had the same colour coats and the same field word[14]. At Cheriton in March 1644, the field sign both sides chose was to wear something white and both sides chose the field word 'God with Us!'. This confusion would save the life of a Parliamentarian commander at the storming of Bolton in 1644.

On 5 March 1642, Parliament issued the Militia Ordinance and Lord Wharton was appointed by Parliament as Lord Lieutenant for Lancashire, but as James Stanley, Lord Strange, was already Lord Lieutenant, appointed by the King, it clearly set both sides at odds, with each attempting to portray itself as the legitimate power in the county. In reality, Lord Wharton was a figurehead and it would be up to the likes of Ralph Assheton and Alexander Rigby to organise Parliamentarian forces in Lancashire.

In April of 1642, the King attempted to take Hull but was rebuffed at the gate, an action which prompted Parliament on 27 May to declare that he had started the war. James Stanley travelled to York to meet with the King, as did George Middleton, who was created a baronet and John Girlington, who was knighted. At York, on 11 June 1642, the Royalist Commission of Array for Lancashire was issued and included the names of James Stanley, Richard Molyneux, Sir Gilbert Houghton, Sir John Girlington, George Middleton, Thomas Tydesley, William Farrington and Edward Rawsthorne among others.

Also in early June, Richard Shuttleworth of Gawthorpe Hall, Ralph Assheton of Middleton, Alexander Rigby and John Moore formed the core for the Parliamentarian committee for the 'preservation of peace of that county' – although mainly they were to put the Militia ordnance into effect and to call out the Trained Bands to suppress Royalist recruitment and confine Catholics 'to their dwellings'[15].

Both sides were seriously lacking in arms and equipment, indeed, the King in York did not have enough arms for his field army and began stripping local militia units. In Lancashire there were four major magazines, stores of Powder and match mainly confiscated from Roman Catholics the previous year, at Manchester, Preston, Warrington and Liverpool and control of them would be vital.

James Stanley, who was charged by the King with raising Lancashire for the Royalist cause, called a public meeting at 'ffullwood moore near unto Preston' on 20 June 1642 with the aim of reading out the Royal proclamations and called on 'all the Gentry and men of best ranke' to attend[16]. Richard Shuttleworth and Alexander Rigby, on their way back to the county, heard of the summons and tried to dissuade anyone from attending but actually attended themselves.

Almost 1,000 people were on the Moor, including most of the leading Royalists' and the King's declarations were read including the Commission of Array, by Sir John Girlington, the Under Sheriff Thomas Danson, and others in the crowd. Alexander Rigby attempted to read the Parliamentary Instructions for the 'Militia of the County'[17] and brazenly demanded that Sir John Girlington give up the Commission of Array. He was shouted down, with some 400 of the crowd riding 'up and downe the moore', crying for the King. In a sign of the times, a Parliamentary account describes them as 'for the most part popish Recusants'[18]. A smaller number cried in opposition for the King and Parliament, but it appears that the Royalists were winning the day even though the majority on the moor apparently took neither side. One Parliamentary supporter felt 'beset by papists' and left the moor, as did Richard Shuttleworth who was one of the first to leave[19].

While the meeting was breaking up, the Royalists acted as William Sumpter, agent of William Farrington, emptied Preston's magazine taking away thirteen barrels of powder and match. Alexander Rigby protested but was in no position to force the issue. This was the first part of the Royalist action to secure all the ammunition in the county and the magazine at Warrington, being predominantly a Royalist town, was taken, as was the magazine at Liverpool, where some thirty barrels of powder and match were also taken – this time personally by James Stanley.

The court records of Prescot stated that on 3 July 1642, a Richard Taylor 'a dissolute young fellow' declared 'Let my Lord Strange Kisse my Arse … for the taking of arms and ammunition from Liverpoole … and (he) was an upholder of Papists', for which Taylor was brought to court in Prescot on the 22nd of that month[20].

Despite this defiance it appeared that Lancashire was falling, almost by default, to the Royalists, with the Parliamentary supporters falling back to the Salford Hundred and the towns of Bolton, Salford and, predominantly, Manchester. The Manchester magazine was at the Collegiate Church of St Mary's College[21] and consisted of 10 barrels of powder and three fathoms of match. The Collegiate rooms where the powder and match was stored actually belonged to James Stanley, but that did not stop Ralph Assheton and Sir Thomas Stanley from breaking in and stealing them away on the same day of the meeting at Preston[22].

When the Under-Sheriff Thomas Danson and others came to take possession of the Manchester magazine for the King, he was rebuffed. James Stanley then moved towards Manchester, and at Bury mustered recruits. Rumours abounded in Manchester regarding these actions, and the shops were shut and the militia called out to drill. With each side edging towards war, messages of mediation went from Alexander Rigby to the Royalists, calling on them to stand down their forces. But this diplomacy was not always well received and a Parliamentary messenger, Roger Haddock of Chorley, was beaten by some Royalists so badly it 'broke his head to the very scull'[23]. Battle lines were hardening, but as yet neither side had actually commenced hostilities, perhaps hoping that events had not yet come that far.

It is somewhat ironic that the event which finally pushed the county into outright conflict may well have been a covert attempt at rapprochement under the cover of a simple invitation to a meal, a banquet, with friends. James Stanley, Lord Strange, was invited to Manchester on 15 July, to the inn house known as the Eagle and Child in the Conduit,[24] just off Market Street[25]. He was invited by Alexander Greene, whose home it was, and it seems this was cover for a meeting to discuss the issue of the Manchester magazine as he was planning to stay until the following Monday, probably with Sir Alexander Radcliffe, at Ordsall Hall. James Stanley called a muster of troops on the morning of the 15th at Bury, where an estimated 2,000 turned out[26]. Later that day he arrived in Manchester for dinner and, as Lord Lieutenant, he came with an armed escort of some thirty horsemen. Other guests included Lord Molyneux and the High Sheriff, Sir John Girlington, each with their own horsemen, adding to the Royalist ranks, which also included Thomas Tyledesley and other 'gentlemen of qualitie'[27].

Approaching the inn, local Royalists, some accounts say about 100, turned out to welcome the guests, swelling their numbers even more. Estimates vary to the numbers of Royalists that evening from thirty, which seems too small, to 400, which seems too high. A number of 120, plus local supporters, seems nearer the truth, but in any event word of their arrival was spreading. Spirits were not dampened by the incessant rain and bravado appears to have got the better of some, with a number of the horsemen riding up and down on the Conduit and Market Street 'with cocked pistols and shouts that the town was their own'. According to some reports, the High Sheriff, Sir John Girlington read out the King's Commission of Array, further raising tensions.

News of the Royalist show of strength travelled fast and Captain John Holcroft, Captain Thomas Birch of Birch and Sir Thomas Stanley of Bickerstaffe called out the Local Trained Bands to muster with pike and musket at the Market Cross. It is not clear what their intentions were at this point. They may have been aiming to keep the peace, given a large and hostile crowd had started to gather, but at least one, Sir Thomas Stanley, was intent on forcing a confrontation. He had been in a property dispute with his relative James Stanley in 1640 and still harboured considerable resentment. His decision to support Parliament was a purely personal one, and he would use any ensuing confrontation as cover to make an attempt to kill his kinsman[28].

The guests had only just sat down to dinner, having been there 'not a quarter of an houre,'[29] when word of this muster reached them and Sir John Girlington left the dinner. Unable to find his own horse, he mounted the horse belonging to James Stanley and went with some of his men to confront the Trained Bands mustered 'neere the Crosse',[30] demanding in the King's name that they 'lay down their armes, keepe the peace and cease the tumult'[31].

Captain Birch and Captain Holcroft had no intention of standing down as they marched on with 'souldiers armed with pikes and muskets, with their matches lighted and cockt',[32] and words and probably blows were exchanged as things turned ugly. Girlington was gone some time and this, and the noise from the growing disturbance, alarmed the other guests, who left the inn to see what was happening.

A large and threatening crowd had by this time surrounded the inn and James Stanley could not find his horse, which had been used by Sir John Girlington. He walked through the angry crowd to the end of the street to take Sir Alexander Radcliffe's horse when at least two pistol shots were fired at him, one of which it appears was from Sir Thomas Stanley, firing directly at his cousin, and 'a musket shot at his Lordship from a shop in the streete, which was seene to hit the wall neare him'[33].

Amid the gunfire, angry exchanges continued as Stanley mounted Radcliffe's horse and at some point Captain Thomas Birch ordered his musketeers to fire, but owing to the rain dampening their powder and matches, or unwillingness even at this stage to fire on fellow Englishmen, nothing happened.

Seeing Birch directly threaten them, some horsemen rode for him with pistols and swords drawn and he only escaped by 'thrusting himselfe under a carte of Gorases', face down in the mud[34], an act for which he forever earned the title 'Carter Birch' from friend and foe alike, a name he despised.

Obviously realising they had to leave, Stanley rode down Market Street with his horsemen pressing the crowd to protect him and force a passage. The crowd tried to bar their way and Richard Percival, a linen weaver of Grindlowe[35], leapt from behind to try and pull one of the horsemen from the saddle and 'cutt a gentleman in the head'[36]. Richard Fleetwood from Penwortham was riding behind this, saw what was happening and shot Percival dead with a pistol[37]. Some accounts claim that Thomas Tyldesley shot Percival at the beginning of the skirmish from a window of the inn, but this does not fit with Tyldesley's character – although legal proceedings were started against him for murder. However, Parliament ordered the judges in Lancashire to 'respire the Tryal and Proceedings' against Tyldesley on 11 August 1642, as they knew there was no truth in the charge. The death of Percival seems to have ended the skirmish, as both sides seem to have dispersed and James Stanley rode on to Ordsall Hall to stay the night with Sir Alexander Radcliffe. Richard Percival was of the Roysten family and was buried at the parish church on 18 July, and was the first known casualty of what would become the Civil Wars[38].

On 29 July, a number of Manchester men calling themselves the 'better sort of townsmen' published a description of the banquet skirmish which blamed Sir Thomas Stanley, Captain Thomas Birch and Captain Holcroft for the disturbance. It is not clear if these were neutrals, Royalist sympathisers or moderate Parliamentarians looking for a reconciliation with Lord Strange, but it appears most people already knew that a line had been crossed. The time for posturing and accommodations had passed, and now both sides prepared in earnest for outright conflict. Battle lines were being drawn.

CHAPTER 4

Early Days:
The First Civil War, 1642–1643

In the two months following the banquet skirmish, both sides set about recruiting and training troops. The Royalist forces had the most success, with James Stanley, still known as Lord Strange, Lord Molyneux and Baron Morley using their power of patronage, family connections and subtle pressure to bring most of their retainers, neighbours and tenants under arms. Buoyed up by most of Lancashire being under Royalist influence, if not control, James Stanley invited the King to raise the Royal Standard at Warrington; however the King declined instead raising his Standard at Nottingham on 22 August. On 26 August, the Royalists mustered 100 musketeers, sixty pikemen and sixteen Horse at Wigan[1], and Thomas Tyldesley called up members of the Trained Bands in Amounderness and 'would not suffer any of them to return home, but compelled and forced them to march with him after the king'.

The Royalist leaders in Lancashire believed, as most people did at the time, that the issue at hand would be decided by the King's army in one decisive battle with the Earl of Essex and his Parliamentary forces, and thus concentrated on raising troops for this critical clash of arms. Over the summer months the Royalists were able to raise troops from most of Lancashire, apart from the Salford and Blackburn Hundreds. They managed to assemble three Foot Regiments, supplemented by Trained Bands of various quality and four troops of Volunteer Horse, as well as accumulating a number of small-calibre field artillery.

Among the Foot Regiments were Charles Gerard's Regiment of perhaps 8–900 men, mostly raised from Lancashire but including elements of men from Cheshire and North Wales. Colonel Charles Gerard of Halsall was born in 1618 and appears to have seen service in the Low Countries, and would go on to be one of the outstanding field commanders of the war. His Lieutenant Colonel was Edward Villiers, and included in the Regiment were Major Cuthbert Halsall, Captains Francis Windebanke, Randle Egerton, Edward Hatton and his cousin Gilbert Gerard[2].

The next Foot Regiment was commanded by Charles' uncle, Sir Gilbert Gerard, which numbered nine companies, some 8–900 men, were raised from

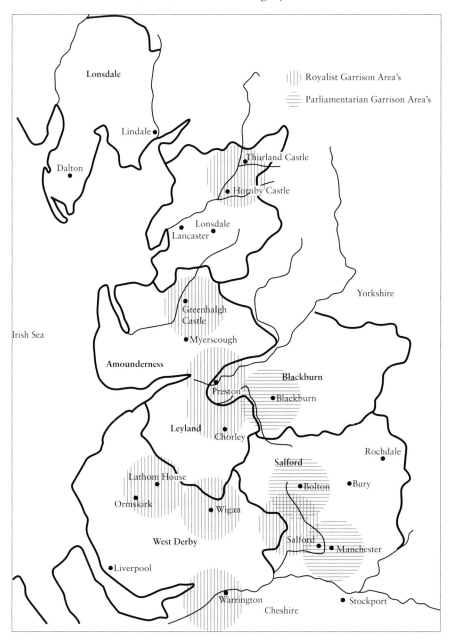

Battle lines in 1642. (Hundreds are shown here in bold text.)

Gerard and Stanley tenants in Lancashire. Sir Gilbert's twin brother, Ratclyffe, was Lieutenant Colonel with Major Richard Bishop and Captains Edward Paynton, Edward Ashton, John Byrom, John Gerard and Hugh Houghton all serving. The last Foot Regiment was commanded by Lord Molyneux and was weaker than the other two, numbering around 4–500 strong and made up of men from Amounderness, some men of the Trained Bands who were essentially press-ganged by Thomas Tyldesley and a band of freeholders, probably local gentry and their tenants from the West Derby Hundred, who were also led Tyldesley[3].

The remaining Foot were a mixed bag of elements of the Trained Bands and less than enthusiastic volunteers, as the better men had been absorbed into the three main Foot Regiments. However, one company from the Leyland Hundred stayed under their own commander, Captain Thomas Standish. This mixed group of Foot companies probably numbered about 4–500 men in total and a small number of mixed Horse and Dragoons that were probably made up of minor gentry, their servants and tenants and would have numbered a few hundred at most. A small artillery train was also put together, which included 'eight or nine Peeces of Ordnance', probably small cannons such as Drakes and Sakers[4]. James Stanley expected to lead this force to join with the King, but it appears a change of plan occurred as when this force mustered at Warrington the aim now was to take Manchester and the magazine and in effect claim Lancashire for the King.

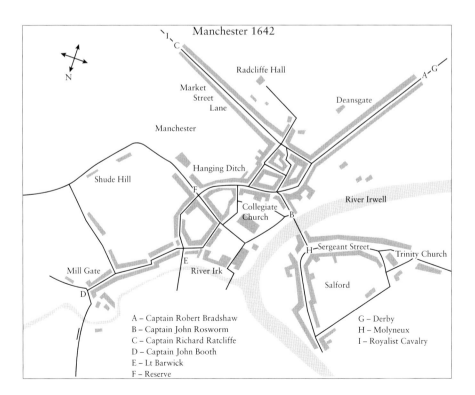

A – Captain Robert Bradshaw
B – Captain John Rosworm
C – Captain Richard Ratcliffe
D – Captain John Booth
E – Lt Barwick
F – Reserve

G – Derby
H – Molyneux
I – Royalist Cavalry

JAMES STANLEY, 7th EARL OF DERBY,
AND CHARLOTTE DE LA TREMOÜILLE, HIS COUNTESS.

From the Original by Vandyke, in the Collection of
The Earl of Clarendon.

James Stanley, 7th Earl of Derby, and Charlotte de la Tremoüille, his Countess.(©
National Portrait Gallery)

The Parliamentarian forces had much less success, as their recruitment was essentially confined to the Salford Hundred. Richard Shuttleworth at Gawthorpe Hall led most of the Blackburn Hundred in sitting on the sidelines awaiting developments, which left the towns of the Salford Hundred, such as Bolton and Manchester, recruiting local militia for their defence. Manchester had resolved to raise a Foot Regiment and Richard Holland of Denton was placed in command. As with the Royalists, the Parliamentarians had a distinct lack of trained and experienced officers and professional soldiers were much in demand. Luckily for the Parliamentarians, one such soldier happened to be in Manchester at the time – John Rosworm[5].

Rosworm was a Dutch or German professional soldier and engineer who had arrived in Manchester around June 1642, and by September was contracted by the Manchester Committee for six months for a fee of £30 to 'endeavour the security of the town'[6]. The very next morning after agreeing this contract, two gentlemen representing James Stanley came to Rosworm with a gift of £150 and a request to go to Lathom House to join the Royalists there. Rosworm, however, declined and set about Manchester's defences, putting up 'good posts and chains to keep out the Enemies horse'[7] at the ends of the streets. Manchester was additionally protected on its northern and western sides by the rivers Irk and Irwell and a potential strongpoint from the collegiate church, overlooking the Salford Bridge spanning the Irwell. Manchester's

Manchester Cathedral.

Salford Bridge.

rudimentary defences were completed on Wednesday 22 September 1642.

Colonel Richard Holland commanded Manchester's defences, which were about 1,000 local militia and a large number of men from the district 'with Musket, Pikes, Halberts, staves and suchlike'[8] who were most likely tenants of local Parliamentarians like Ralph Assheton.

The Royalists set out from Warrington on 24 September, heading for Manchester, but were bogged down by prolonged wet weather, poor roads and a broken gun carriage that caused considerable delay, and it was not until 9 a.m. on Sunday 25 September that outposts at Manchester sighted 'sundry companies on their colours … in open view'[9]. The Royalists had approached along the Irwell and split into two divisions at Stretford with these forces approaching through Salford and on either side of the river.

Church bells were rung, calling out the defenders who manned positions at the end of the streets and Salford Bridge. Captain Robert Bradshaw of Bradshaw Hall near Bolton commanded 150 tenants of Ralph Assheton, well armed and drilled, at the end of Deansgate. Bradshaw was the younger brother of John Bradshaw, Sheriff of Lancashire, and was described as 'a very moderate man and of good parts'[10] and as his position was considered the most vulnerable, he had the town's single piece of artillery. John Rosworm and fifty musketeers covered Salford Bridge, while Captain Richard Ratcliffe of Ratcliffe Hall, south of Market Street Lane, commanded a company of the Manchester Trained Band who took post at the end of Market Street

Lane. Captain John Booth, son of Sir George Booth, Lord of the Manor of
Warrington, led another company of Manchester's Trained Band holding
Millgate and Lieutenant Barwick commanded a company posted at Hunts
Bank. The reserve was placed at Shudehill and appears to have been under
no commander, while other small contingents would have attempted to guard
minor entries and lanes. Many of these defenders would have been armed with
scythes, rakes and clubs as there were more men than weapons, while William
Bourne, an elderly, ailing preacher from Chadderton moved from position to
position, leading the singing of psalms to encourage the troops[11].

The Royalists had strong support in Salford and, led by Lord Molyneux,
had no difficulty moving through the town, where they headed towards the
stone, three-arched Salford Bridge. James Stanley, on the other side of the
river approached Manchester with his division and came to Alport Lodge,
belonging to Sir Edward Mosley[12], heading for the end of Deansgate. The
positions taken by the defenders meant that they held the advantage, with
the Manchester bank of the Irwell steeper at Salford Bridge while the small
River Tib had reduced the area around Mosley Street to a waterlogged marsh
impassable to cavalry. The most obvious approaches were along Deansgate
and a quarter of a mile away, at Salford Bridge.

Seeing the army at its gates, the Manchester authorities, probably directed
by Colonel Holland, sent two envoys out to discover the Royalist intent. James
Stanley then sent Major Windebank, of Charles Gerard's Regiment, with his
demand that his troops were to be allowed to freely enter the town. The day
ended with fruitless negotiations.

The following day, Monday 26th, further demands were sent in, this time
insisting on the surrender of all arms. No reply came and at midday, in heavy rain
the Royalist cannon at Salford Bridge and 'a drake' at Alport Lodge, opposite
Deansgate, opened fire and 'played fearsly against the townee'[13]. Royalist
Foot, commanded by Thomas Tyldesley, attacked the entrance to Deansgate,
where the 'fight was hot on both sides', with the defenders 'constantly charging
and discharging'[14] their muskets. The position was under so much pressure
that Rosworm at Salford Bridge sent twenty of his fifty musketeers to assist
Bradshaw on Deansgate. During the fighting Captain Robert Bradshaw was
brushed on the arm by a flying cannon shot, but otherwise was unharmed.

Beaten back by Bradshaw's men, the Royalists 'burnt a great Barne with
much corn and hay' belonging to a Mr Greene and also set fire to 'some houses
of Master Foxes'[15] and under cover of the flames and smoke, attacked again.
The wind at first was with the assault, blowing in the faces of the defenders
to their 'great annoyance and endangering of the Towne', but the wind turned
and the 'rage of the fire was abated' and the attack was beaten off with 'divers
… souldiers being slaine there'[16].

Later that afternoon the attack came across Salford Bridge, where John
Rosworm had his thirty remaining musketeers. The opening cannon barrage

had unnerved the defenders, but as the attack was uphill and over the exposed bridge they managed to stand firm and halt the Royalists. Some of the attackers did, however, gain entry to a house at the foot of the bridge, from where they kept up desultory musket fire throughout the night. At around the same time, a diversionary attack by cavalry to the east of Manchester was easily beaten off.

Musket fire continued from the house until nightfall, and around midnight the Royalists at Salford crept down the riverbank. Throwing lighted faggots across the river, they tried to set fire to the houses on the Manchester side with little effect. In the day's fighting, the defenders admitted to losing three men killed but claimed an unlikely 120 of the attackers, including 'Mr Mountaine, A Colonel of Horse', most likely one of the horsemen in the diversionary attack and a 'Captain Skirton'[17].

The next day, no attempt was made on Deansgate, while Salford Bridge felt the first assault. The opening cannon bombardment Rosworm described as 'being a strange noise and terror to my raw men',[18] causing sixteen of his musketeers to take to their heels, while Rosworm claimed that he had to then draw his sword to convince the remaining fourteen to stay at their posts. No attempt was made to force passage over the bridge and Rosworm was reinforced with fourteen men, probably from Shudehill and Millgate reserves, while the attack shifted to the Manchester side of the river, in particular at Market Stead Lane, held by Captain Richard Radcliffe and a company of the Manchester Trained Band. The attacks were not pressed home, and as they died down towards evening the defenders sent out several sorties, cutting off Royalist stragglers and capturing seven troopers and a quartermaster for the loss of only two men[19].

A truce was called overnight when Stanley sent several proposals, each more moderate than the last. The reply was negative to all these overtures, with the defenders stating they 'would not give him so much as a rusty dagger'[20]. Despite their defiance the defenders were wracked with division, with Colonel Richard Holland, Robert Hyde of Denton and John Booth advocating capitulation, while Rosworm, Bradshaw and Radcliffe, the men who had commanded the defenders who had repulsed the Royalists, wanting to fight on. Rosworm went as far as accusing Holland of cowardice but supplies were running low with Rosworm, his musketeers being down to six pounds of powder and eighteen fathoms of match[21].

At this time a relieving force of 150 men from Bolton were intercepted by the Royalists, who drove them off, killing three[22]. The Manchester Parliamentarians were on their own and would receive no help from outside. During the uneasy truce, the Royalists repositioned two of their cannon in Salford and continued a desultory fire that only resulted in killing a bystander, 'a strange boy looking about him but not in armes' who 'stood gazing upon the top of a style'[23].

The following day, Thursday 29 September, 200 musketeers of the defenders sallied out from the end of Deansgate, aiming to capture a house used by Royalist marksmen. The Royalists counterattacked with 100 musketeers of their own supported by a troop of Horse. The exchange of fire lasted about an hour before the Royalists broke and fled, some of the troop of Horse being cut off and being forced to cross the river, resulting in three being drowned, including a Captain Snell. Snell's body was looted with 'two rings on his hands worth £20' being taken[24].

Parliamentary musketeers occupying the high ground around the collegiate church used their commanding position to put harassing fire on the two re-positioned Royalist cannon, forcing them to retreat to a safer position. High on the top of the church steeple, a Parliamentarian marksman pulled off a remarkable shot that dealt a fatal blow to the Royalist morale. Captain Thomas Standish of the Leyland Trained Band was quartered in Robert Widdow's house on the north side of Salford, 'well upp towards the Chappell', was 'was washing his hands in the morning at the dore' when a sniper from the church steeple shot him dead. This must have been at what the Royalists considered a safe distance because morale plummeted, as it was reported 'his souldiers' fled[25].

Hopes of a quick victory for the Royalists were washed away in the wet weather and the Royalists in the open were suffering considerably in the rain, and the steady downpour had swelled the river so that the fords would have been difficult, if not impassable, leaving the two halves of the Royalist forces cut off from each other. News had reached James Stanley that his father had died, making him the 7th Earl of Derby, and, influenced by the realisation that the King's army needed his three best Foot Regiments, he decided he could not spend the time reducing Manchester in a drawn out siege.

There was only scattered ineffectual firing on Friday 30 September, the cannon making 'holes in divers houses, and battered downe a piece of chimney, but did little harme',[26] while the most activity was at the end of Deansgate where the Royalists began to dig a large ditch and bank, making it look as if they were settling in for a long siege. On Saturday 1 October, a prisoner exchange was agreed when eighty-five Royalists were exchanged for a similar number of what the defenders claimed were local civilians seized purely to be part of the exchange.

Using the cover of the bank thrown up on Deansgate, the Royalist army marched away. The rivers and tributaries of the Irwell, Irk, Tib, Mersey and Medlock criss-crossed Manchester and the incessant rain had turned much of the ground to a waterlogged swamp. Little coordination appears in the attacks as communication between the Royalists in Salford and at the end of Deansgate was hampered by the Irwell in flood; indeed men and horses drowned trying to cross, one of whom may have been Andrew Homerson[27]. The swampy ground may well have forced the assault on Manchester to be made on the strongest part of the defence, especially at Salford Bridge. The assault had come perilously close to succeeding but had failed, with the defenders such as Captain Robert Bradshaw being noted to 'hath behaved himself most valiantly to his everlasting renown'[28]. No such accolades were given to the Royalists for although the attacks, notably by Thomas Tyldesley at Deansgate, were bravely delivered, the rain, or poor leadership, meant they lacked any co-ordination, subtlety or tactical awareness. Perhaps it was not just the swampy, difficult ground, as it would not be the first time that the local Royalist forces in Lancashire showed tactical naivety and fragile morale. Casualties are difficult to ascertain as the Parliamentarians claimed 220 of the attacking Royalists killed, including eighty-five taken prisoner, while admitting losing just nineteen of their own men. These figures seem too one-sided but the Royalist losses were heavy, including some senior officers such as Colonel Cuthbert Clifton,[29] who was killed, and Lawrence Holker who was captured and had his estates sequestered[30].

The best Lancashire Royalist Foot Regiments of Charles Gerard, Sir Gilbert Gerard and Lord Molyneux left for the King's army during the second week of October to join in what was hoped would be the deciding clash with the Parliamentary army of the Earl of Essex. James Stanley, now Earl of Derby, was apparently snubbed and ordered to remain in Lancashire with the most ill equipped and badly motivated Royalist troops. With the Regiments that marched south went the best equipped and trained troops, the best officers like Charles Gerard and Thomas Tyldesley, and the best junior officers and NCOs, the backbone of any army. If, as everyone hoped, this single clash resulted in the end of the war, this would not matter, yet any prolonged conflict would result in the weakening, perhaps fatally, of the Royalist forces in Lancashire. For without experienced officers and NCOs, the task of turning raw recruits into disciplined soldiers would be almost impossible. The Parliamentary forces, though lacking in number, stayed firmly in Lancashire.

While the country awaited the decisive encounter of the main field armies, in Lancashire peace talks were tentatively being arranged.

Richard Shuttleworth and others proposed a meeting at Blackburn on Thursday 13 October with a view to discuss peace in the county. Colonel Holland and Peter Egerton declined to meet outside their own hundred but suggested Bolton at any date convenient. Letters passed between both sides with the Royalist Roger Newell of Read, a relative of Shuttleworth, as a middleman. The suggestion was for a 'meeting upon Tuesday next at Boulton' at 'about tenne of the clocke in the afforenoone', on the condition that 'such security for our safe going and cominge backe from Boulton as shall be thought fitting'[31] was ensured.

It was tentatively agreed that the meeting of the 18th should take place at Bolton with Richard Holland, Peter Egerton, John Bradshaw, Richard Shuttleworth, John Braddyll and John Starkie representing the

Parliamentarians, while Saville Radcliffe of Todmorden, Sir Thomas Barton and Robert Holte represented the Royalists. Word of this local rapprochement had reached London and Colonel Holland and Peter Egerton received commands in writing from Parliament stating 'how much it is against their liking to have any treaty'. Richard Shuttleworth wrote on the 16th that due to the letter from Colonel Holland outlining Parliament's resistance to any peace talks, 'the meeting att Boulton upon Tewsday next cannot hold' and ends the letter 'and soe we rest'[32]. Thus, the meeting never took place and with it went any chance for peace in Lancashire.

The Lancashire Royalist Regiment's joined the King's army at Shrewsbury sometime after 10 October. The King's strategy was to march on London and, if possible, force an encounter with the Parliamentary army commanded by the Earl of Essex and with this in mind, they set out on 12 October, moving south-east. By 22 October, the Royalist army was quartered at Edgecote and received news that Essex's Parliamentary army was marching on nearby Kineton. The King ordered his army to muster on the escarpment of Edgehill the following morning to await events.

Essex's outposts reported the deployments of the King at about 8.00 a.m. on the 23rd and Essex consequently deployed his army in the cover of some hedges half way between Kineton and the Royalist positions.

It was before this battle that Sir Jacob Astley composed the lines, 'O Lord thou knowest how busy I must be this day, If I forget thee, do not thou forget me'.

The Royalist army deployed with Prince Rupert, Lieutenant General of Horse, commanding the right wing with John Byron in support, while on the left wing Sir Henry Wilmot was in command with Lord Digby in support. In the centre the Foot Regiments were commanded by Sir Jacob Astley supported by five brigade commanders, one of whom was Charles Gerard. The Lancashire Regiments of Sir Gilbert Gerard, Charles Gerard and Lord Molyneux were stationed in the front lines with the Welch Regiment of Sir Thomas Salisbury[33].

The Earl of Essex was Lord General of the Parliamentary forces with Sir William Balfour commanding the Horse on the right wing. The left wing was commanded by Sir James Ramsey, while Sir John Merrick commanded the Foot Regiments in the centre.

Essex showed no signs of advancing as he was hoping for reinforcements so the Royalists started to advance down the slope to Radway Field. This movement, and the sight of the King's entourage, goaded the Parliamentary cannon into opening fire, precipitating an ineffective artillery exchange. While the cannon of either side pounded away, Royalist Dragoons drove back the Parliamentary Dragoons on both flanks, leaving Prince Rupert the opportunity to charge.

The Prince charged and drove Ramsey's brigade from the field, with the Parliamentarian Foot brigade adjacent to Ramsey also breaking and fleeing. On the other flank, Wilmot also charged and drove into Fielding's outnumbered

Regiment. Both Prince Rupert and Wilmot chased the broken Parliamentarian Horse on into Kineton to loot the baggage train, leaving the Royalist Foot Regiments to fight on at Edgehill.

The Royalist Foot advanced in the centre within musket range of Essex's army and a firefight began. Reserves were brought into the Parliamentary line as both sides closed to the push of the pike. Now the reserve Parliamentary Horse Regiments of Stapleton and Balfour, held in the centre behind the Parliamentarian Foot, rode through gaps in the line and with no Royalist Horse to oppose them, ran straight into the exposed Royalist Foot, two Regiments breaking completely. With no reserves, the Royalist Foot gave way and Ensign Arthur Young captured the Royal Standard, carried by Sir Edmund Verney, who was killed.

Only on the right did the Royalist Foot hold while the left and centre collapsed. Returning Royalist Horse rallied the breaking Royalist Foot Regiments, particularly on the left, and Captain John Smith recovered the captured Royal Standard. As night fell, both sides had fought to a standstill and broke off for the night. As dawn broke the following morning, the Earl of Essex withdrew to Warwick Castle, leaving the field to the King.

The losses of the Lancashire Regiments are difficult to assess but Molyneux lost his Major Henry Byrom, who was killed, as was Captain John Assheton of Curdale, and Captain Henry Ogle was captured[34]. The battle of Edgehill was not the decisive result both sides had wished for and instead of trying to force the issue by marching on London, the King's army trudged back to Oxford. It would be a long war.

After Edgehill, the Lancashire Royalist Regiments of Sir Gilbert Gerard and Lord Molyneux fought under Prince Rupert at Brentford on 12 November when he attacked Denzil Holles' Regiment in his drive on London, and although the attack was successful the march on London stalled. Sometime that winter, Lord Molyneux and Thomas Tyldesley left the main Royal Army and returned the Lancashire as it appears Lieutenant Colonel Roger Nowell was the field commander of Molyneux's Regiment that, with Sir Gilbert Gerard's men, had occupied the strategic garrison at Brill on the Hill. On 27 January 1643, Parliamentary forces under Colonel Goodwin tried to dislodge the Royalists from Brill on the Hill[35]. Behind earthworks encompassing the remnants of Brill Castle, the Royalists sheltered from the initial Parliamentary cannonade and then set fire to damp straw creating, a wall of choking smoke. The Parliamentary forces pulled back without attempting to take Brill and the Lancashire Regiments settled in as the garrison, with Sir Gilbert as Governor.

With the promise of an early end to the war, both sides in Lancashire consolidated and the weaker Parliamentarians set about recruiting 'faithfull honest and knowing gentlemen' in the Royalist areas, such as Joseph Rigby of Aspull and Alexander Thompson of Wigan, to act as spies. Nor were the Royalists reticent in recruiting and sending spies – Henry Haddock was detained by the Parliamentary Captain Starkie and found to be in possession of the suspicious 'note or Wryteinge'[36].

Sir Gilbert Houghton lit the beacon at Houghton Tower after he returned from the attack on Manchester and raised perhaps 300 men, mostly from the Fylde and Leyland, and marched to the Militia store at Whalley and carted it back to Blackburn on 17 October. This raid stung the Parliamentarians into action and Richard Shuttleworth led a two-pronged attack on Blackburn, along Darwin Street and from the bottom of Church Street, which was on the guards posted at the parish church before they could react. In a few hours it was all over, and Sir Gilbert only escaped by leaping onto his horse and riding off into the darkness towards Preston.

Parliamentary spies had been at work assessing the Earl's forces and a memorandum dated 26 October 1642 noted:

> That att Warrington are billeted between 300 and 400
> Att Preston..300
> Att wiggin.. 200
> Att Ormskirke..300
> Att Eckleston...100
> Att Pressberye..100
> 1400

This information was no doubt provided by the likes of 'Alexander Tompson, who liveth in Wigan Town', 'Thomas Smythe ... well acqueynted' with the town of Warrington and 'Henery Asshurst ... who lives not farr from Ormskircke', all named in a letter, dated 18 October, to Richard Shuttleworth as 'honest knoweing gentlemen' willing to provide 'ifformation' to the Parliamentary cause[37].

Skirmishing and raiding continued around the boundary areas, and on Sunday 27 November the inevitable happened. Chowbent lies a few miles north east of Leigh and while the villagers were going to church, a 'post rode through the country' informing them that the 'Earle's troopes were comming towards the Chowbent'. By 1.00 p.m. over 3,000 Horse and Foot were gathered and attacked the Royalists, driving them back towards Leigh. The 'young youths, farmers sons' of the Parliamentary Horse troop 'over-rode our foote' and left them behind and found the Royalists had reformed on Lowton Common. Checked by this stand, the Parliamentarian Horse had to fall back to wait until the Foot companies arrived, only then driving off the surviving Royalists. The Parliamentarians claimed a very unlikely 200 Royalists were killed in the running fight for the loss of only three wounded on their own side.

A few days later, Parliamentarian companies under Captains Venables and Rupert Bradshaw, with many men from Bolton, led a raid to 'plunder a Papists house neere Wigan'. The Royalists from Wigan sent a party after them, forcing the Parliamentarians to leave 'their plunder and take to their Armes' to enable them to get clear[38].

The return of Lord Molynuex and Thomas Tyldesley had galvanised the Earl of Derby into reorganising his forces for the coming campaigns, and on 10 December a meeting was held at Preston to decide how the new recruiting drive was to be financed and what administration would be needed to facilitate this influx of recruits.

On 15 December, three companies of Parliamentary troops 'marched forth of Bolton'[39] under the command of Captain Venables, Captain Bradshaw and Captain Risley Browne, heading again towards Westhoughton 'to plunder another Papists house'[40], but this time the Royalists were better prepared and were aware of their movements. Marching along Manchester Road, the Parliamentarians came to 'a close of ground upon the side of Houghton Common' where they met the Earls of Derby's forces from Wigan, 'about a thousand horse and foot'[41]. The area of the close, that is land already enclosed from the Common, covered Warcock Hill and Commercial Fields. In this enclosed space the Parliamentarians claimed the battle went on for three hours, until the Parliamentarian ammunition wagon caught fire and with it the chances of fighting their way out went up in smoke. Serjeant Major Dacres of Venables, company was mentioned as being killed in the action[42], but it appears there was little actual fighting and perhaps the Parliamentarians, seeing they

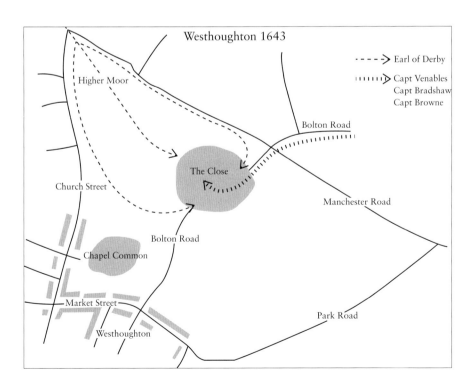

had little option but to surrender, fired their own ammunition wagon. It was reported that 'eight score' soldiers were marched off into Royalist captivity but Captain Bradshaw, wounded or sick, died soon afterwards.

Next it would be the Royalists, raiders that were surprised. On Christmas Eve they were ambushed at Leigh by the Manchester Parliamentarian garrison, which included John Rosworm, who claimed 'we shattered the Enemy'[43]. On the same day, Sir Gilbert Houghton attacked Blackburn with around 1,000 men down the lane from Mellor and Salmsbury. Settling in for a siege, they set up their only field piece at the house of a man who went by the name 'Duke of the Bank'[44]. From this position they fired off a number of desultory shots, the only result being one 'entered into a house upon the south side of the churchyard and burst out the bottom of a fryen pan'. In reply the defenders retuned fire with muskets and even sallied out, but they must not have gone far as no casualties were recorded. After the great victory of bursting a frying pan, Sir Gilbert and the Royalists slipped away 'upon Christmas Day night', so that 'they myght eet theyr Chrystmas pyes at home'. The whole episode was a complete farce and the unfortunate 'Duke of the Bank' had all this 'provision of Meale and Beefe and the like' eaten by the Royalists, and before they commenced the 'burning of his barne doors with his Carts wheels and other husbandry stuff'[45].

With the departure of the three Regiments for the King's army, the Earl of Derby organised his remaining resources on 30 December, with 'Leigh to be kepte with 20 men and 2 horses' commanded by a 'Liefftennante' and '2 dragooners'. Warrington was to have '300 men, whereof the welch Companies to be parte'. At Wigan were '300 men', including the companies of Captains Chernoke, Captain Chisnall and Captain Barrow 'alsoe 100 dragooners & a troope of horse', and at Preston '200 men under the Command of Captaine Houghton and Captain Farrington'[46].

At the end of 1642, the total forces available to the Earl of Derby were a little over 1,000 men, the majority infantry, many of whom many were lacking arms and were in under-strength formations. The loss the Lancashire forces fighting with the King had weakened the Royalists to such an extent that their early strong position in the county was now in considerable doubt.

In January 1643 a professional Scottish soldier, Sir John Seaton, arrived in Manchester to co-ordinate Parliamentary forces in Lancashire. On Monday 6 February, Sir John led three Foot companies from Manchester and, marching via Bolton where three more joined him, had by the evening of Tuesday reached Blackburn.

Joined by more troops led by Captain Nowell, the Parliamentary forces were 'about 900 or 1,000 firemen, Horse and Foot, and about 600 Bill men, Halberdiers and Club men'[47]. The Royalist forces were likely to be Sir Gilbert Houghton's dragoons and some companies of Foot, Thomas Tyldesley's dragoons then being raised under Captain William Blundell, and two troops of Horse under Major Anderton and Captain Radcliffe Houghton. By the Wednesday night the Parliamentary force had reached Preston, and sympathisers led some of Seaton's troops into the town via 'Fryers Gate Barrs'[48] while the main force assaulted from 'up at a lane at the East Barres where the Watter voides the towne' before dawn[49]. Captain Booth led the Parliamentary assault, shouting 'Follow me or give me up forever'. The Royalist defenders had loopholed the walls surrounding individual houses and plots of land and fired their muskets through, only to have their muzzles pushed aside by the attacking Parliamentarians, who had crept up close to the walls. An earthen bank defended by pikemen was circumvented by the simple expedient of a group of attackers breaking into a nearby house and emerging from the back door to take the defending pikemen from behind.

Seaton led his men on the strongpoint of the church, where 'our musquiets beat them from their centeryes and from the steeple'[50]. Preston's Mayor, Adam Morte, killed one of the attackers 'with push of his pike', but 'came up to the souldiers very fearsley but was slayn in a short space'[51]. Radcliffe Houghton, Sir Gilbert Houghton's brother, led his troop of Horse, the last Royalist reserves, in a charge, but some twenty Parliamentarian musketeers had taken position in a house and fired a volley which downed many of the horsemen and killed Radcliffe Houghton, thus ending Royalist resistance. Sir Gilbert had fled from Preston so fast he left his hat behind. Within an hour it was all over and Preston had fallen to the Parliamentarian forces; among the prisoners was Richard Fleetwood of Penwortham, whose pistol shot had killed Richard Percival at the Manchester Banquet skirmish[52].

With Preston taken, the Parliamentarian forces turned their attention to Houghton Tower, Sir Gilbert's fortified home and headquarters. Three companies, about 300 men, marched on the tower, whose garrison of only about thirty musketeers soon surrendered. Captain Nicholas Starkie and his company were first to enter the Tower and found 'good stores of armes and powder strewed upon the stairs' and while continuing the search, the tower exploded. The explosion 'blew both him and his men, with the top of the house up' leaving many 'without armes and some without legges, and others frearfull spectacles to looke upon'[53]. The Parliamentarians blamed treachery by the Royalists, but another account speaks of a 'fearfull accident' by some of the men carelessly setting the powder alight with their own muskets' match cord or their pipes during a drunken celebration. Those who knew the truth probably died in the explosion. The Royalist prisoners took advantage of the confusion in the explosion to make their escape, with the Parliamentarians keeping only six 'in hold the rest got away'[54].

The opening skirmishes of the war in Lancashire had resulted in losses on both sides and a number of prisoners. With each side unable or unwilling to think in terms of a long-drawn-out conflict, both looked to solve the prisoner problem with a number of exchanges and Bolton, being a front-line town, saw its fair share.

Some of those taken at Westhoughton were part of the prisoner exchanges organised involving Bolton for, on 27 January 1643, J. Bradshaw wrote 'the Major generall is pleased they upon the release of Peter Rylands, late Lieftenant to Captaine Browne, Phillip Norris late lieftenant to Captane Stevenson now prisoner at Boulton shallbee delivered'. The exchange was 'perfected' on 30 January.

A note on 1 February 1643 mentions sixty prisoners returned to Bolton and the following exchanges:

Thomas Seddon exchanged for John Bayliffe	Jan 31st
James Deane exch. for James Howell	Jan 30th
John Collier for Richard Rydings	Jan 22nd
James Sale for Christopher Whittle	Jan 22nd
Thomas Skellorne for James Horneby	Jan 31st
John Boardman for William Hasleden	Jan 18th".

The note also mentions a further 254 'muste goe to morrowe'.

The exchanges continued into March, for on the 1st of that month John Harpur wrote regarding Thomas Cheetham 'of Stopforth, serjeante'[55] that 'The committee at Boulton is pleased that if Thomas Cheetham now prisoner at Wigan may be released Henry Whaley now prisoner at Boulton Shalbee delivered & upon sight of the first at Boulton the other shall be sent to Wigan.'

But things did not always go smoothly, as John Harpur was yet again to write, 'Sir, Fletcher who was sent with Captain Browne to Boulton, I heare (since the writing of my last letter) is with his wife at Prestwich parish it seems he is a Knave, I pray bee pleased to release the messenger you have in Wigan detained for him & use your best means to Plague the man who hath dealt falsely with you.' It seems that Mrs Fletcher was far more formidable than either army[56].

The holding of prisoners gave a perfect excuse for a little more espionage. Edward Hulme, a Bolton Fustian weaver, was among those captured at Lowton Common and was held at Warrington. His wife, Margaret, travelled from Bolton to see him there but before she left, she was asked by Mary Morris, daughter of John Morris of Bolton, to carry a letter to Mr Wooley of Warrington. After visiting her husband, and delivering the letter, she travelled back in the company of William Aspull from Hindley, a travelling salesman known as a badger. He carried her basket on one of his pack horses and they stayed at his house at Hindley before being stopped by a Royalist patrol on Friday 13 January 1643. She was found with a letter and £100[57] on her person, so was promptly detained and taken to Wigan for interrogation by James Stanley.

She admitted taking a letter from John Morris at Bolton to Mr Wolley at Warrington but claimed she was ignorant of its contents. When asked where she obtained the money, she admitted it was from Mrs Wooley to John Morris but the contents of the letter left little doubt that her journey was not just a visit to her husband. Although the top of the letter was torn, it appeared to be addressed to Mr Morris and listed Royalist strength, morale and troop movements. The writer of the letter, presumably Wooley, admitted to almost giving away his Parliamentarian sympathies, but that 'such a suspicion is now growne upon me that I dare not be seene in any such business'. The letter also stated that he would 'provide a gyde to lead you in' in such a way that 'you may enter quickly and besides I have meanes to make way to the magazine'. Margaret Hulme's fate was sealed with the line that said he should follow any directions given by the bearer of the letter, as 'shee is free from all suspition'[58]. The fate of Margaret Hulme after the interrogation is not recorded but it is unlikely that she ever returned to Bolton or saw her husband again.

CHAPTER 5

The First Assault:
18 February 1643

The sleepy market town of Bolton had, by the 1640s, become one of the prosperous commercial centres of east Lancashire, along with Manchester, Salford and Blackburn. Nestling in the Croal River Valley on the West Pennine moors, Bolton, still known then as Bolton-le-Moors, had by that time a population of around 1,500 who lived along the four main streets emanating from the market cross in the marketplace[1]. The houses were timber-framed lath and plaster, with the odd stone or brick building, and while most were thatched, some had slate roofs. The main thoroughfare to the north was the narrow and steep Windy Bank, leading from the marketplace, down the steep embankment, over the Croal river, to the hamlet of Little Bolton and beyond[2]. The wind still whistles up that street, giving ample evidence for its name. Heading east from the market cross, and encompassing the old marketplace, is Churchgate, from the Old English word *weg,* meaning road or track, and church for the fourteenth-century St Peter's Church which stood at the end of Churchgate, on a high, steep bank over looking the Croal river. Hence, Churchgate obviously means the road that leads to the church[3]. The Croal river itself gets its name from the Old English *croh,* meaning crooked or winding, and *wella,* meaning stream, and the Croal certainly earns its name as it's a winding stream that snakes round the town on the northern side before turning south to run along the eastern side[4]. The river, and in particular its steep bank, effectively protected the settlement from attack to the north and east. Along Churchgate, as well as dwellings, were a number of public houses serving the market, including Ye Old Man and Scythe, established in the 1100s, whose landlord was James Cockerill. Cockerill also owned the Silver Well, adjacent to Silverwell field and Silverwell meadow to the south of the church, behind the pub, no doubt using the water in the brewing of his ale. On the corner of Churchgate and Bradshawgate sat another large public house, called the The Swan[5].

Leading south from the market cross is the old medieval thoroughfare of Bradshawgate. The meaning comes from 'Brad' from the Old English *brad,* meaning broad, Shaw, from the Old English word s*ceaga,* meaning a small wood or

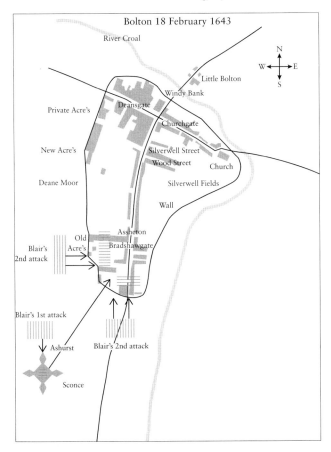

Bolton from the river, *c.* 1700.

copse and, gate, from the Old English word *weg*, meaning road or track – therefore Bradshawgate was a track into or from a small, broad wood[6]. The last main street leading west from the marketplace was a narrow lane called Deansgate, meaning a track that leads to the Deane valley[7]. At the end of Deansgate, on the edge of town, stood the great house and orchard of John Oakey[8].

After the abortive attack on Manchester in September 1642, other Parliamentary towns such as Bolton looked to their defences. Colonel Ralph Assheton of Middleton, upon his appointment as Parliamentary colonel in October 1642, ordered the garrisoning and building of the mud and chain defensive wall at defenceless Bolton.

John Rosworm, the German mercenary who had led, with Captain Bradshaw, the defence of Manchester had also, perhaps more importantly, directed the building of Manchester's defences. He would have been an ideal choice to direct the construction of the defences at Bolton and was in the area at the time. However, it is unlikely Rosworm did direct the construction of the fortifications as he was at the action at Chowbent on 24 December, and by 2 January 1643 had received a commission of lieutenant colonel to Colonel

Ralph Assheton.

Assheton. In this capacity, he was with Colonel Holland's Regiment with Sir John Seaton in the taking of Preston on 6 February and stayed to direct the building of fortifications there. His later account of his activities in the pay of Parliament makes no mention of him being in charge of the building of the defences of Bolton, and had he been there he would certainly have mentioned it. Although he was not directly responsible, he no doubt influenced the engineers that constructed Bolton's walls as they used the same mud and chain configuration Rosworm had used at Manchester[9].

The advances in the destructive power of artillery in the preceding two centuries had proved that high medieval walls made of brick and masonry were no match for the new cannons and their iron shot. However, an earthwork that could absorb the destructive power of cannon shot would be more effective and this, coupled with the haste in which the fortifications were needed, made a mud wall the best choice. The mud wall was in fact an earth bank over two yards thick (6 feet or almost 2 meters) and perhaps the same height, covered with turf to bind the earth together and limit erosion. On the top of the wall would be a wooden palisade, and perhaps horizontal storm poles, positioned to hinder anyone attempting to climb up. Outside the walls would have been a graff or ditch, which was commonly six feet broad (2 meters) and four to five feet deep (1.2 to 1.5 meters), and this would certainly have been to the west and south of town but perhaps not to the east and north, where the wall sat on the embankment above the River Croal[10].

The walls ran along the crest of the embankment of the River Croal to the north of town and followed the embankment round as it snaked southwards around the church. As the bank was so high and steep, it made sense for the wall to follow it on the crest and encompass the church, churchyard and Silverwell field and meadow. As the embankment depth lessened the further south it went on the east of town, the wall probably pulled back from the edge to line and include the back of the houses at the southern end of Bradshawgate. Turning at the end of Bradshowgate and now heading north, the wall encompassed and included the houses at the end of the road, just filling in the gaps between the buildings. However, the odd house and farm at Old Acres was too far west to be in the perimeter, as it followed the western edge of the main built-up area of town to New Acres. At New Acres, the wall turned west to encompass the end of Deansgate, ending at the house of John Oakey at Private Acres and turning north to meet up with the northern embankment of the Croal.

At each of the major thoroughfares out of Bolton, at Windy Bank, Deansgate and Bradshawgate, heavy chains were strung across the road to hinder the movement of attacking cavalry. There may have been a precipitous track down the river embankment and across the Croal east of the church, but it seems the wall ran round the bank at this point, denying easy access.

Outside the walls were three sconces. Sconces were earthwork defences, or forts, which varied in size and were either rectangular or polygonal in shape, with bastions, most likely at each corner. The bastions projected from the wall of the sconce, commanding the foreground and the outworks providing flanking fire to the adjacent walls and bastions. These fortifications, with the bastions, provided covered fire from the flanks, giving the maximum field of fire for all round defence. The sconce, or sconces, at the southern (Bradshawgate) end of town were actually described as 'a great worke'[11]. This may mean that the three sconces mentioned were part of one large defensive earthwork. The sources are not clear as to where exactly the sconce was; they merely state that it was south of the Bradshawgate end of town, within 200 yards (183 meters) of the defensive wall. The most likely position for the sconce is the higher ground where Trinity Church now stands on Crook Street. This raised position dominates the track south to Manchester and provides enfilading fire across the roads to Wigan, Westhoughton and Chorley to the west of the town – there was also 'another worke, at Hardmans, of the crosses', a location, which, thus far, has not been identified[12]. With the defences in place, Colonel Assheton garrisoned the town with the local companies of Sergeant Major Leighs, Captain Bulkley of Oldham, Captain James Schofield of Schofield Hall, Rochdale, Captain Hoult of Bury and Captain Ashurst of Radcliffe Bridge, totalling about 500 men[13]. It seems they did not have any cannon[14].

The loss of Preston had been a serious setback for the Earl of Derby and exposed the left flank of his defensive line across Lancashire. Many of the Parliamentarian troops in the attack came from Bolton and as this intelligence filtered in to the Earl of Derby at Chester, where he was planning a possible joint venture with Earl Rivers, he and his advisors saw an opportunity. If he could take Bolton which, he assumed, was denuded of the troops now at Preston, he would have a morale-boosting victory and, in addition, capture the centre of the Puritan heartland of the county. More importantly, should Bolton fall, the road to Manchester, the ultimate prize for the Royalist cause in Lancashire, would be open and a successful attack against the centre of Parliamentary strength there could well, he reasoned, secure the county for the King.

The Earl ordered his commander in Wigan, the Scot Sergeant Major General Blair to call up all able-bodied men between the ages of sixteen and sixty with a proclamation stating that they 'be and appear at the towns of Wigan upon Monday next with their beste and complete armes, weapons and habilments of Warre and likewise with provision of victuals'[15].

One of the main sources claims that Sir Gilbert Gerard commanded the force to be sent against Bolton, however this is extremely unlikely[16]. Sir Gilbert and his Regiment had marched south with the Regiments of his nephew Charles Gerard and Lord Richard Molyneux to join the King's army in time for the battle of Edgehill on 23 October 1642. Sir Gilbert and his Regiment stayed with the King's army and fought, with Lord Richard Molyneux's Regiment, in the battle of Brill on the Hill on 27 January 1643, protecting the King's

Trinity Church.

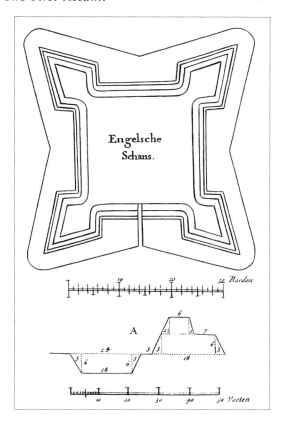

Engelsche
Schans.

A

A 1627 Sconce.

position in Oxford, and it is likely he stayed with his men in this strategic position as he was made governor of the town. A protégé of Prince Rupert, he commanded an infantry brigade at Newbury on 20 September 1643 and there is little evidence he left the King's army and returned to Lancashire in the meantime.

Sir Gilbert had a nephew by his brother Radcliffe, also called Gilbert Gerard, however this Gilbert served as a major in his uncle's Regiment and would have been with him at Brill on the Hill. It is thought he did not return to Lancashire throughout the Civil War, so it is unlikely to have been him in command[17]. The source may be referring to Sir William Gerard of Bryn, a cousin of Sir Gilbert who was known to be with Earl of Derby when he re-organised his forces on 22 December 1642, but there is no definitive evidence[18]. A different source said 'the Earles Major Generall' commanded the force and this may well refer to Sergeant Major General Blair, and he seems altogether the more likely commander of the Royalist forces[19]. The only certain fact is that the Earl of Derby did not join this attack.

The force the Royalists started to assemble to take Bolton that Monday consisted mainly of eleven colours of Foot supplemented with those men newly called up, two companies of dragoons, some under-strength troops of

Horse and a small artillery train. The Foot Regiment had somewhere between nine and eleven companies, some 800-900 men, raised mainly from the Earl of Derby's tenants and those brought in by the proclamation of Sergeant Major General Blair[20]. Some of the officers in the Royalist force included Captain Christopher Anderton of Lostock, Captain Anderton of Burchley[21], John Ashton of Penketh[22] and Hugh Houghton of Childwall House.

The two companies of dragoons were probably an *ad hoc* unit of mounted retainers of the Earl of Derby, while the troops of Horse were made up of local gentry, their servants and their tenants, perhaps as many as 180 mounted men at the most. How many cannon the Royalists had is uncertain, but there were probably one or two sakers that had a barrel of 10.5 foot (3.2 m), a calibre of 3.25 inches (8.25 cm) and fired shot weighing 5.25 lb (2.4 kg). The sakers would require three *yoak*, or pairs, of oxen or horses each to pull their 1,400 lb (635 kg) weight[23]. The Royalist force marching on Bolton numbered just over 1,000 men, perhaps a third of the total Royalist forces under arms in Lancashire at the time[24].

The Royalists left Wigan, nine boggy miles away by road, early in the morning of Thursday 16 February 1643 and approached Bolton by way of what is now Wigan Road[25], across Deane Moor by way 'of the Picks'[26]. Surprising the town's scouts, they came within a mile of the town 'about nine of the Clocke' in the morning and caught the Town garrison at prayer in the parish church[27]. Had they launched an assault immediately, it is likely they would have caught the garrison unprepared and captured the town with minimal casualties. As it was, they decided to invest the town and guided by locals, worked their way south by way of Great Lever and Bishop Bridgeman's House, an action described by a chronicler as 'fetching a compass that they may come on in a more ominous way'[28]. While the Royalist Horse and dragoons invested Bolton and the surrounding area, the companies of Foot moved to the southern end of town and formed up for the assault. While the attacking forces were making their dispositions, the Royalist saker cannons arrived and were set up on the higher ground on Deane Moor, to the south of their line of march from Wigan, overlooking the town's west and southern approaches. This was probably on what was for a time called Cannon Row, but, now known as Cannon Street, off the present Deane Road, where the remains of the earthworks for the battery could still be seen as late as the 1800s[29]. The delay in forming for the assault allowed Colonel Assheton and the garrison to man their defences at the walls and a small company of musketeers under Captain Ashurst to take post in the sconces at Crook Street. Colonel Assheton also had opportunity to send messengers to Middleton, Oldham, Rochdale and Manchester for assistance, but it would take time for these reinforcements to arrive.

The first assault by the Royalist Foot companies, supported by 'muskets and great cannon', came against the sconces, or more probably the single 'great Worke' at the Bradshawgate (southern) end of town[30]. The Royalists sent their musketeers in first, supported by cannon fire from Cannon Row. A single block of musketeers fired first with more blocks of musketeers being fed in to keep up the fire on the Sconce.

Captain Ashurst and his men resolutely held on, as the musket fire was more to break their nerve than cause casualties, and this failed to dislodge them. The attackers had no option but to assault the fortification directly, and the Royalist Foot attacked the defenders in the Sconce 'so resolutely that they beate them from their workes', forcing Captain John Ashurst and his twenty-four men defending the sconce to run with 'muche difficultie and hazard' back to the main defensive wall. Some sixty Royalists barred their retreat, and Ashurst and his men had to batter their way through with the butt end of their muskets; one solder 'thrust another through with his pike' and Ashurst dispatched 'one with his skeane'[31]. Losing a number of his men, Ashurst and his party reached the walls and threw themselves over[32].

The cannons placed at Cannon Row 'played sore' upon the walls, shooting their five and six pound shot straight through, with one shot running on and breaking a defender's leg[33]. The cannons fired at least fourteen times at the walls and the sconce during the battle, though little damage seems to have been done apart from the one broken leg already mentioned.

After taking the sconce, the Royalist Foot formed up to assault the town at its southern end on Bradshawgate, and from the south-west at Old Acres. Approaching the walls at Old Acres, the Royalists set fire to a house 'outside the chaine'[34], where the 'winde served them to carry the smoke' in among the defenders[35]. Using cover of the smoke, they approached the walls so close a defender reported that they came 'up to the mouthes of our Muskets,'[36] but the wind turned to blow the acrid fumes back at the Royalists to 'darken and smother the fire kindlers'[37]. In the smoke and confusion, the Royalists did gain access to a house that was part of the defensive wall. The house was said to have belonged to a Royalist sympathiser that let them in freely, but they may just have battered their way in[38]. Climbing to the upper floors, the windows overlooked the walls and it enabled them to fire down directly on the defenders, driving them from that part of the perimeter wall. With the wall unmanned, more attacking Royalists stormed over, led by a soldier called Rigbie who cried out, 'A Towne! a Towne!' before he was slain by the defenders[39]. Rigbie and these soldiers were probably part of Captain John Ashton of Penket's company, which led the assault. A chronicler described the fighting as 'such sharpe service for a great while together that I think has seldome beene heard of'[40]. Colonel Assheton led his men from the front, firing a musket 'with his owne hand as fast as he was able' in the fierce fighting to hold the Royalists back[41].

The house the Royalist had occupied also had a stable, which gave access behind the wall onto Bradshawgate, and the door was forced and the attackers streamed in behind the defenders standing beside Colonel Assheton[42]. The attackers could not press this advantage; as the defenders reformed to face them, they were 'so faced and feared by our men that they turned their backs and shut the doore'[43]. While this action was taking place the Royalists also got into some other houses along the row, set fire to a second house 'on the backside', possibly outside the perimeter of the walls, and then set fire to a third house and barn, where the hay sent smoke billowing across the battlefield[44].

The Parliamentarian defenders stood firm and then formed up to fight bitterly to gain control of the houses. During the close hand to hand fighting, the Royalists used a 'new invented mischievous instrument' called, contemptuously a 'Roundhead'. It was said to be 'a head about a quarter of the yard long, a staffe of two yards long or more, put into that head, twelve iron pipes round about and one in the end to stab with'[45]. Undoubtedly a local home made version of a Morning Star spiked mace, another example of the lack of weapons available to the Royalist forces of the Earl of Derby at this stage of the war.

The Royalists fired muskets from the houses they occupied into the ranks of the Parliamentarian defenders trying to batter their way back in. During this fighting for the houses, two of Captain Buckley's men of the garrison were shot dead and Sergeant Major Leigh's horse was shot from under him and killed. As he was remounted to lead his men, he was shot in the arm but continued to lead the charge to retake the houses. One of Leigh's men, named Scoles, shot and killed the two men who had wounded Leigh and his horse, and then two other Parliamentarian soldiers finally gained entrance to one of the houses, using the butt ends of their muskets to batter a way in. More of the garrison streamed into the house and, clearing it, charged on into the next where there was 'such a threshing as never was heard before' as troops fought hand to hand in the confined rooms[46]. Three times the Royalists holding on to the houses grasped the ends of the garrisons muskets in an attempt to wrench them away only for them to go off in their faces. A Parliamentary chronicler claimed, 'our men fought like lyons'[47] to drive out those Royalist troops occupying the houses on Bradshawgate. Captain John Ashurst and sixteen men, possibly the remnants of the defenders of the sconces, broke through one of the houses behind the Royalist attackers and started to volley fire into them to drive them back. They fired 'such storms of bullets into the houses as to powdered them to purpose' as the timber and plaster construction collapsed under the heavy fire of lead shot[48]. This sustained fire broke the momentum of the attack and the Royalists retreated from the walls under cover of the smoke dragging away their dead and wounded. The defenders pulled down one of the burning houses so that fire would not spread to the other buildings and started to repair and reorganise the defence.

During the assault the Royalist Horse 'prevented assistance' reaching the town from the surrounding districts as the ill-armed clubmen militia had little chance against the cavalry in the open[49]. Whenever they saw any coming to the town's aid, they rode them down and disarmed them of 'pitchforks and the like', as these were the only weapons they had[50]. The Royalist Horse went a little too far at one point as troops of Horse and what were described as Foot but were probably dragoons 'went a plundering' in Little Lever, over three miles (5 km) from Bolton, but did not stay long enough to 'do any great harme'[51]. Yet despite the cavalry roaming the area, some 1,500 clubmen militia from Middleton, Oldham, Rochdale and 200 trained soldiers from Manchester under Captain Radcliffe marched to aid the town from different points and the Royalists, 'perceiving the shouts of the country people', drew back and, putting their wounded and dying in a number of requisitioned farm carts, set about retreating wearily back to Wigan[52]. The parish church clerk, Robert Welch, wrote in the burial records that 'the Rebells of Wiggan were beaten back abowte 4 of the clock in the afternoone'[53]. The surgeons would have much work to do in Bolton and Wigan that night. The hard-fought assault on Bolton had lasted seven hours, but had failed.

Royalist casualties were undoubtedly heavy; the Parliamentarian defenders claimed over one hundred were killed, with 'two or three cartloads of dead bodies' taken back to Wigan in addition to the twelve dead and many 'others mortally wounded' left behind in the shattered houses and earthworks[54]. Among the dead carried back to Wigan was Captain John Ashton of Penket, the highest-ranking casualty of the assault. It is also claimed that a woman and child were killed in the fighting and subsequently found in one of the burnt-out houses. This would have been Alice Rothwell, daughter of Nathaniel Rothwell, who the Parish Burial Register states as being killed in the battle and was interred in the church on 17 February[55]. The Parliamentarian casualties were claimed to be very light, some 'eight or ten at the most, but never a commander'[56]. Certainly seven local men and soldiers were killed, as the Parish Burial Register records the following:

17th Feb – John Rothwell, James Coop, John Greaves, Edmund Taylor, soldiers; John Seddon, John Nuttall, Robert Dandy, yeomen and six rebelles, killed 16th.

Undoubtedly more were killed or mortally wounded in this fierce action and as many of the companies in the garrison came from elsewhere in Lancashire, they may well have carried their dead back to their home towns for burial.

The action firmly closed the back door to Manchester and the Earl of Derby soon had further bad news. The jubilant Parliamentary forces had tasted success at Preston and Houghton Tower and had repulsed the Royalist counter attack at Bolton. They now had the momentum and the men to carry on their offensive and looked towards Lancaster, hitherto safely a Royalist stronghold, as their next target.

CHAPTER 6

Struggle for Lancashire: Early 1643

With the successful defence of Bolton, the Parliamentarians decided to seize the initiative. The capture of Preston and Houghton Tower had split the Royalist forces into north Lancashire, which appears poorly garrisoned, and south-west Lancashire with the major Royalist centres of Wigan, Lathom and Warrington. Tentatively approaching Lancaster, Sergeant Major Birch and Parliamentary forces from Preston, 'finding no great opposition', entered the town and soon afterwards found that the garrison in the castle, including Sir John Girlington, had melted away[1]. The capture had expanded Parliamentarian influence over half the county, but Lancaster in particular lacked artillery.

In early March, the grounding of the *Santa Anna*, a Spanish ship from Dunkirk, at Rossall with 'twenty peeces of brasse and iron Ordnance'[2] seemed to be an answer to their prayers. Sergeant Major Sparrow and four companies set out from Preston to capture the ship and cannon but word had also reached the Earl of Derby at Lathom, who set out at the head of a troop of Horse on a similar mission.

Sergeant Major Sparrow heard of the Earl's approach while at Poulton and, unaware of the Royalist strength, sent out scouts to discover the Earl's whereabouts. By the time the Earl's troop of Horse was spotted, he had slipped past Sparrow and was riding through Layton Common, heading for the ship. Reaching the stranded vessel, the Earl realised he had neither the men nor the wagons to move the cannons and, aware of Sparrow's force in the vicinity, set the ship afire and retreated back to Lathom. Although the ship was 'burned down to the watter', the Parliamentary forces eventually succeeded in salvaging twenty-two guns, of which '8 were brass, 2 demi-cannons, one minion, five sacres'. Of the crew, the officers and ladies were carried away with Derby but the ordinary crewmen were left and 'died in the Country of extreme povertie of Body'[3].

The Earl decided that he had to reclaim Lancaster to secure north and west Lancashire and to recruit men for an eventual move on Bolton and Manchester. On 13 March, the Earl marched from Wigan at the head of 1,000 men and 'a litle piece of Ordnance'[4] and within 48 hours was at Lytham Hall. While at Lytham, the Earl summoned those in the Fylde for the King, issuing warrants for all those from sixteen to sixty 'upon payne of death' to appear at Kirkham the following morning, fully armed and ready for the King's service. The quality and willingness of their muster is questionable and two captains, John Hoole of Singleton and John Ambrose of Plumpton, were set to lead this motley addition to the Earl's forces. Although this force was sizable, with an estimated 3,000 answering the call, the majority were clubmen militia, also known as billmen, armed with whatever agricultural tools they could get. Thomas Tydlesey and Sir John Girlington brought more men, many armed with muskets, to add the Earl'~s sizable force.

Sir Thomas Tyldesley. (© National Portrait Gallery)

On 18 March, this force arrived outside Lancaster and summoned the town to surrender. The reply the Earl received was 'so slight an answer' from the Mayor that he was 'enraged to see their sauciness' and ordered an attack[5]. Sergeant Major Sparrow most likely had his four Parliamentary companies in the town and refused the summons and manned the defences. Volley after volley swept the Royalists ranks as they attacked, and it was said 'bodyes lye on heaps',[6] driving the remainder to take cover behind the hedgerows and outlying houses. Setting fire to some of the houses as cover, the Royalists attacked again and burst into the town at several points. Sparrow's men conducted a fighting retreat to the castle where Captain Richard Shuttleworth was killed right at the gates. The Royalists did not get off lightly either as William Blundell, the twenty-two-year-old Captain of the Dragoons, had his thigh shattered by a musketball. He was so badly injured, he claimed later, that he lost three inches in height and walked with a limp from then onwards[7]. In later years, Blundell was known as 'William the Cavalier'.

The victorious Royalists then set about the town, looting and killing indiscriminately with 'all barbarous crueltie'. Although it is unlikely the massacre became general, the town was certainly plundered and 'divers of the most eminent houses [and the] long street from Whitcroft was all burned'[8]. The Earl claimed that 'no woman or child suffered or any but those who did bear arms', but in the same letter admitted 'except some three of four that I think likely to be killed'[9]. No attempt was made to take the castle and discipline was lost and buildings set on fire; 'the dwelling houses that were burned were in number fourscore and ten' along with eighty-six barns, stables and outhouses[10]. This loss of control turned what should have been a victory to a strategic blunder. Word reached the Royalists that a relief force under Major General Seaton and Colonel Assheton had set out from Preston, and this news forced the Earl to withdraw.

In the failure to take the castle the Royalists had failed to secure the town and in burning a community that was in many ways neutral or indeed sympathetic to the King, the Earl had playing into the hands of his enemies. The view that the Royalists were lawless, unprincipled robbers who cared little for their friends, never mind their enemies, was burned deep by the sack of Lancaster.

The Parliamentary relief force was made up of little more than 1,000 men of eleven companies of Foot and a few Horse, who had actually mutinied against Seaton's heavy handedness a few days before. Because of this, Seaton was forced to leave behind in Preston, under Colonel Holland, four companies of Foot, 500 clubmen and a troop of Horse under Captain Duckenfield. The castle itself could not have withstood any sort of siege, so if the Earl had awaited this smaller force and met it in open battle, he could have secured a sizable victory and could have then turned his attention to securing the castle.

However, it seems the Earl had his sights set on Preston just as Seaton was intent on relieving Lancaster. Each heading the opposite way, the Earl and Seaton's forces passed within two miles of each other. The scouts would most certainly have located each army, so it seems both were avoiding battle.

The Earl's eyes were firmly on Preston and he approached during the night of 20 March, and the Parliamentarian troops' morale melted away in the darkness. Many of the locally raised forces had been for the King scant weeks before, so the staunch Parliamentarians would have been increasingly uneasy, while the townspeople who would have heard of the fate of Lancaster and would not have wanted to join their fate.

Colonel Shuttleworth thought, once again, that discretion was the better part of valour and headed off on his horse, as did many others. The Earl approached by the Fryers Gate and fired 'that little peece of Ordinance they carried with them divers times'[11] and the Royalists stormed in to little resistance, their Horse riding to the east end of Ribble Bridge to block any further escape of the defenders. Most of the town avoided being plundered, apart from the homes and shops of those, notably Edward Wearden and Henry Tailor, who had 'showed themselves favourers of the Parliament'.[12] After taking Preston, many of the Royalist clubmen were discharged to head home with their booty. The loss of Preston and the burning of Lancaster marked the end of the local Parliamentarians' belief in Major General Seaton and with the mounting disquiet of the troops in Lancaster, Sergeant Major Sparrow advised him to leave for Clitheroe, which he promptly did. Back in Manchester by 25 March, Seaton was afraid to go out of his lodgings for fear of being attacked and consequently left Lancashire while he could.

In 1643 the Royalists held Durham, Northumberland, Cumberland, Westmoreland and the Vale of York, as well as being dominant in Wales. Parliament held sway in East Anglia, the south-east and Devon, while in the Thames Valley and the Midlands both sides were striving for control. The King looked for more territory to hem in the Parliamentarians, but faced a number of new armies being raised. Sir William Waller was appointed 'Serjeant Major General' of all Parliamentary forces in the county of Gloucester with orders to raise 'Five Regiments of Horse and Five of Foot,'[13] while the Eastern Association, under the Earl of Manchester with Oliver Cromwell as his second in command, were also raising forces.

The King was hoping for more men and arms to force the issue, and one source claims that the Earl received word from the King to release the Regiments in Lancashire for service further south. Subsequent actions do not seem to support this, and perhaps this was a convenient fiction to cover the events that were to unfold in the county in 1643. The Earl would soon have a considerable force at his disposal and his campaign to dominate Lancashire was far from over.

CHAPTER 7

Stanley's Attack:
28 March 1643

James Stanley, the Earl of Derby, had assumed the leadership of the Royalists in Lancashire out of a sense of duty, honour and position. He was well read, thoughtful and of superior intelligence, but hampered by what Lord Clarenden describes as 'having lived so little among his equals that he knew not how to treat his inferiors'. He no doubt realised his lack of experience and appears to have become anxious and brooding about his limitations, particularly as the best troops and junior officers had gone south to the King. He appears not to have know how to manage men or lead his troops, and these limited leadership skills would be put to the test in the coming months – his first challenge was again at Bolton.

The forces the Earl of Derby had at his disposal for the attack on Bolton were large but varied in quality. The core of his forces were his 'regulars' of Foot and Horse Regiments such as Sir John Girlington's Foot Regiment, including Captain Thomas Greene and Ensign Bryan Burton[1]. Also he had Thomas Tyldesley's and Lord Molynuex's recently recruited weak Foot Regiments and Thomas Tyldesley's Dragoons, a combined force of perhaps 600 Foot and 400 Horse.[2] The problem was the bulk of his forces were clubmen militia, mostly from the Fylde coast, and these numbered up to 3,000.

These recruits to the clubman levies of the Earl's forces were increasingly being coerced, as the number of tenants with ties of fealty, and those committed Royalist supporters, grew thin. Many undoubtedly wanted to remain neutral and forced conscription could have the opposite effect. Adam Martindale, a nineteen-year-old from Prescot recounted that his twenty-four-year-old elder brother, Henry, 'knew not where to hide his head' from the Earl's summoning officers who required men 'upon pain of death' to appear at general musters. Henry, as well as many more 'yoeman's sons', went to shelter at Bolton to avoid the Earl's conscription and 'took up arms there'.[3] The forced conscription of these clubmen began pushing people to make a choice and some were choosing the Parliamentarian side.

The Earl's forces approached Bolton by the same boggy track they used the previous month, across Deane Moor. The only account of the action does not give any indication of the forces defending the town, other than 'most of them were townsmen', but accounts of the other assaults indicate a garrison of around

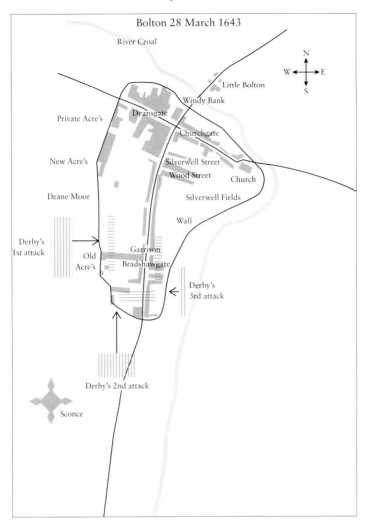

500 men and this seems to be a likely figure[4]. However, this time they did have cannon, most likely drakes or sakers, added to the defences. No mention is made of the defensive 'great worke', the sconce, at the end of Bradshawgate during this attack, so the earthworks had either been damaged beyond repair in the first assault in February or deemed to be too vulnerable a position and had been abandoned. Whatever the reason, 'the great worke' was not defended.

The Royalists did not approach close to the walls until 'three of the Clock' in the afternoon, as they began to form up into Regiments for a proposed assault on the western side of town on Deane Moor. A Parliamentarian gun crew manning a saker, placed in a 'Croft on the backside of towne', opened fire. This was most likely on the higher ground near the market cross, and its second shot killed two horses 'neare a mile off'[5]. Realising they were under cannon fire, the Royalist forces must have drawn back and decided to try negotiation.

A messenger was sent to summon the town's submission, but the defenders decided 'not to change the tenure for King and Parliament'[6] and declined to surrender. The Royalists, no doubt wary of the cannons now in the town, decided to wait until dusk, when a company of defenders were at prayer. In the fading light the Royalist Foot attacked, most likely to the south-western side of town. Adam Martindale claims that the clubman militia were forced forward first, armed with little more than pitchforks, with troopers behind with 'commission to shoot such as lagged behind'[7]. Using the cover of the fading light they 'came on desperately', some getting onto the walls and fighting hand to hand with the defenders, where a chronicler claimed 'Club-Law' reigned, before the Parliamentarians managed to repulse the attack. Pulling back, the Royalists left ten men dead behind[8].

The reinforcements for the defenders arrived from Bury while the Royalists regrouped, and these men bolstered the defence. Possibly unaware in the darkness that the defenders had been reinforced, the Royalists moved to the southern, Bradshawgate, end of town and once again moved forward. In the darkness they came up to Mud wall and set fire to some buildings on the outskirts, attempting to force the defenders back, but all this did was illuminate the battlefield and silhouette them in the flames. Under fire from the defenders and clearly out in the open, the Royalists 'fled for safetie' back into the darkness[9].

Regrouping again, the attackers marched to the east, looking to try and gain a foothold, but found it a 'busie and warm corner' and could not even get close to the walls due to musket and possibly cannon fire. Broken by this third repulse, the Royalist force pulled back into the gathering gloom and marched back towards Wigan, leaving 'upon the ground … three and twenty men'. The defenders claimed not to have lost a man, apart from 'one youth shot through the arme'[10].

The casualties appear very one sided and more would have been wounded, possibly on both sides, and the Parish Burial Register records the following:

29 March – 23 of the Earle of Darbeyes men all in one cave.
4 April 2 solders slayne
10 April Roger Dixon a soldier.

Certainly the Royalist dead were interred in a mass grave, while the others listed may well have been wounded in the attack and died later as those buried on 4 April infer they died in some sort of action.

With the repulse at Bolton, the Earl's offensive ground to a halt. Over the last few weeks he had raised an army, taken and lost Lancaster, retaken Preston and been repulsed at Bolton. With no assistance from the Royal army at Oxford, the Earl's immediate resources of men and materials has run their course and the Royalists needed time to recover.

CHAPTER 8

Brother Against Brother:
1643–1644

With the momentum of the Earl's offensive spent, the Parliamentarian forces in Manchester took the initiative. At the end of March Colonel Holland led, according to John Rosworm who joined the expedition, 2,000 Foot, 200 or 300 Horse and as many as 'eight peeces of ordnance'[1] from Manchester, heading for the Royalist stronghold of Wigan. Upwards of 500 musketeers of Colonel Assheton's men were sent to reinforce Bolton at the same time. The Parliamentary expedition reached Wigan on 1 April, where Colonel Assheton led the assault, which immediately came under cannon fire from the defenders, killing two of the attackers on the approach. Undaunted by the fire, within an hour Assheton and his men had forced entry into the town, taking many prisoners. About 100 of the defenders who had previously 'for a refuge observed and fitted the Church and Steeple' fell back into the building and fired on the attackers from there[2]. An account stated that the galling fire from the church killed 'more men, after the taking of the town, than we had lost in the whole assault'.

Royalist cavalry appeared on the scene, which the Parliamentary Horse led by Rosworm moved out to counter, and rumour spread that the Earl's forces were about to descend on the Parliamentarians still fighting in Wigan. Rosworm encountered 'three slender troops of Horse', who instantly took 'to their heels' at his approach[3].

On his return to Wigan, Rosworm states that he found Colonel Holland shaking with fear and ordering a withdrawal. Rosworm also claimed he remonstrated with Holland to attempt an assault on the church but Holland would not be swayed, so Rosworm demanded the Royalists in the church 'wholly to surrender … otherwise in one houre blowe them up'[4]. Ironically, as the main Parliamentary force under Holland was pulling out, the Royalists in the church, some eighty-six men, finally surrendered.

Rosworm was sorting out the prisoners when he realised that Holland had gone with the main body of troops, leaving him with a mere company of musketeers to guard 400 newly disarmed Royalists and a town of angry people whose homes had just been ransacked. He was then 'forced first to run to find my Horse and then to flie for my life'[5].

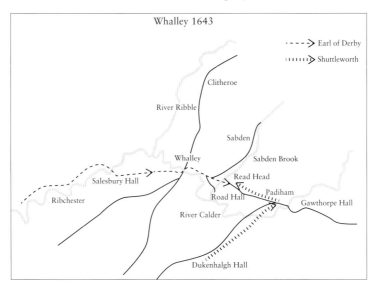

The Parliamentarians did not leave empty-handed. Meting out the same medicine as Lancaster had suffered, they sacked part of the town, carrying away 'goods to the value of twenty thousand pounds' taken from those they claimed were papists. The Cloth Hall was looted and heaps of linen, wool and fustians littered the marketplace, and the town records were scattered to the four winds. The church itself was ransacked and the records destroyed as the stalls were wrecked and the church valuables stolen.

The next Parliamentarian target was the Royalist headquarters at Warrington. Warrington's importance lay in the fact that it was the lowest point that the Mersey was bridged, and it was the Earl's headquarters. He had a garrison of 300 men, with a large proportion being Welsh[6]. Fortifications had been built on and off throughout the winter and were now quite formidable.

The Mersey, skirting the southern end of town, was spanned by a bridge with four arches and a gatehouse in the middle with an 'engine devised and placed' on the bridge to 'stop the passage over it'[7]. Earthworks ringed the town with outlying sconces possibly at Longford in the north, Mersey Mills to the south[8] and one east of the parish church. The Earl of Derby reinforced Warrington after the sack of Wigan and it is likely that Lord Molyneux's Horse Regiment, Thomas Tyldesley's Horse and Foot Regiments and an unknown number local militia Clubmen, perhaps 2,000 men in total, garrisoned the town. They may also have had up to fourteen cannon[9].

An ambitious co-ordinated plan of attack by Lancashire Parliamentarians and those from Cheshire under Sir William Brereton was put into effect. Brereton, who was related to both Colonel Holland and Colonel Assheton, was made chief of Parliamentarian forces in Cheshire in March and it was his companies, under Captain Arden of Alvanley, who first approached

St Mary and All Saints Parish Church.

All Saints Parish Church, Wigan.

Warrington from the south on 3 April. Brereton's forces are unknown for definite, but probably included his own Regiments of Foot and Horse and the Foot Regiments of Sir George Booth, Robert Duckenfield, John Leigh and Henry Mainwaring, around 2,000 men in all.

For once Derby, 'perceiving their strength to be small',[10] showed considerable tactical skill, or perhaps his officers did, and the Royalists marched out of Warrington and caught Arden and his men unprepared and attacked them at Stockton Heath. Brereton and his force arrived to join the battle, and although the Parliamentarians had lost men and Colours in the initial action, Brereton had managed to place a battery on Moot Hill, little more than a mile from the town. In 'the duske of the evening',[11] the Earl sent some of his own Royalist troops under Brereton's captured colours forward across the Mersey by the Old Latchford ford. In the gloom the Parliamentarians mistook the Royalists for their own men and moved forward to be met, and were 'charged very hotly upon' and defeated with 'great slaughter and little labour'[12].

Brereton pulled back, awaiting the Lancashire Parliamentarians coming from Wigan. Colonels Holland and Assheton, with 500 musketeers, joined Brereton and at 4 p.m. on 4 April, they 'fiercely and vyolentlye assaulted' Warrington, capturing Sankey Bridge, east of the town. The Lancashire Parliamentary troops attacked near the parish church and 'making a strong assault against it, scales some workes about it', but were forced to 'bear off' and retreat at some loss[13]. The Parliamentary troops then pulled back from Warrington 'after they had lyen against ytt three days' to regroup.

Overall the fighting had proved largely inconclusive in the early spring of 1643, with neither side achived a breakthrough. The Earl of Derby resolved to change that and set about rebuilding his forces. In mid-April a general muster of Royalist troops was called at Preston, when the Earl called to the King's colours every man he could. The Royalist force amounted to eleven troops of Horse, 700 Foot and a large contingent of clubmen, a force of at least 3,000, perhaps as many as 5,000. Led by Derby, Lord Molyneux, Sir Gilbert Houghton and Colonel Tyldesley, the army was one of the largest fielded by the Lancashire Royalists, but not the best armed, trained or disciplined.

Marching east from Preston, along the north bank of the Ribble, the Royalists reached Ribchester around noon on 19 April. Crossing the river towards Salesbury, they turned left to Whalley, 'plundering in most of the townes they passed'[14]. Two troops of Parliamentary Horse at Dukenhalgh Hall raised the alarm and fell back towards Padiham. Colonel Shuttleworth at Gawthorpe Hall heard of the approach and had a few hours grace as the Earl's army dawdled. His natural caution coming to the fore, the Earl's unwieldy and ill-disciplined force occupied Whalley, the Earl himself taking Captain Assheton's home at Whalley Abbey, while with remarkable speed Colonel Shuttleworth mustered musketeers, clubmen and cavalry of between 500 to 1,000 men in total[15]. Even this force was greatly outnumbered and should

Gawthorpe Hall.

have withdrawn from Gawthorpe Hall; indeed it appears that Shuttleworth, true to form, wanted to do just that.

His troops, however, did not. Perhaps aware of the fate their homes would have under a rampaging Royalist army of clubmen intent on plunder, they resolved to fight. The area around Read Bridge remains very much as it was in 1643, where Sabden Brook runs along a steep-sided valley. Across the bridge from Whalley, the old Roman road climbs and bends away to the left with trees and dry-stone walls hemming in the road on both sides. In the Royalist van, Colonel Thomas Tyldesley's Regiment of Horse crossed the bridge and slowly made their way up the road out of the depression, unaware they were being watched.

Tydesley stopped by Read Head, the house of Roger Nowell. Nowell had been involved in the abortive peace negations that never took place at Bolton the previous year, and had succeeded Tyldesley as lieutenant-colonel in Lord Molyneux's Foot Regiment. Stopping at the house, Tyldesley apparently asked a local woman where he was. Why he did this is uncertain and he must have known where he was, as he knew Roger Nowell well. Perhaps he wanted to engage the woman in conversation to find out where Shuttleworth's men were, who were actually hiding within earshot. The woman only said he was at Read Head and nothing else, so the disappointed Tyldesley spurred on his horse[16].

Tyldesley and his troopers continued up out of what they described as 'hollow dingle', where they were engaged by a light force of Parliamentarian

The old Roman road.

Sabden Brook.

cavalry. Seeing what they thought was a weak force ahead, Tyldesley's troopers moved forward in a tight formation along a narrow defile, right into a killing ground.

The Parliamentary musketeers had 'planted themselves in the fields' and lined the walls either side of the road 'with their muskets readie charged'[17]. A Parliamentary officer said he 'shot off my pistol' as a sign for the musketeers, who 'discharged with a great showt'. Firing at such close range, from cover behind a dry-stone wall, into the closely packed ranks of Royalist Horse meant the results were devastating. Reeling from the fire, Tyldesley's Horse broke and fled back down the hill, taking the following Foot Regiments with them. The Parliamentary musketeers, flushed with the sudden rout of Tyldesley's Horse in front of them, rushed forward, 'against all sense and reason'. What should have been a setback turned into a rout as the Earl's army melted away under the charge of the heavily outnumbered Parliamentarian musketeers. Tyldesley, separated from his men, 'for haste took the lane that leads to Mr Shutelworth's house at Ashterlee'[18] and was forced to 'leap over a yate and passed down by Partfield to Whaley'[19]. He was more fortunate than one of his captains, James Collier, who was captured. Some Royalists tried to stand but most fled, pursued by the Parliamentarians, towards Whalley. The Earl and his officers finally brought some semblance of order at Whalley, where a stand was made at the abbey, where a Royalist cannon was brought into action, firing 'twise or thrise'[20]. This cannon fire bought enough time for some of the Royalist Foot to form up near the river, and in the church and tower. This stand had hardly started when a Royalist officer was killed by a shot through the eye and the clubmen militia's shaky morale finally broke and they fled. With the army disintegrating about him, the Earl's shortcomings as a military leader were brutally exposed as he himself fled on horseback, ending up at Mr Fleetwood's house in Penwortham.

On the other hand, the Parliamentary officers were struggling to hold their men back, some wading the river with water 'to the chin' to get at the fleeing Royalists. The small Parliamentary Horse completed the rout by pursuing the fleeing Royalists though Salisbury Park and as far as Ribchester.

It is difficult to ascertain casualties as the Parliamentarians claimed 300 Royalists killed, although this certainly an overestimation. The Parliamentarian losses would have been light, but it was the psychological impact of the disintegration of the Earl's army that would resonate across the whole of Lancashire. In a few short hours, the largest army the Earl had commanded in Lancashire had for all intents and purposes fallen apart. The Earl was 'dismayed and disconsolate' and in a 'sad pensive condition by reason of the dastardlines which appeared in his Army'[21]. It would appear this depression was not only in his men but his commanders, in particular Lord Molyneux. At this critical time the leaders of the Lancashire Royalists were at breaking point, and there appears a serious split between them. Perhaps the younger

Molyneux and, possibly, Tyldesley were disdainful of Derby's lacklustre leadership, for Derby himself is apparently to have said that Lord Molyneux gave him 'as much trouble as the enemy'[22]. The Royalist Lancashire leadership appeared as fractured as their army.

Colonel Assheton and the Parliamentarian forces in Manchester soon took advantage of the defeat at Read Bridge. Two days after the battle, on 22 April 1643, he led '22 hundred horse and foot' to Wigan, where Thomas Tyldesley commanded '9 troops of Horse and 700 foot'[23]. Tyldesley's men did not stand at Wigan but withdrew to Lathom, leaving the town to be occupied by Assheton's troops, who 'demolisht all the outworks and fortifications, burnt the new gates and posts that had been set up' and set about looting whatever they could.

Tyldesley and Lord Molyneux retired on to Ormskirk, then across the Ribble northwards, crossing below Preston. Molynuex was at Clifton and Tyldesley at Kirkham, while the Earl went to York in an attempt to persuade Queen Henrietta Maria, who had landed at Bridlington in February, to support a campaign in Lancashire. The Queen had no assistance to give and Derby went back to Lancashire, and with a small entourage of horsemen 'passed by Clifton with little or no speech' to Molynuex or Tyldesley 'and so onto the North of Whitehaven and Taking shipping there to the Isle of Man'.

The battered Royalist Regiments headed out of Lancashire, with Tyldesley making for Yorkshire after refitting at Broughton-in-Furness. Tyldesley and Lord Molyneux appear to have given up on Lancashire, or perhaps they were giving up on the Earl of Derby. However, the Queens army, with the Earl of Newcastle, was marching south. Sir John Girlington's Foot remained with Newcastle's army while two small Regiments of Horse, commanded by Colonel Thomas Dalton, and Tyldesley's Foot and Horse Regiments joined the Queen's escort marching via Newark to Burton-on-Trent[24]. Here, on 2 July 1643, while Charles Cavendish led the Royalist Foot across the fords, Thomas Tyldesley charged his Regiment of Horse across the bridge of thirty-six arches, forcing entry into the town. For this gallant action he earned a knighthood and remained with the King's army fighting at Bristol, Gloucester and Newbury. Molynuex also headed south through Lancashire crossing the Mersey at Hale Ford into Cheshire.

The position for the Royalists in Lancashire worsened as the Parliamentarian forces continued their offensive. The next target was Warrington, now commanded by Colonel Edward Norris. Norris was a Catholic and had some limited experience as a captain in the trained bands of the Derby Hundred, so he must have downplayed his religion to gain this commission. Norris' Regiment was incorporated into the Welsh troops already in Warrington and his officers were probably Captain John Lancaster, and the Welshmen Captain Henry Vaughan and Drum Major Richard Roberts[25]. As Governor, Colonel Edward Norris issued a summons on 14 May for all able men 'within the age of 60 yeares and above the age of 16 yeares' to come to the town's defence 'by 9 of the clock on the 15th day of this instant May'. Ordered to appear with their 'best armes', but with the lack of proper arms and equipment, at best this would have amounted to an ill-armed militia stiffened with a few better-equipped troops. The Parliamentarians left Manchester on 20 May, meeting up with the Cheshire forces of Sir William Brereton. Creeping up to the town, the advance guard moved, under cover of a windy night, within 'half a musket shot of the town', and on the following morning of the 22nd the Parliamentary cannon outside Warrington opened up. Aiming, it seems, for the church, the cannon fire must have caused some casualties, as a number of those killed were mentioned in the parish burial records. Norris had around 1,600 men and between 10 to 14 cannon[26] available. No attempt was made to storm the town but with the casualties inflicted by the 27th, the defenders, short of supplies and learning of Fairfax's Parliamentary victory at Wakefield, destroying any hope of support, sued for terms. Surrendering early, Colonel Edward Norris managed to agree good terms, and his officers were allowed to depart with 'his horse and pistols' and his men 'to pack away unarmed, and leave al the arms, ammunition and provision behind'[27].

The virtual collapse of the Royalist cause in Lancashire had some senior Royalists calling for the removal of the Earl of Derby. His military prowess left much to be desired but his loyalty was without doubt, so the King resisted calls

Sir William Brereton.

to remove him. Perhaps there was also a little fear that if he was dismissed, his influence and support in Lancashire would be lost to the cause. In leaving for the Isle of Man, the Earl claimed he was following instructions to secure the island against the Parliamentarian navy and to guard against any rising for Parliament, but before departing Lancashire he stopped at Lathom House to leave some experienced troops and made what provision he could to defend his home.

Around this time, Colonel Alexander Rigby returned to the Preston area with a commission from Parliament to raise troops. With him he brought officers from outside the county, such as Edward Robinson who had raised a troop of horse which served with Colonel Shuttleworth[28]. In Yorkshire things were not going so well for Parliament, for on 30 June the Earl of Newcastle defeated Sir Thomas Fairfax at Adwlaton Moor. Fairfax had perhaps twelve companies of Lancashire Parliamentarians fighting in Yorkshire at the time and Adwalton was a serious set-back, and meant that Royalist Yorkshire would remain a threat to the Lancashire Parliamentarians for some time to come.

However, in Lancashire itself there was little resistance to the dominant Parliamentarian forces. Colonel Assheton marched from Lancaster with three companies to take Hornby Castle. Launching a diversionary assault on the main gate, the real assault was round the other side, aiming through some relatively undefended glass windows. A chronicler stated 'it was a great adventure the windows being very high from the ground'[29]. Caught behind as well as in front from the main gates the garrison 'speeded the cry ... for Quarter',[30] which was quickly granted and the gates opened. In the assault, which lasted two hours, the Parliamentarians claimed to have lost 'but two Common soldiers, a third dangerously wounded'[31] – the Royalist losses were not stated. Hornby Castle had fallen but Thurland Castle, a mere five miles away, held out.

Thurland Castle had been in the Girlington family since 1605, and 'Sir John, his wife and many disperat cavaliers'[32] had no intention of giving it up. In early August Colonel Alexander Rigby led a large Parliamentarian force of at least four Foot companies, including men from Bolton, 200 Horse and 'some pieces of ordnance' against Thurland. Surrounding the castle with his cannon to the east 'in a very fair plot betwixt Cansfield and it,'[33] Rigby settled in for a siege. The defenders 'shot desperately when they spyed occation' and 'killed many that aduentured to near it'[34].

Soon afterwards, Rigby learned a relief force, some '200 fire men, and the rest clubmen' commanded by Colonel Huddleston of Millom, were heading out of Cumberland, intent on lifting the siege. Leaving a small force to keep Thurland penned in, Rigby marched with '500 foot, 2 Drakes and 3 small Troopes of Horse' to meet Huddleston. The two forces met on Sunday 1 October at Lindale, some three miles from Cartmel.

The Parliamentary Horse went onto 'Lyndal cotte' and drew up facing Huddleston's Horse, who were on the top of Lyndal close. Both forces spent an hour throwing little more than insults at each other, during which time the Parliamentary Foot had marched up. The Parliamentarian troops then charged, and Rigby claims that the Royalists broke before the two forces had even come to blows, 'their foot dispersed and fled; they all trusted more to their feet than their hands'[35]. Riding down the fleeing poorly armed clubmen, the Parliamentarian troops captured Colonel Huddleston, two captains, an ensign and 400 soldiers, as well as 'four of five Ensignes of Cullers of brave silke' and one Horse colour[36]. The Royalists had a handful killed while Rigby did not lose a man.

On hearing the news, Sir Philip Musgrave, Royalist commander in Westmoreland and Cumberland, promptly surrendered Thurland Castle. Rigby had it demolished, while Sir John Girlington and his wife were fortunate to be allowed to leave for Yorkshire. The fall of Hornby and Thurland had left Lathom House the only Royalist stronghold in Lancashire and while the string of Parliamentarian victories had also freed up troops to support the cause of Parliament in Cheshire, the thorn in the side that was Lathom would soon have to be tackled.

CHAPTER 9

'A better Souldier':
The Siege of Lathom House

Lathom House, the seat of power of the Stanley family in Lancashire, originally started life as the manor house of the de Lathom family and lay approximately 3 miles (5 km) north-east of Ormskirk. However, by 1385 there was no male heir to the de Lathom estate and all their lands, power and possessions, including Lathom Hall, passed into the hands of the Stanley family through the marriage of Sir John Stanley to the heiress, Isabel de Lathom[1]. Sir John laid the foundations of the Stanley power by the adroit, and timely, transfer of loyalty to King Henry IV, for which support he was granted the Kingdom of the Isle of Man in 1405. But the true architect of the rise in power and prestige of the Stanley family was his grandson Sir Thomas, Lord Stanley.

During the dynastic civil wars between the houses of Lancaster and York known as the Wars of the Roses, Sir Thomas Stanley appears a reluctant participant throughout. The Stanleys had traditionally supported the House of Lancaster, but Sir Thomas had married the daughter of one of the leading Yorkists, Lady Margaret Bueamont, as his second wife in June 1472; thus he became Henry Tudor's stepfather, and had little desire to fight against his wife's family. He managed to steer a successful course during those troubled times, always seeming to end up with the winning side.

However, his most audacious duplicity came at the Battle of Bosworth Field in 1485, where despite solemn promises to support King Richard III, he remained resolutely on the sidelines until it was clear which side was winning, then threw in his lot with his stepson, and soon to be King, Henry Tudor. He is said to have discovered the royal crown hanging on a hawthorn bush and presented it personally to Henry Tudor. For this service, the new King Henry VII created him Earl of Derby. Despite his brother, Sir William Stanley, losing his head in February 1495 for supporting the pretender to the throne Perkin Warbeck, the Stanley family retained such power and authority as to be virtually regal in Lancashire and the Isle of Man. As such, they needed a regal residence and extensive additions and alterations were made to Lathom Hall, now also known as Lathom House, in particular for the King's visit in 1496[2]. In fact, it appears the manor house was little but a ruin prior to this, as an old ballad states:

When place, and weete, and wisdom call'd
Home this Earle to rest,
He viewed his ancient seat, and saw
The ruins of his nest,
And pulled it down, and from the ground
New builded Lathom Hall,
So spacious that it can receive
Two kings, their trains and all.

The imposing new structure was so impressive the King ordered his architects to model his palace at Richmond, then under construction, on Lathom.

It is somewhat ironic that Lathom House, so grand a King used it for a model of one of his palaces, has only the vaguest of descriptions surviving, and no original paintings or engravings[3]. However what sources that do exist, when collated, give a good idea of what the House, a fortress as well as a home, looked like. Lathom House stood on what was described as 'moorish, springy' ground in a shallow, saucer-like depression, described as being like the palm of a man's hand. Surrounded by an earthen embankment, it was set within the summit of a plateau of high ground with the ground beyond steeply sloping away[4]. It was surrounded by a strong wall thirty feet high (9.1 metres) and six feet thick (1.8 metres), with earth and sod piled up behind to deaden the effects of any shot. There were eight flanking towers, each with six 'pieces of ordinance', three facing one way and three the other. Some of the towers were named, such as the Tower at Kitchen Bridge, presumably the sally port[5], or a postern tower[6] on the north-east side of the estate, on the opposite side of the house to the gatehouse. A small tower stood next to Kitchen Tower, and next to that the larger Corner Tower, the Tower of Madness, and the Chapel Tower containing a belfry, and a small private tower. There were two smaller towers possibly as part of a turreted gatehouse, which most likely straddled the moat leading to an inner courtyard[7]. This gatehouse appears to have been a barbican, with a gate set into an arch beneath the gatehouse and built as an imposing grand entrance to the house. Lastly, towering majestically above them all, was the Eagle Tower in the middle of the house, at least four stories above, giving a total of nine towers in all[8]. Surrounding the walls was a moat 'eight yards wide and two yards deep', that is over 7 metres (24 feet) wide and 2 metres (6 feet) deep, and on the brink of the moat between it and the wall sat a strong row of wooden palisades[9]. Recent geophysics on the site estimate the internal diameter of the moat as 150 metres (490 feet), with additional defences a further 25 metres (82 feet) further out[10]. Lathom House itself was renovated when brick was in fashion for high-status buildings and the lower stories may well have been in brick rather than stone; however, the upper stories would have been of timber-framed lath and plaster, with the buildings arranged in a series of courtyards and quadrangles. The first courtyard lay within the gatehouse; the next was an inner or central court, which gave access to the Eagle Tower, and at least one was disused, in an old part of the house[11]. The main house had a Banqueting Hall, a Great Hall, domestic apartments and living quarters for the family and guests, and any number of out buildings; kitchens, storehouses, stables, sheds and at least one formal garden[12]. The house itself, being on 'moorish, springy' ground, suffered from damp. This is known because extensive Wainscot panelling was used between the skirting board and dado rails to cover the lower walls and cover the damp[13]. The impression of Lathom House is of a once grand residence, now past its best, uncomfortable and suffering from damp. The Earl of Derby, James Stanley, and Lady Charlotte certainly preferred their homes in Knowsley and the Isle of Man to it, but as a defended position it was second to none of their properties in Lancashire, and as such a powerful base for the Royalist cause.

After the fall of Warrington and the exodus of the Royalist leaders, the Earl of Derby, Sir Thomas Tyledesley and Lord Molyneux, from the county, the Parliamentarian Colonel Alexander Rigby took it upon himself to reduce the last few Royalist strongholds in Lancashire. During the summer he moved troops close to the Royalist enclaves, and was rewarded when the castles at Hornby and Thurland surrendered. Lathom ignored his presence, although the garrison was penned into the grounds of the estate apart from foraging missions, for which Rigby described them as 'a nest of brigands'[14]. Rigby's appeals to the Manchester Committee were ignored until January 1644, when Sir Thomas Fairfax came west of the Pennines to counter the threat of Royalist troops from Ireland coming ashore in Chester. That month a troop of Rigby's Horse, commanded by Captain Hindley and Lieutenant Dandy, came across a party of locals trying to smuggle provisions into Lathom House and

The most Excellent Sr Thomas Fairfax
Captin Generall of the Armyes etc

Sir Thomas Fairfax.

arrested them. Escorting their prisoners to detention, they themselves were surprised by a larger party of soldiers from the Lathom garrison who freed their prisoners and captured many troopers, the cornet and the unfortunate Lieutenant Dandy, who was wounded in the action[15].

Rigby went personally to Manchester to browbeat support. The appeal and the presence of the Northern Commander was a godsend to Colonel Holland and the Manchester Committee, and on Saturday 24 February 1644 orders were issued to Sir Thomas Fairfax, aided by Colonel Rigby, Colonel Moore of Banckhall and Colonel Assheton of Middleton, to take a force of 3,000 men and a train of artillery and seek the submission of Lathom House, by negotiation if possible, but by force if need be. Fairfax seems to have been reluctant to commit to a mission of limited military value, but he had come to aid the Lancastrian Parliamentarians and orders were orders.

Sir Thomas Fairfax was born on 17 January 1612 at Denton Hall, near Otley, into well-connected Yorkshire gentry. Tall, thin and dark, Fairfax, known as 'Black Tom', learned soldiering in the Low Countries, joining English forces under Sir Horace Vere in 1629. He earned his knighthood leading a unit of Dragoons called the Yorkshire Redcaps against the Scots in 1639–40 in the Bishops' War. At the start of hostilities in the Civil War in 1642, his father, Lord Fernando Fairfax, was appointed General of the Parliaments forces in Yorkshire, such that they were, and Sir Thomas was appointed General of the Yorkshire Horse, although due to their small number he was in effect little more than a troop commander. A gallant and courageous commander, he was

Lathom House.

routed at Seacroft Moor in March 1643, but by May had won a spectacular victory at Wakefield. Beaten again at Adwalton Moor in June 1643, the Fairfaxs retired to Hull. On the move again, Sir Thomas was at Winceby in October 1643 and in December helped recapture Gainsborough. In January 1644, he led the relief force to Nantwich to counter the Royalist reinforcements from Ireland before finding himself tasked with reducing Lathom House.

Lady Derby heard of the meeting in Manchester on the morning of Sunday the 25th and dispatched a messenger to her 'secret friend, one acquainted with the determinations'[16]. Undoubtedly there was a spy in the Parliamentary ranks sufficiently highly placed to be particularly useful to the garrison, and Lady Derby no doubt requested further information. This spy confirmed on Monday that Fairfax was already on the road by way of Bolton and Wigan, and the Parliamentary forces duly arrived before Lathom House on Tuesday 27th. They soon took the outpost at the 'The Stand', the highest point on the estate, and the Windmill[17]. Fairfax and his senior officers based themselves in Ormskirk while the army camped in the Tawd Valley, described in a journal of the siege as 'the distance of a myle – 2 or 3 att the furthest', with a forward base at New Park House, three quarters of a mile (1.2 kilometres) from Lathom[18].

The forces ranged against Lathom were substantial. Sir Thomas Fairfax was in command, assisted by the three colonels, Alexander Rigby, Ralph Assheton and John Moore. Many of the 3,000 men came from the Leyland and Amounderness Hundred, and under Rigby's command were Captain Duddell of Wood Plumpton and Captain Richard Davie of Nuton in Poulton, with most of their companies. Also in Rigby's companies were Captain William Dandie of Tarleton, with his son Lieutenant Dandie, and Major Edward Robinson[19]. One who came with Fairfax was Major Thomas Morgan, born in Lianrhymny in South Wales. In 1604, he had been with Fairfax at Nantwich and now joined him as artillery officer. Of great service to Major Morgan would be Captain William Bootle, an ex-servant at Lathom House, who knew the layout of the buildings inside the walls intimately, Captain George Sharples

Cromwell's Stone.

of Lythom and Captain John Ashurst, from Ashton Hall in Dalton, a bare two miles from Lathom House, both of whom no doubt knew the surrounding area and where to place the siege cannons to best effect. The besieging soldiers were divided into watches to be on duty every third day and night[20].

Charlotte de la Tremoille, Countess of Derby, was aged about forty-one at the time of the siege and was described as 'a well built woman having large eyes, heavy eyebrows and a prominent nose'[21]. After being raised on the continent, she probably found the provincial life as the wife of the diffident James Stanley somewhat staid and tedious and appears to have relished the challenge the siege presented.

Lady Charlotte had a small garrison at her disposal at Lathom compared to her besiegers; the odds were around ten to one against. Her principal advisors throughout the siege were her Chaplain, Reverend Samuel Rutter, and William Farrington of Worden. Reverend Samuel Rutter came from the family that owned the mill at Burscough and was a contemporary of James Stanley. He must have been a man of talent, as the Stanley family sponsored him to both Westminister School and up to Christ Church, Oxford in 1623, both well above what his family could afford. He was ordained and became the personal Chaplain to the Stanley family, and eventually personal tutor to their first born son. Portly and habitually wearing dark clothing, he looked like the cleric he was, and he played a crucial part in the early part of the siege[22].

William Farrington of Worden Hall in Leyland had been Sheriff of Lancashire in 1636 and one of the King's Commissioners of Array. His loyalty to the Crown cost him dear, as he lost his house and lands to Parliamentary sequestrators and ended up in Lathom as a refugee. His wise counsel appears to have steadied the Countess throughout the coming siege.

The Lathom House garrison comprised of 300 soldiers that consisted of a mixture of mercenaries hired as a professional defence, refugees from Parliamentary action elsewhere and the remnants of the Earl's army that he had left behind when ordered to the Isle of Man by the Queen. Of the professionals, foremost was Captain William Farmer, a Scot and veteran of the Thirty Years War described as 'long in the school of Mars' who commanded the garrison as Major of the House[23]. Five further captains were chosen of the gentlemen of the house for their 'courage and integrity'[24]. They were Henry Ogle of Whiston, Edward Chisnall of Chorley[25], Edward Rawstorne of New Hall near Preston, Molyneux Ratcliffe of Ordsall and Richard Fox of Prestwich, all of whom had most likely served previously with the Earl[26]. In addition, each chose a junior officer to be under their command and these were Lieutenants Brethergh of Childwall, Penketh of Penketh, Walton of Wigan, Key of Bury, Worral and Heap. Edward Halsall, aged only seventeen, was also there as an Ensign[27]. The watches were split so that one hundred and fifty men would be on watch every second night, apart from sixteen marksman, generally under the command of Captain Rawstorne, who manned the towers all day[28].

In addition to the soldiers, there would have been the household staff, under the Steward, Mr Broome, which could have numbered upwards of 100, of which the huntsmen and gamekeepers were particularly useful[29]. Some would be used as the marksmen in the towers with screw muskets and early rifles, which would be used to good effect to target officers and gunners of the besieging Parliamentary forces[30]. Lastly would have been the Countess and her family and household, any number of Royalist refugees from the surrounding area and an indeterminate number of dependants such as officers' and soldiers' wives and children.

The garrison had limited armaments. In addition to muskets and pikes, there were six sakers, small cannon and two sling pieces, and a wide-mouthed cannon, which fired stone rather than lead shot. For close-in defence they had a number of 'murderers', also known as swivel guns, small calibre and used to fire on attackers at very close quarters[31]. Hardly a fearsome arsenal, but the main concern was a lack of powder and shot that could cripple any defence.

Parliamentary Captain Markland arrived at the gates of Lathom House on Wednesday morning to present a copy of the Parliamentary ordinance to surrender Lathom House and a personal letter from Fairfax to Lady Derby. Lady Derby calmly read the message and played for time, asking for 'a weeks consideration both to resolve the doubt's of her conscience and seek advice'. Fairfax was no fool and rejected this request, inviting Lady Derby and her officers to New Park House to discuss the matter face to face. She declined and with more verbal sparring, suggested 'it more knightly that Sir Thomas Fairfax should wait upon me than I upon him'[32]. This continued with messages passed to and fro until Fairfax lost patience and on the evening of Friday 1 March, demanded two of his colonels have safe passage to discuss this matter directly with Lady Derby.

Thus, on Saturday 2 March colonels Rigby and Assheton and entourage walked through the gatehouse of Lathom House to find the entire garrison on parade, fully armed and manning cannon on the walls and inner courtyard. Lady Derby met them in the Great Hall in all her finery with her ladies in waiting and advisors beside her, and her two daughters at her feet.

The colonels issued Fairfax's four conditions. Firstly, she was to surrender all arms and ammunition in the house immediately to Sir Thomas Fairfax. Secondly, Lady Derby and the garrison were to leave Lathom House but were free to go to Chester or any other place in Royalist hands they so wished. Thirdly, the Countess herself could also go to Knowsley or rejoin her husband in the Isle of Man, whichever she chose, and lastly the Countess could keep her lands and revenues, subject to the approval of Parliament. She prevaricated and Rigby, not overawed by the garrison's display and with his enmity of the Stanley family evident, argued with her at length, but to no avail. The meeting ended with an agreement that she would table counter proposals the following

Monday and that although Colonel Assheton would be welcome to receive them, Rigby would not.

During these discussions, Lady Derby's Chaplain, Samuel Rutter, noticed Captain Ashurst from Ashurst Hall among the Parliamentary delegation, and it was said later they 'had not only received their education together and were not only well acquainted – but intimate and familiar with one another'[33]. Ashurst had opportunity to speak to Rutter privately and asked him why Lady Derby was so stubbornly refusing reasonable terms when she faced the overwhelming force now camped in her grounds. Rutter, either by design or just taking the opportunity that presented itself, tried an astonishing bluff. As one of Lady Derby's advisors, he knew that with odds of ten to one the garrison could not withstand a direct assault, but due to provisions already at hand, and sympathetic locals willing to smuggle goods in, they could survive a siege almost indefinitely. He decided to switch the circumstances round completely. He pointed to the assembled soldiers and cannon on view and said that Lady Derby would welcome an attack, as she knew she had the strength to defeat it, but had 'but little provision of victuals in the house'[34] and would not be able to resist more than fourteen days, for want of 'bread to supply the number of her soldiers'[35].

Monday and Tuesday slipped by in fruitless negotiation, when first Colonel Assheton and then Major Thomas Morgan tried to convince Lady Derby to accept surrender terms. A meeting was held of the Parliamentary leaders on either that Tuesday, 5 March, or the following day to decide on how to proceed. Captain Ashurst no doubt relayed the substance of his conversation with Chaplain Rutter and this probably influenced the decision to lay siege to the house rather than storm it, just as Rutter had hoped. But it would not be Sir Thomas Fairfax that led the siege, for he had been recalled to Yorkshire and it is with undoubted relief that he handed over command to Colonel Peter Egerton of Shaw.

The garrison were unaware of these developments, so their spy must have been elsewhere. Over the next three days local people, perhaps at gunpoint, were conscripted to assist the Parliamentary soldiers in digging the trenches and earthworks that would eventually surround Lathom House. The forward base was located in 'stooping declining ground', protected from gunfire from the House[36]. The likely spot is Spa Brook, where earthworks have been discovered and which could be used as a protected route to go from the main camp in the Tawn Valley to any forward positions.

On Sunday 10 March six local men of standing approached the house, asking Lady Derby to accept the terms of surrender to which she, believing it to be a Parliamentary trick, refused. Captain John Ashurst took a new set of final surrender proposals to the house on Monday 11th, which were even more favourable than before to the defenders, but they too were rejected.

So far neither side had taken any action, other than the digging of trenches, but this was to change. On Tuesday 12 March, Major Farmer and Lieutenant Brethergh of Childwell, covered by Captain Ogle and a small group of solders, led 100 men out of the main gates towards the trenches, some sixty to one hundred yards away. At the same time Lieutenant Kay led the only cavalry in the house, some twelve troopers, out the postern gate at the Kitchen Tower, covered by Captain Rawsthorne and a small party. Major Farmer's command marched unchallenged to the lip of the trench, halted and fired a volley, forcing out the Parliamentary soldiers who were probably unarmed, having stacked their weapons while digging. As they ran from this assault they were taken in the flank by Lieutenant Kay and his small band of cavalry and routed completely. The besiegers lost thirty men, forty arms and six prisoners while the garrison lost none. From these prisoners, Lady Derby learned of the success of Rutter's bluff in propagating the siege and of Fairfax's departure.

Lack of shot and powder meant the garrison could not build on this success, but had to rely on the marksmen in the towers to harass the besiegers in their trenches for the rest of the week.

The attack had unnerved the Parliamentary besiegers considerably. At 3 a.m. on the following Monday, Captain Chisnall, Lieutenants Prethergh and Heap and thirty musketeers crept out of the postern gate at the Kitchen Tower to surprise the night watch in their trenches. However, the slow-burning fuses, the slow matches, used to fire their muskets, gave them away in the dark and they were spotted. The night sentries raised the alarm and then took to their heels, running into the nearby wood faster than Chisnall and his men could follow them so, seeing his birds had flown, he returned to the house.

The besiegers redoubled their efforts on the Monday and Tuesday to complete the trenches and earthworks and mount their cannons. Casualties were mounting from marksmen in the towers, so a wooden framework on wheels that straddled the trench and had thick planks facing the walls was constructed so the work could be completed.

The completed siege works, overseen by Ribgy's engineer, a man called Browne, consisted of three concentric lines with communication trenches connecting them. The forward position was a deep, open, zigzagging trench consisting of 'a yard of ditch and a yard or raised turf' sixty yards (55 metres) from the house[37]. The next line, some one hundred yards (92 metres) from the house, consisted of a ditch three feet deep (0.9 metres) with eight sconces with six feet (1.8 m) high earthen ramparts strengthened with wicker gabions, with the ditch circling them. The final position was another hundred yards back, consisting of an earthen wall. Recent geophysical surveys suggest these siege works comprised an area over 600 metres (1,970 feet) in diameter[38].

That same Tuesday, the besiegers mounted their first cannon, to the south-west facing the main gatehouse. This was their heaviest armament, a demi-cannon and a culverin. The demi-cannon typically had a barrel 9–10 feet (2.7–3 metres) long, a calibre of 6.5 inches (16.5 cm) and fired iron shot of anything from 24 lb to 34 lb. A culverin had a longer barrel, perhaps 13.6 feet long (4.1 metres), with a smaller calibre of 5.5 inches (14 cm) and fired a smaller shot weighing anything between 8 lb to 16 lb. They also had three sakers, named after the Middle Eastern saker falcon, which had a barrel of 10.5 feet (3.2 metres), a calibre of 3.25 inches (8.25 cm) and fired shot weighing 5.25 lb (2.4 kg)[39]. Where their three sakers were placed is uncertain, as they likely moved positions throughout the siege.

The realisation was dawning on the besiegers that they had been tricked into expecting the surrender due to lack of provisions and on Wednesday 20 March the demi-cannon fired 24 lb iron shot three times at the walls. The defenders had not been idle and had strengthened the walls by building an earthen bank behind them, which meant the cannon had little effect. Seeing this, the gunners raised their aim at the turrets and pinnacles surmounting the house. Reinforcements for the besiegers were still arriving including Captain William Paterson and his company, recruited only seven weeks previously, which came in from the Fylde[40].

After this initial round of hostilities, negotiations resumed. A letter was sent into the house under a flag of truce. It was actually from the Earl of Derby to Sir Thomas Fairfax, asking him to intercede on his wife's behalf and to allow her to leave the garrison. It was essentially the Earl offering to surrender the house as long as his family gained safe passage. Lady Derby played for time once more and that night sent a messenger through the besieger's lines to her husband in Chester. The contents of this message are unknown, but can be guessed at: namely, Lady Derby was resisting the besiegers and that the matter could be left in her hands, without her husband's unwanted assistance.

Over the next four days the besiegers brought up, placed and dug in their cannon, and on Monday 25th the demi-cannon and culverin were fired seven times, their only success being a lucky ricochet breaking down the gate. The defenders rushed to barricade the remnant of the gates with furniture, beds and anything else to hand. The fact that the besiegers failed to repeat this feat and concentrate on this vulnerable spot must mean the topography of the ground shielded it from a direct shot.

Once again, the besiegers did nothing for two days, enabling the defenders to draw breath and no doubt secure the gate further. It was not until Thursday that the cannons spoke again, firing five times at the house, but something was not right, for twice that afternoon the cannons were discharged harmlessly into the air. Friday saw a change in tactics as a fierce exchange of musket fire from marksmen on the walls and those in the trenches continued most of the morning. One of the defenders, showing a little too much of himself on one of the tower walls, was shot dead[41]. In the afternoon the demi-cannon and culverin were fired four times at the small cannons mounted on the gatehouse towers, where one shot 'struck the battlements upon one of marksmen …

and crushed him to death'[42]. It seems likely the besiegers were clearing the gatehouse battlements in preparation for an assault at the smashed gate, a spot made vulnerable the previous Monday. The attack never came, for there was dissention and division in the Parliamentary ranks.

A fierce disagreement broke out in the Parliamentary leadership, with Colonel Rigby and Colonel Egerton on one side and Colonel Assheton and Colonel Moore on the other. It is not clear what it was about, but most likely it was regarding a tax being levied across the whole county to help pay for the siege. The amount was to be £4,627 6s 4d, the exact same amount that the Earl of Derby levied when he was Lord Strange for the Bishops' War in 1639. At that time, Alexander Rigby argued it was illegal and had James Stanley impeached in Parliament for attempting it. Now the shoe was on the other foot, and Assheton and Moore no doubt pointed out the hypocrisy of Rigby's position. The rift was sufficient for Assheton and Moore to stay in Ormskirk and take no further part in the direction of the siege[43]. The attempt to force the gate went with them.

At this stage the excellent information the garrison had been getting on the besiegers intentions' dried up, so it is safe to assume their spy was an officer attached to Assheton or Moore and withdrew with them to Ormskirk. Despite this loss of their primary intelligence source, information and messengers continued to pass in and out of Lathom. Reverend Rutter, not content with spreading disinformation to Captain Ashurst, organised at least one local spy. Loyalty to the Stanley family was strong and Rutter selected and persuaded a widow named Read who lived close by to carry dispatches. She would slip in and out of Lathom by making a 'private signal', which would tell the garrison to send out a small party of soldiers so she could slip in with them. She was, however, captured with dispatches 'in cipher', and according to Royalist sources was tortured with lighted matches applied to her fingers, causing three to be 'burnt off'. This poor woman died under this torture[44].

The garrison did not just have human messengers. One of the garrison, a local man, had a dog which was seen to 'go betwixt his master' at Lathom and the man's wife, three miles away. A message was sent to her that whenever the dog came home, to check around its neck to find 'a thread with a little paper wrapt about' with dispatches for the King, and to use the same method to send messages into Lathom. For some months this 'hound dog' was used to run though the besiegers' lines with dispatches tied around his neck, but this canine spy was shot by one of the sentries on one journey too many and died on reaching the gates[45].

The change in Parliamentary leadership and activity became evident, as by Sunday the demi-cannon and culverin had been remounted to fire two shots over the wall, into the upper rooms of the house. On Monday 1 April, the besiegers began to fire chain-shot and iron bars, sometimes known as hailshot, which did little damage but kept the defenders' heads down while the cannon positions outside were changed. The main change was the placing of a huge mortar, lent to the besiegers by the Cheshire Parliamentarian Sir William Brereton, to the south-west of the house. This was just beyond the ditch, at the point where the ground rose, so the battery was raised eight feet above the ditch so the gunner could see the fall of shot. Rigby had asked Brereton for the Mortar and 'half a dozen or more shells for grenadoes'. He even, optimistically, offered to return any that were unused 'at the end of the work'[46]. The short mortar, also known as a perrier, fired massive stone, or hollow explosive-filled grenades, on an indirect trajectory high over the walls to plunge down on the defenders below. The muzzle was a massive 13 inches (33 cm) and could fire stone missiles weighing 80 lbs (36.6 kg), but because it fired its shot at a lower velocity than other ordinance this used less propellant powder and this, in turn, meant the barrel could be thinner than the other cannons. Mortars were usually cast of bronze, a copper and tin alloy, but confusingly were usually referred to as 'brass'[47]. That Tuesday, the mortar fired three stone ranging shots into the house[48].

Using Wednesday to fine tune his calculations, the gunner waited until Thursday 4 April before firing another stone shot and then a grenade. The hollow grenade, being lighter than the stone shot, sailed over the house to burst harmlessly beyond but with the introduction of the mortar, the momentum of the siege swung the besiegers' way. The demi-cannon and culverin had made little impression against the 30-foot walls, and the topography prevented them getting a good shot at the walls base in any case. Sappers had attempted to undermine the walls and divert the water supply, but these attempts had also failed. But the introduction of the mortar, with its high trajectory plunging stone shot and grenades into the bowels of Lathom House, put the defenders in serious trouble. The only countermeasures the garrison could make were to have men on fire watch with untanned and dampened hides to douse any flames, but this could not hope to contain the damage of a sustained bombardment.

With the garrison at the besiegers' mercy, they now did a very strange thing. Nothing. For a whole six days nothing happened. The only explanation would be a lack of grenades; perhaps Brereton had none to supply, or perhaps the tax, which caused such disruption and ill feeling, was to pay for this ammunition. While the besiegers waited, the defenders planned an all-out attack to turn the siege back in their favour.

At eleven o'clock on the morning of Monday 10 April, they struck. Captain Farmer and Captain Molyneux Ratcliffe, supported by Lieutenants Penketh and Worrall, poured out of the postern gate at the Kitchen Tower on the north-east side of the house, leading one hundred and forty men. Captain Chisnal and his men guarded the postern gate while Captain Ogle guarded the main gate with his. Captain Rawthorne and some sixteen marksmen, the best they could muster, manned the gatehouse towers while Captain Foxe, high atop the Eagle Tower, co-ordinated the attack using signal flags. The postern gate was used yet again for this sally as the besiegers' guns opposite could not be brought to bear due to the ground and captains Farmer and Ratcliffe were able to charge the gun battery under the muzzles of the cannon and drive off the gunners with little difficulty. They then set about clearing the trenches and sconces, some men driving along the trenches in hand to hand combat while the remainder fired volley after volley into those besiegers that were driven out by their comrades below. Captain Ratcliffe, aided by just three soldiers, cleared two sconces and personally killed seven Parliamentarian soldiers. But the besieging army had started to reorganise and fifty of them attacked Lieutenant Worral, who had managed to capture a sconce by himself. He managed to hold them off until Captain Farmer and the rest of the assaulting force relieved him. Having captured their objectives, the defenders started to nail up all the cannons, that is to drive a nail with no head into the touch hole, stopping the charge being lit or, in this case at least, to drive nails into the barrel. They tried a similar tactic with the huge mortar but the mouth was too wide, so they had to settle for turning it over and trying to batter the bore out of true. Having driven off all opposition, they took the opportunity to march triumphantly round the perimeter to enter through the main gates to rousing cheers under the covering sixteen marksmen of Captain Ogle. They claimed fifty besiegers killed, captured sixty small arms, one colour and a drum, all for the loss of one mortally wounded and an indeterminate number less seriously injured. In a departure from previous raids, they only took one prisoner, an officer, as an agreement with Rigby to exchange prisoners had not been honoured by the Wigan MP. Captives had been released from Lathom but no corresponding release of Royalist prisoners elsewhere in the county had occurred. The garrison could not keep captives so had adopted a no prisoners policy, apart from those that could give them intelligence. The siege had turned ugly.

One of the besiegers' saker cannons fired twice before nightfall, but there was no disguising the extent of the defeat. It took a few days for the Parliamentarian gunners to unspike their cannon and on Friday the 12th the mortar was back in action, firing twice to no effect. A chance shot from a saker in the north-east battery penetrated Lady Derby's bedchamber but the shot was spent and caused little damage and did not 'fright her from the lodging'[49]. The demi-cannon was back in action the following day, but was only test fired to ensure that it had not been 'poisoned' during the raid, that is to say booby-trapped with an extra charge of power to burst the barrel in the gunners' faces[50].

The real bombardment commenced again on Monday 15 April, with the mortar flinging five stone missiles into the house. On its sixth shot, it fired a grenade that fell onto a walkway between the walls and the Chapel Tower. Blasting two-inch (5-cm) thick shrapnel from the casing in all directions over the whole house, it destroyed the clock on the Chapel Tower; the besiegers no longer heard its chimes[51]. The effective firing of a mortar was a skilled job. Not only did the gunner have to judge the right charge to fire the stone, or lighter grenade, into the target, he had to ensure the fuse for the explosive grenade detonated at the right time. Too early and the grenade would explode harmlessly in the air, too late and it ran the risk of defenders getting to a safe distance or actually putting out the fuse. Indeed, at Gloucester, when a Royalist grenade fell near the south gate, a woman 'with a payle of water, threw the water thereon, and extinguished the phuse thereof'[52].

If this was not enough to think about, the fact that the fuse had to be lit at the same time as the charge propelling the grenade from the mortar caused further difficulties. There were two ways of overcoming this problem. The first was to use a circular bung of wood, called a tampion, with a hole in the middle allowing the fuse to project back into the propellant powder. When the priming powder ignited the main charge, the fuse itself would be lit. The second required considerable nerve and coordination. The gunner reached in the mouth of the mortar to light the grenade fuse; once this was done he would, with the other hand, or with the help of an assistant, set off the main charge. Get this wrong, and the gunner would either fire an unlit and expensive grenade, explode the grenade in the mortar barrel, killing those close by, or lose an arm[53]. It is unknown which method the gunner at Lathom used but whichever one it was, he was beginning to get it right.

The following day, the barrage intensified with cannon fire interspersed with musket fire. At eleven o'clock the mortar dropped a stone missile into the heart of the house, followed by a grenade, which fell into an old courtyard in an older part of the house. Digging a crater 2 feet deep (60 cm), it bounced back into the air, bursting and blasting down the 'glass, clay and weaker buildings near it, leaving only the carcase of the walls standing'[54]. Two women nearby burnt their hands putting out the ensuing flames.

The besiegers once again suspended the barrage, but this time the morale of the defenders had taken a severe battering, worse than the physical damage to the house. The soldiers refused to sleep in the upper floors with walls of lath and plasterer unless the officers quartered in the stone and brick lower floors joined them[55]. The only victory for the garrison that day was when a marksman spotted one of Morgan's gunners at the mortar who had climbed too high on the rampart to see the fall of the grenade, and shot him dead.

Both sides observed a brief truce on Maundy Thursday and Good Friday. Colonel Peter Egerton was called back to Manchester around this time, leaving Alexander Rigby in sole charge of propagating the siege. His enmity for the Stanleys became evident as the intensity of the bombardment increased from Saturday 20th. The demi-cannon and culverin at the north-east battery fired thirty times in a clear attempt to batter down the walls at the Kitchen Tower, where there were no palisades[56]. As the postern gate at the Kitchen Tower had a bridge across the moat this was a sound plan, but as before, the topography ensured the cannon could not depress enough for the base of the walls to be struck and the attempt failed. It did, however, destroy the battlements and remove a yard from the top of the walls, damage the defenders repaired that night. Again, the marksman in the towers scored a hit, shooting and killing a gunner 'through the porthole', presumably a gap or loophole in the embankment to enable the gunners to see the fall of their shot[57]. That afternoon the mortar lobbed five more missiles into the house and continued after dark, firing two more stones and a grenade after last light.

The usual Sunday truce was observed, but Easter Monday was a wakes holiday for the county and local people crowded around to watch a free show. Rigby, ever the politician, put on a display with half an hour's musket fire followed by nine shots from the cannon and two stone missiles from the mortar. An eyewitness described the firing of the mortar, saying the 'stone would fly so high that almost a man could not see them and then the falling was so ponderous that they break down all where they lighted'[58]. The crowd cheered and shouted with every hit, although little real damage was done to Lathom House.

Tuesday, another holiday, brought more spectators and Rigby did his best not to disappoint them. The demi-cannon and culverin at the north-east battery, which had problems depressing their muzzles to hit the walls, had no such difficulty raising their aim to hit the Eagle Tower. Someone with intimate knowledge of the inside of the tower, probably the ex-servant, Captain William Bootle, directed fire at the weakest spot where a staircase ran up within it. A constant pounding of this spot, with some twenty-three iron shot being fired at it, created a large breach in the tower, opening up the staircase to the elements[59]. The gunners put more two more shots through the breach into Lady Derby's bedchamber, forcing her to find a bed elsewhere.

The besiegers did not have it all their own way as marksmen in the Eagle Tower picked off two gunners who were firing at them. But the barrage had done its job, not breaking the Eagle Tower, but giving those watching taxpayers forced to contribute to the siege their money's worth. Flushed with success, Rigby invited them all back that Friday, when he would level Lathom House for their amusement. Not only did he invite the locals, he also invited the Manchester Committee and all the local dignitaries to enjoy the show. He wanted as many witnesses to his moment of triumph over the Stanleys as possible.

The Stanley intelligence system continued unabated and that night two musketeers with firelocks sneaked out of the garrison, possibly to cover a messenger bringing news into the garrison. The musketeers were spotted due to their glowing slow-matches and the besiegers, thinking a large assault was underway, fired the mortar, two cannon loaded with chain shot and a hail of musket fire into the darkness to repel the non-existent attack. The following night, the night sentries in the trenches again saw slow matches glowing in the darkness, and raised the alarm amid cannon and musket fire. Once the confusion had died down, it was discovered that the slow-matches had been fixed to balls of clay and thrown out of the house, much to the sentries' chagrin. The garrison continued with this trick in various forms for the rest of the siege, always prompting a reaction, much to their amusement and embarrassment for the besiegers.

With no crowds to please on the Wednesday, Rigby's men contented themselves with firing the mortar three times and the cannon twice. A grenade from the mortar fell 'near the place where the Lady and her children, with all her commanders, were seated at dinner, shivering all the room, but hurt no body'[60]. A full supply of grenades arrived that day, and it appeared the end was in sight.

On Thursday, Rigby sent a messenger to the house demanding its unconditional surrender. In a studied insult he sent a drummer, not an officer. Lady Derby read the note, couched in no doubt arrogant terms, and called the messenger and said 'a due reward for his pains would be to be hanged from her gates', a threat that may well have resonated at Bolton within a month. Regaining her temper, she told the messenger that he was just a foolish instrument of a traitors pride and, tearing the note in two in the messengers face, told him to take this message back to Rigby. 'Tell that insolent rebel he shall have neither persons, goods, nor house. When our strength and provisions are spent, we shall find a fire more merciful than Rigby; and then, if the providence of God prevent it not, my goods and house shall burn in his sight; and myself, children, and soldiers, rather than fall into his hands will seal our religion and loyalty in the same flames'.

Her men, hearing this, took up that they would rather die for his Majesty and her honour. Cries of 'God save the King' echoed around the garrison as the messenger took the reply back[61].

Despite her open defiance, Lady Derby and the garrison were well aware of their predicament. The occasional mortar grenade had caused considerable damage and consternation bordering on panic and a sustained bombardment would surely see the fall of Lathom House. They knew from messengers and the ultimatum from Rigby that their continued defence might be counted in hours not days. It was, as the chronicler of the diary of the siege said, 'kill or be killed', and they must venture out and risk all[62]. Everyone in the garrison who could fight or be of service would take part in a desperate throw of the dice. Rigby must have known that some kind of attack was imminent, but it is not clear if the besiegers made any special arrangements. It appears they did not and Rigby, once again, shows poor military judgement.

The garrison was roused from a fitful sleep at four o'clock in the morning of Friday 26 April, well before dawn. Captains Ogle and Rawsthorne and their companies took up position to guard the main and postern gates respectively. Captain Ratcliffe and his marksmen quietly took position in the towers and gatehouse and Captain Farmer stood by with the reserve in the central courtyard to support anyone who got into difficulty. Captain Chisnall and Captain Fox divided all the remaining soldiers into two companies and made ready. Captain Chisnall and his men, including Lieutenants Brethergh and Penket, were first to move, streaming out of the postern gate and charging the battery at the north-east which held the demi-cannon. Keeping under the muzzle of the cannons, they gained the earthworks, driving out the gunners, killing many and capturing some, and secured the sconce. Fox's company, including Lieutenants Worril and Walton, also came out of the postern gate and moved through Chisnall's position and worked their way, clearing through the trenches, right round the perimeter from the east to the south-east towards the battery at the main gate[63]. This battery contained the main target, the mortar that by now was defended by fifty men, well dug in. The battery was eight feet (2.4 m) above the surrounding trenches and Fox and his men had great difficulty getting at them, resorting to throwing stones at one point, possibly as their powder and shot ran low. After fifteen minutes, desperate fighting Captain Fox and his men captured the position. He stationed a company of musketeers in the battery to defend it; at the same time, Captain Ratcliffe and his marksmen on the gatehouse spotted the Parliamentarians massing to take back the position. Musket fire from Fox's men in the battery and marksmen on the gatehouse drove off this counter attack.

The first phase of the attack had succeeded in capturing all the major earthworks of the siege lines, and Fox and Chisnall's men stood by to cover phase two. Captain Ogle and the defenders at the main gate ran out to cover Mr Broome the steward and the household staff, who streamed out with spades, shovels and pulling a low sled. Broom and the servants feverishly reduced the battery ramparts, filled in the ditch and manhandled the heavy mortar onto the sled. Covered by Captain Ogle's company and Captain Ratcliffe's marksmen, Captain Fox, Mr Broom and the soldiers and servants dragged the mortar over the filled-in ditch and through the gatehouse, the repaired great gates slamming shut behind them.

Captain Rawsthorne and his company at the postern gate then went out to aid Captain Chisnall at the north-east battery in a similar attempt to pilfer the demi-cannon and culverin. However, shielded by the wooded Tawd valley, the Parliamentarians were able to approach the captured battery under cover. Captain Rawsthorne and Captain Chisnall defended the position, but when the attack was pressed by the Parliamentarians they had not yet filled in the ditch and the heavy cannons could not be manhandled out of the earthworks in time – the demi-cannon alone could weigh up to 5,600lb (2540kg). Seeing the counter attack coming close, Rawsthorne decided to the poison the guns, roll them into the ditch and retire back to the House with Chisnall and the last of the garrison. The entire sortie lasted barely more than an hour[64]. The garrison claimed 120 besiegers killed for the loss of only two men mortally wounded, five or six injured, and five prisoners captured by Captain Chisnall, one of whom was the engineer Major Browne's assistant[65].

The mortar sat, like a slain lion, in the central courtyard amid wild celebrations of 'ale and Bagpipes'[66]. Soldiers took turns to place a foot on it like some fallen hunting trophy. Despite the cannons not having been captured, the main threat to the garrison had been removed. Lady Derby and Chaplain Rutter then led the garrison in a service of thanksgiving.

Alexander Rigby's standing was now at its lowest ebb. He had promised the Manchester Committee and local dignitaries the fall of Lathom House, and all he could show were dead and wounded, damaged siege works, his cannons nailed and his loaned mortar stolen right out from under his nose. He was said to be 'sick with shame and dishonour' and the morale of his men must have plummeted[67].

The Manchester Committee obviously now doubted Rigby would be able to reduce Lathom and withdrew all the cannon bar one, which, to keep it out of the reach of the garrison, was placed too far away to do any damage. During May, Colonel Rigby tried another strategy and had the engineer, Browne, build a sluice to attempt to tap in to the water supply and drain the moat, and also a tunnel to undermine the walls. Captain Ratcliffe's marksmen on the battlements kept the work under constant sniper fire and the sluice to the moat ran so close to the House as to be 'the death of many poor honest men'[68]. In any event, the garrison knew all about the plans, having captured one the Browne's engineers in the action of the 26 April, and dug a countermine from within the house. The never-ending rain that spring ended any tunnel work as the ground turned to mud with the consistency of porridge and the besiegers' tunnel collapsed, burying three miners alive[69].

The constant rain drenched the besiegers in the trenches and the failure of the tunnel, the loss of the mortar and the constant sniping of Ratcliffe's marksmen sapped morale. By this stage, it is likely only Rigby's companies from Aroundeness were involved in the siege as Assheton and Moore's withdrawal probably included their own men. The garrison continued with the slow match trick at night, even sending poor dogs out with lighted matches on their backs to spread alarm. In a letter to the Manchester Committee, Rigby admits to having to raise the alarm 'five or six times in one night'[70]. Rigby's poor showing as commander was never more evident and desertions increased. One even tried to join the garrison, but this was thought to be a trick by Countess Derby and his offer was declined. The other problem was pay, or lack of it, for the besiegers. Even Colonel Rigby ordering the doubling of the guard failed the stem the tide and desertions continued, and to add to Rigby's problems the tax levy, which had caused the split between the colonels, had failed. Rigby had no choice but to pay the soldiers' arrears out of this own pocket, to the tune of £2,000[71].

Rigby was called to Manchester to account for his failure to take Lathom House on 15 May, and returned on the 20th with Colonel Holland. Redundant of ideas, they drafted yet another letter to Lady Derby asking for the surrender of Lathom House. Gone was the vindictive nature of Rigby's letter of 25 April, as this note, carried by Captain Edward Moseley to the House on 23 May, contained no threats or sanctions, just a demand to surrender. Lady Derby rejected the terms, and Moseley then said she could have the terms she offered to Sir Thomas Fairfax at the start of the siege. It was a clear admission of defeat and Countess Derby and her advisors knew it. She advised Moseley that colonels Rigby and Holland should contact her husband and negotiate with him, and summarily dismissed the browbeaten captain.

The besiegers' sentries were few and far between at this stage, and that night a messenger got into the house by using a pistol to shoot the single sentry in his way. The messenger brought the news that the Earl of Derby and Prince Rupert were poised to enter Lancashire at the head of a sizable Royalist army. Relief was at hand and the siege was as good as over.

On Sunday 25 May, when the besiegers changed watch, the garrison noticed how few men the new watch had. They reasoned that morale had finally cracked in the besieging forces and Captain Ogle and Rawsthorne gathered two hundred men to attack the following morning. When first light came that Monday morning, the lookouts on the Eagle Tower reported the Parliamentary trenches were empty. Captains Ogle and Rawsthorne rode out to find the besieging army gone like thieves in the night. Lady Derby, described by her Parliamentary enemies in comparison with her husband as 'of the two a better Souldier', called for her carriage and made a triumphal inspection of the surrounding earthworks[72]. The defence of Lathom House inspired the following verse:

> Where they raised midst sap and siege
> The banners of their rightful liege
> At their she-captains call,
> Who, miracle of womankind,
> Lent mettle to the meanest hind
> That mann'd her castle wall[73]

The siege was over, but where had Colonel Rigby and his army gone?

CHAPTER 10

The Gathering Storm: Rupert's March through Lancashire, May 1644

The word that Prince Rupert was leading an army into Lancashire sent fear and trepidation throughout the whole of the Parliamentarian supporters in the county. But just who was this prince whose very name caused fear in his enemies? Prince Rupert of the Rhine was born on 18 December 1619, the son of Frederick V, elector palatine of the Rhine and his wife Elizabeth. In the political turmoil that was the Thirty Years' War, his family was exiled to the Hague in 1620 and Rupert was brought up in the court of the Prince of Orange, Frederick Henry. His elder brother drowned in 1629 and his father died just three years later, putting Rupert second in line to his elder brother Charles Lewis. The family had to rely on the largesse of the house of Orange and Elizabeth's brother, Charles I of England. Rupert grew up badly behaved, impetuous, headstrong and with a quick and ungovernable temper, earning him the nickname Robert *le diable*, Robert the devil.

He arrived in England in 1636 with his brother, and became feted everywhere, but Rupert was called back in 1637 to learn his trade as a soldier. He fought at the battle of Breda and the following year, in October 1639, with a little army of mainly English mercenaries that was overwhelmed by the Imperialist forces on the River Weser, where he was captured. He spent the next three years as a prisoner at the castle in Linz, on the Danube in Austria. He did not waste his incarceration, but used the time to study the art of war, and diplomatic moves by his uncle, Charles I of England, obtained his release in October 1641.

He arrived with his brother Maurice and a large entourage of soldiers and military experts in England in time to join his uncle, who had raised his standard at Nottingham starting the Civil War.

Due to his family ties to Charles, and despite his tender years, Prince Rupert was appointed to command of the Royalist Horse. His preferred tactic was to rely on shock, with his horsemen three ranks deep, and to charge home with sword in hand rather than halt and discharge pistols. This worked spectacularly on the slopes of Edgehill but he lost control, his Horse sweeping on the plunder of the baggage train, leaving the Royalist Foot to fight to an inconclusive standoff.

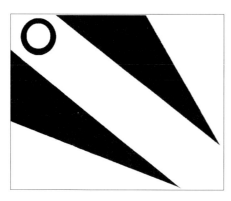

Prince Rupert's Regimental flag.

It did show that cavalry could be a war-winning arm of the army, and the Prince broke through at Brentford and threatened London. Now a new element came into play: the printed word. Widely circulated printed propaganda was a new and unfamiliar phenomenon in England, and as such had a huge impact. In pamphlets throughout the land, the Prince was portrayed as a 'Robber Prince', a foreign mercenary, the ultimate Royalist bogeyman.

While this character assassination in the Parliamentarian press continued, the Prince proved himself not only an impulsive, brilliant cavalry leader but an organised, meticulous, hard-working field officer as well. In the early months of 1642, he extended Royalist control from Oxford to the south and West Midlands and in July took Bristol for the King. At Newbury in September 1643, the Earl of Essex and the London trained bands withstood Rupert's Horse, although he retained the King's support and was raised to the peerage as Earl of Holderness and Duke of Cumberland in January 1644, which was soon ridiculed in the London pamphlets as the 'Duke of Plunderland'. Ordered to raise the siege of Newark in March 1644, with his characteristic energy he raised a scratch force from surrounding garrisons and, after a series of forced marches, surprised and attacked the besieging force of Sir John Meldrum. In the midst of the confused fighting Price Rupert was almost killed, but his forces won the day and Newark was relieved.

Word was now circulating that the Prince would be moving north, as on 18 June Colonel Ralph Assheton reported to Colonel John Moore that he had heard 'the Princes forces are joined and fear their objective may be Lancashire'. The reasons for the Prince coming to Lancashire were part of the Royalist national strategy, outlined at a conference at Abingdon in April of 1644. The King's Oxford army would remain where it was, defending what was in effect the King's capital while Prince Maurice would take Lyme. Prince Rupert would strike north with a large force to link up with the Earl of Newcastle, raise the siege of York and secure the north for the Royalist cause.

While Alexander Rigby was preoccupied at Lathom, the remainder of Lancashire was weakly garrisoned and a move into the county could win back at a stroke what had taken the Parliamentarians months to gain. In addition, the Earl of Derby appealed for assistance in lifting the siege of Lathom House so that on the way to meet the Earl of Newcastle at York the Prince would move through Lancashire, securing the strategic towns of Warrington and Liverpool as well as relieving Lathom. Also, it was hoped that in taking Lancashire and joining forces with the Earl of Newcastle, the Prince would counter any move by the Scots in the north and perhaps swing the war in the Royalists' favour.

Rupert left Oxford on 5 May and, via Worcester and Ludlow, was at Shrewsbury on 8 May when he was joined by the Chester forces under Lord Byron and his second in command Sir John Urry[1].

The army the Prince now commanded was formidable but the makeup, particularly Regiments classed by the Parliamentarians as 'Irish', would have serious repercussions at the walls of Bolton. The Royalist leadership had for some time been looking for help from English troops serving abroad, in particular those stationed in Ireland. These were a mixture of old army units and those raised and sent in 1641 and 1642 to combat the rebellion of the Irish Confederates. All had gained considerable combat experience, but before they could be released a truce with the Irish Confederates would have to be agreed. Individual officers had been filtering back to England since the summer of 1642, but negotiations with the Confederates were in full swing by 1643 and a truce, or cessation, was agreed on 15 September 1643, negotiated by the Earl of Ormonde, 1st Lord Deputy in Ireland, enabling units to be freed for service in England.

Consequently, troops began to arrive from October 1643 in England and North Wales, many of them with new native Irish recruits added to the hardened Regiments. They had to dodge the Parliamentary patrols in the Irish Sea who had no mercy for any Irish captured attempting a crossing. Brereton described the Parliamentary patrols as 'the Liverpool ships and there be 6 of them'[2]. They were armed merchantmen of some 100–200 tons, a crew of between forty and sixty and some fifteen or twenty guns. In 1644, Anthony Willoughby's Foot Regiment was intercepted as it was shipped over and at least 150 of his 400 men were captured. On 23 April seventy of these prisoners, and two women, were tied back to back and thrown overboard to drown by Captain Richard Swanley 'under the name of Irish rebels'[3]. To many Parliamentarians these Regiments, many of whom were in Prince Rupert's force, were classed as Irish irrespective of their make up, and treated with contempt as a result. The Parliamentary vessels in the Irish sea, the half a dozen armed merchantmen based at Liverpool, were effectively countered somewhat by the Royalist vessels from Dublin, the naval fifth rate named *Swan* under the command of John Bartlett and the armed merchantman *Providence* under the command of Thomas Bartlett[4]. These kept the sea lanes open for the bulk of the Irish reinforcements for Lancashire to arrive[5].

The Prince's Royalist army now consisted of a varied mix of experienced and recently raised units, some strong some relatively weak. The cavalry contingent was particularly strong, some 2,000 men, made up of the following units. Firstly, Prince Rupert's red-coated Lifeguard and Regiment, who had been raised in 1642 and numbered at most 550 men altogether, had fought under the Prince throughout the war[6]. Lord Byron's black-coated Regiment of Horse was raised in 1644; they seized Oxford and fought in many engagements including Edgehill, Roundway Down, Bristol, Gloucester, Aldbourne Chase Newbury and Middlewich[7].

Sir William Vaughan's Regiment was originally raised in 1640 as Lord Lisle's Horse and sent to Ireland in 1641. The Regiment, of some 160 men[8], landed at Chester in December 1643 and served under Lord Byron[9]. Sir John Urry's Regiment of Horse were a small unit raised in 1643 as part of the Oxford army, and had seen action at Adderbury, Aldbourne Chase, Newbury and Newark[10].

Lord Molyneux's Regiment of Horse, with his brother Caryll as lieutenant-colonel, had an uncertain beginning, but were known to be at Campden House in late 1643[11]. Sir Thomas Tyldesley's Regiment was raised in Lancashire in Christmas 1642 and, after the debacle at Whalley, had crossed the Pennines to march south with the Queen. They fought at Burton-on-Trent when Tyldesley won his knighthood at their head, and were also at Bristol and Newbury[12].

Colonel Marcus Trevor's Regiment was originally raised in 1642 in the Welsh marches by Lord Capell, and was taken over by Colonel Marcus Trevor in 1643[13]. Sir William Pelham's Regiment was raised in Lincolnshire and served in the Newark garrison, as did Colonel Rowland Eyre's Regiment, which was raised in Derbyshire in 1644 as part of Loughborough's forces[14]. Colonel John Frescheville's blue-coated Regiment of Horse was raised in Derbyshire in 1643 and was initially based at Stavely House and had fought at Newark[15]. Colonel Thomas Leveson's Regiment of Horse had been raised in 1641 as part of the garrison of Dudley Castle, and was drawn out to fight at Newark and to join the Prince's army[16].

The Foot Regiments, some 5–6,000 strong, consisted of Prince Rupert's Regiment, who had been raised in Somerset in 1642 as Sir Thomas Lunsford's Regiment. They fought at Edgehill and the storming of Bristol, after which the Prince took command. This blue-coated Regiment took part in the closing stages of the siege of Gloucester and fought at Newbury. For the forthcoming campaign Lieutenant-Colonel John Russell was in actual command[17].

Clad in coats of green, Colonel Henry Tillier's Regiment was made up of detachments from various units from Ormonde's army in Ireland such as Hunck's, Goote's, Tichbourne's, Lambert's and Borlace's. They had joined Lord Byron's forces after Nantwich and had fought at Newark[18].

Colonel Robert Broughton's Regiment was another of Ormonde's Leinster army, raised originally by William Cromwell, possibly as a Welch Regiment. This green-coated Regiment landed in North Wales in February 1644 and fought at Newark. Tillier's and Broughton's Regiments numbered together around 1,000 men[19].

Sir Michael Ernle's green-coated Regiment was raised in 1640 and sent to Ireland as the Dublin garrison in 1641. Returning the England via North Wales, they numbered some 400 men[20] and in late 1643 they fought at Bathomley and lost much of their strength at Nantwich[21].

Colonel Robert Ellis' Regiment of Foot were raised in North Wales in 1642 and served entirely in Wales before joining the Prince's army. Lord Byron's Foot Regiment was raised in Ireland for him by Colonel Thomas Napier, a professional soldier, and had previously served mainly in Cheshire[22].

Colonel Robert Byron's red-coated Foot Regiment was an Anglo-Irish Regiment raised at Drogheda, with Sir Henry Tichbourne in command and Byron as lieutenant-colonel. At the end of March 1643, Byron was ordered to raise 1,000 musketeers from various units of Ormonde's Lienster army, with the nucleus being Tichbourne's men. They arrived in North Wales in December 1643 and had fought at Barthomley, Middlewich and Nantwich[23].

Colonel Henry Warren's Regiment was originally raised in 1640 and sent to Ireland as the Lord Lieutenant's Regiment, under the command of Colonel Monck. It returned to England in late 1643 and was badly mauled at Nantwich, losing Monck in the fighting[24].

Colonel Richard Gibson's Regiment had originally been raised in 1640 by Sir Simon Harcourt and sent to Ireland in 1641. In 1642, as part of the Dublin garrison it was taken over by Richard Gibson and landed in North Wales some 700 strong[25]. After which it had fought at Hawarden and Nantwich[26].

Sir Thomas Tyldesley's red-coated Regiment of Foot was raised at Christmas 1642 in Lancashire, at the same time as Tyldesley's Horse, and were tumbled out of Preston in February 1643. After Whalley, it followed Tyldesley's Horse over the Pennines and on to fight at Burton on Trent, Gloucester and Newbury[27]. Colonel Henry Cheater's Regiment of Foot was apparently an Irish Regiment in the garrison of Bolton le dale Castle before joining the Prince's army[28]. Colonel Rowland Eyre's Regiment of Foot was a small unit raised in Derbyshire in 1644.

Colonel John Frescheville's Regiment was a small unit that was raised in the autumn of 1643 and had fought at Newark[29]. Colonel John Millward's Regiment was raised in 1644 and seems to have not seen action as yet[30]. Henry Washington's Dragoons, about 500 men in total, were raised in 1642 by Colonel James Ussher, and were taken over by Washington after Lichfield. They had served in the Oxford army in 1643 and garrisoned Evesham and Worcester before joining up with the Prince's army[31].

The colonels in the Prince's army were also a diverse group. John Byron, 1st Baron Byron, was born in 1599 at Newstead Abbey, Nottinghamshire. He attended Trinity College, Cambridge, was knighted in King Charles I's coronation honours list and sat as an MP in 1624 and 1628 for Nottinghamshire. He served a Lieutenant of the Tower of London from December 1641 to 1642 before joining the King's army as a colonel of a cavalry Regiment. He fought at Edgehill and, in the fight at Burford on 1 January 1643, was struck in the face by a halberd leaving a prominent scar on his left cheek. He commanded the Royalist cavalry on the right wing at the battle of Roundway Down and was created Baron Byron of Rochdale in October 1643, after Newbury. On Prince Rupert's recommendation he was appointed commander of Royalist forces in Cheshire, Lancashire and North Wales.

Henry Tillier was of French extraction, his family being Huguenot refugees. He was a member of the London Trained Bands, and in 1642 was an officer in the army sent to Ireland. By June of 1642, he was a major in Sir Fulk Hunck's Regiment in Dublin before raising his own Regiment for service in England.

Sir John Urry was born in Aberdeenshire and learned his trade in Germany and Flanders. He returned to Scotland in 1639 to serve as a lieutenant-colonel in the Army of the Covenant and when fighting broke out in 1642, joined the Parliamentarian army. He fought at Edgehill and Brentford and was nominated a major of Horse under the Earl of Bedford in early 1643. Apparently disappointed at what he considered this low rank he deserted to the King's army and rode with Prince Rupert at Chalgrove Field, after which he was knighted. Marcus Trevor was born in Ireland in 1618 and served as a captain in County Down in 1641 before coming to England with his Regiment after the cessation in 1643.

Lieutenant-Colonel John Russell, in command of the Prince's Foot Regiment, was born in 1620, the third son of Frances Russell, Earl of Bedford. He had served as lieutenant-colonel in Thomas Lord Wentworth's Dragoons at Marlborough in December 1642 and Cirencester in 1643. He left to take over the Prince's blue-coated Foot Regiment in the summer of 1643 and although retained his rank of lieutenant-colonel, he was de facto commander.

John Frescheville was born into the Derbyshire gentry in 1606 and had served as a cornet in the Bishops' War in 1639. He had fought with the Prince at Powick Bridge in 1642 and Newbury in 1643, where he was wounded.

On 16 May, the Prince and his army advanced north to Whitchurch, living off the land, taking resources along the way. William Davenport of Bramhall was eaten out of house and home, stating, 'besides victuals and other provisions they ate me three score bushels of oats'[32]. To add to this, no sooner had the Princes' men left, the Earl of Derby's cornet, named Lely, and twenty of his troops 'hastened their return to plunder me of my horses which the Prince had left me'[33]. Davenport, like many others, would also suffer at the hands of the Parliamentarian sequestrators for being a Royalist supporter.

Swelled by new recruits, and no doubt pressed men, the Prince's army reached Knutsford on 24 May. The Parliamentarians aimed to stop the march into Lancashire at the Mersey crossing at Stockport and mustered 3,000 men, mainly local militiamen, under colonels Henry Mainwaring and Robert Duckenfield to block the crossing.

The first Royalists on the scene were a reconnaissance force of cavalry, which were repulsed with little loss to either side. As evening drew in, about

6 p.m., the Royalist Foot Regiments were arriving and the Parliamentarians withdrew from the crossing to line the hedges with musketeers. The Prince sent 'Colonell Washington and some Dragooners to scour those hedges', which soon had the Parliamentarian musketeers 'in great affright' and they fled into the town, hotly pursued by the Prince's forces. The town soon fell, as did the Parliamentarian cannons and the way to Lancashire was open.

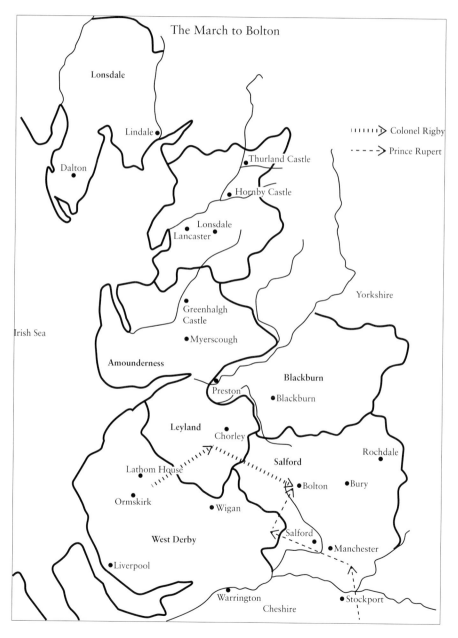

The March to Bolton. (Hundreds are shown here in bold text.)

News of the Prince's army's swift, almost contemptuous, brushing aside of the blocking forces at Stockport spread across Lancashire. On Monday the 27th, the army had reached Eccles, skirting Manchester, which was garrisoned by local forces and a Scottish Regiment under Sir John Meldrum, and the following day were heading towards Bolton. In the lead was Colonel Henry Tillier, who was scouting for supplies, and when he and his men came over the high ground of Great Lever above Bolton they were astounded to find the town teeming with Parliamentary troops.

News of the Prince's advance had reached Alexander Rigby outside Lathom on Sunday 25 May, and he made immediate plans to withdraw. It was obvious that Lathom and the besieging Parliamentary forces would be a target and Rigby and his fellow colonels were overawed at the prospect and pessimistic as to the future in Lancashire. The Parliamentary companies started to pull out immediately, the weakened numbers in the trenches being noticed by the garrison, and the last of them had left under the cover of darkness as night closed in. They split into three forces, Colonel Moore heading for Liverpool, Colonel Holland for Manchester and Alexander Rigby, with around 2,000 men of the Amounderness companies, marching the six miles to Eccleston Green, near Chorley[34], 'standing there in a great suspence which way to turn'[35]. Rigby does seem to be unsure of his next move; from Eccleston he contacted two companies of Amounderness men under Captain Pateson and Captain Swarbrick based at 'Toye House' in Preston. Twice he ordered these companies to join him and twice countermanded the decision[36]. Finally deciding on a course of action, he ordered these companies, and the fifty Royalist prisoners guarded by Roland Gaskell with them, to march to Lancaster and join Colonel Dodding in the castle there. He also sent word to his wife and family to pack up what they could and head into Yorkshire. Rigby decided that his force would be no match for the Prince's army and the likelihood of blundering into the Royalists was too much, so he headed for the nearest defended outpost – Bolton.

CHAPTER 11

Massacre:
The Storming of Bolton,
28 May 1644

Colonel Alexander Rigby and his 2,000 men of the Amounderness companies marched into Bolton early on the morning of Tuesday 28 May 1644. They were, for the most part, new recruits and no doubt dispirited at having to abandon the siege at Lathom and fearful of the future with the Prince's army in the vicinity. The town itself had a militia of around 500 men and 'Troop of horse under ye Command of one Shuttleworth'[1]. It is not clear if this was Colonel Richard Shuttleworth or his son Nicholas. Other officers mentioned in the garrison were Captain Willoughby and Captain William Bootle[2].

The Bolton clubmen militia contained most of the able-bodied men of local families. There were at least three Rothwells, three Norres, two Lightbownes, two Wights, two Cromptons and John Bradshaw, known as a gentleman so probably one of the Bradshaw's from Bradshaw Hall. Typical was the Mason family, Alexander[3], Robert and Samson all serving. Alexander was likely the eldest, with his younger brother Robert being born around 1598. Robert married Hannah in 1620 and had seven children, one of whom, Thomas, died when he was four. Samson, the eldest son, was born 10 March 1626, so two generations of the family served in the militia.

The Bolton militia would not have been particularly well armed and had a variety of weapons, including those made by Issac Crompton, a blacksmith in Churchgate who was employed 'making pikes to enable the people of Bolton to withstand interlopers who might present themselves opposing their barricades'[4]. Those barricades had seen little repair since the previous year and 'the Workes about the Towne being decayed'[5]. The sconce in particular seems to have been slighted and was in no fit state to be defended[6].

Prince Rupert was unaware of the movements of Rigby and had sent 'Col Tillyer wth a Regm^t of horse & foot' to Bolton to 'make Q[uar]ters there.'[7]

Tillier came over Slack Fold Lane to Lever Edge Lane and probably rested here, on the high ground of Great Lever Moor, which was out of sight of the town, before moving over the crest and down into the broad valley[8].

Tillier may have come in sight of the town as the last of Rigby's men were entering, as an account stated he 'found y^e Enemy there before him, getting

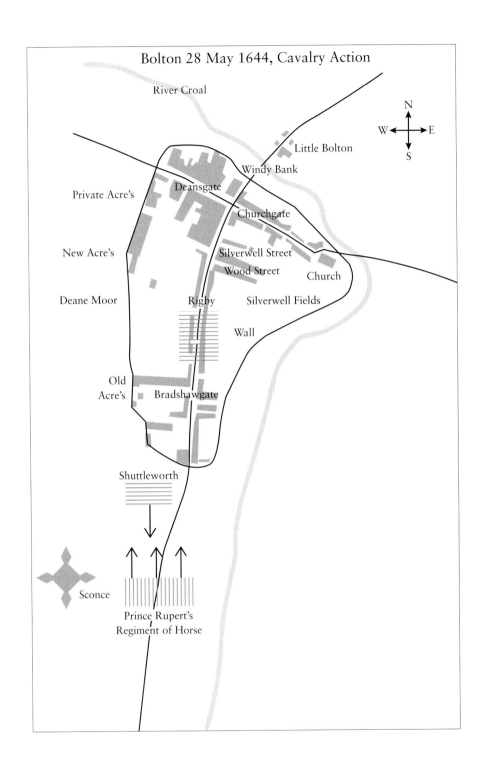

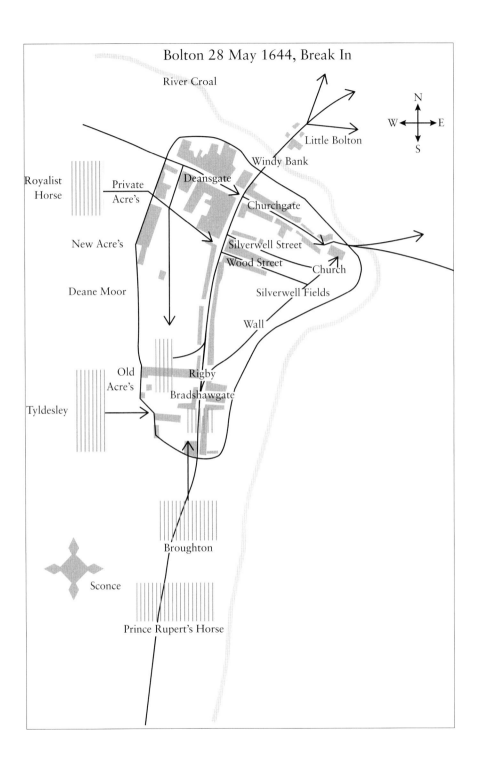

Bolton 28 May 1644, Break In

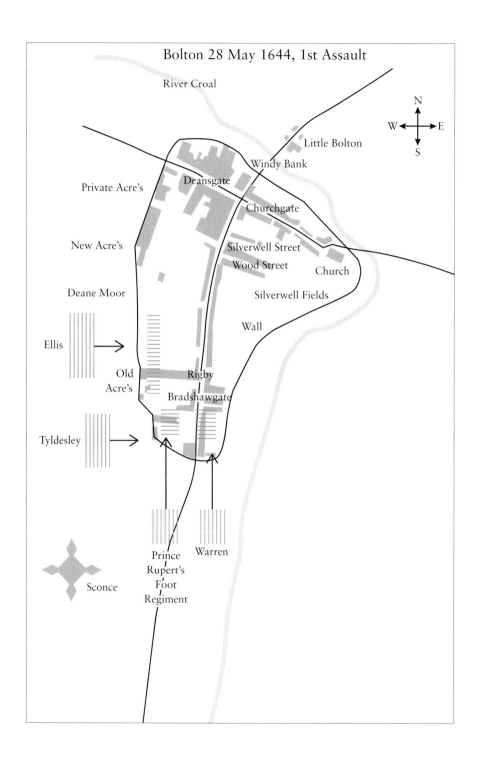

Bolton 28 May 1644, 1st Assault

Slack Fold Lane.

Prince Rupert,
Count Palatine.
(© National
Portrait Gallery)

into q^rs in disorder'[9]. Seeing the forces in the town, he immediately called for the Prince's full army to come up to join him.

At 'about two of the clocke in the afternoon', the full forces of the Prince's army came over the high ground and were 'discovered about a mile off'[10] by the town's defenders. The Prince's forces numbered upwards of 12,000 men and 'appeared at first like a wood or a cloud'[11] as they moved forward, but 'presently were cast into severall bodies, divers Scouts approached to discover the way for their entrance with most advantage.'[12]

The main body 'approaches to the Town on the More South West from the Town'[13] to the end of Bradshawgate, as the previous assaults had done for the same reason: it was the easiest approach. An account from the Prince's army described 'ye Enemy having drawen a good line round the Town wth four or five thousand men in it and a Troop of horse under ye Command of one Shuttleworth',[14] and with the sconce in disrepair 'onely gates and highwayes fortified lightly.'[15]

The Parliamentary troop of Horse under Colonel Shuttleworth 'braveringly issued out of the towne to disorder and vexe our foote in the assault'[16]. This charge was met by 'part of the Princes owne horse' which, according to the author of *A Journal of the Siege of Lathom House*, included the Earl of Derby. He was probably serving as a gentleman volunteer as the Prince had refused him a command. The same account claims 'hee chact to the very walls, where he slewe the cornett, and with his owne hand took the colours, being the first ensigne taken that day'[17]. No more is heard of Shutttleworth and the Parliamentary Horse, and they may have taken the opportunity to escape what was to follow.

With the Parliamentary Horse scattered, the main assault went in. The Prince 'attaqued ye Place' sending in four Regiments of Foot, Colonel Robert Ellis' Welshmen, Sir Thomas Tyldesley's red-coated Lancastrians', Colonel Henry Warren's Regiment from Ireland, and the Prince's own Foot Regiment under the command of Lieutenant-Colonel John Russell.

The assault troops would probably be led by firelocks and possibly dismounted dragoons with flintlock muskets, swords and grenadoes. These attackers would be backed up by matchlock-armed musketeers firing at the defences to either side of the assault, and by pikemen directly attacking the defenders as the height of the walls at Bolton were less than the length of a pike. The Regiments probably assaulted in battalion, with a centre of pike and two wings of shot and with the assault troops carrying ladders sheltered behind the pike. On braving the fire to reach the wall, the pikemen attacked the defenders to drive them back from the palisade while the musketeers fired on the defenders to the sides of the assault point. The pikemen would hope to open up a gap which the assault troops would aim for, placing their ladders against the walls. The initial assault would be with men armed with their swords and with their muskets slung on their backs. The pikemen would follow into the breach, leaning their pikes against the wall and climbing the ladders.

The pike then formed a defensive block while the remaining musketeers fired on the enemy with their muskets[18].

The Parliamentary defenders 'sore engaged stood to it manfully',[19] and 'in the first encounter gave them about halfe and hours sharpe entertainement'[20]. During the assault 'the rayne was so immoderate that it cost an howre or two dispute'[21] and the fighting was hand to hand and 'close in discharge'[22].

Colonel Robert Ellis' and Sir Thomas Tyldesley's Regiments were repulsed before the walls and Colonel Henry Warren's Regiment and the Prince's Regiment 'after entering ye Town were beaten out again'[23]. In the assault, Laurence Hardman of Buckfold was 'struck down and would have been slain … but for the timely interference of a friend name Scholefield'[24].

A Parliamentary account states that the defenders had 'repulsed them bravely to the enemies great loss and discouragement and in their retreat cut them down in great abundance, and they fell like leaves from the Tree, in a Winters morning'[25]. The Royalists reported 'of ye Ps Regt L[ieutenant]:C[olonel]: John Russell hurt, his Major a Prisoner & 300 men lost'. The Major was Dominic Mitchell[26].

At this point, the defenders, flushed with success, made a fateful error as a Royalist eyewitness reported: 'During ye time of ye Attaque they took a prison^r (an Irishman) and hung him up as an Irish papist'[27]. Reported to be an officer, this may have been Captain Gilbert Ashton, possibly of Tyldesley's Regiment, who was listed as being killed at Bolton in the *Royal Martyrs* in 1663. However, this is not certain as John Ashton was known to have been killed in the first assault on Bolton in 1643 and the two might be the same person. In any event, the cold blooded murder of the captured officer in sight of the Royalist army was an act of suicidal folly, particularly if he was a local Catholic of Tyldesley's Regiment. It is not clear who ordered this or which of the defenders carried it out, but it is unlikely to have been the local militia; Rigby and his companies were in charge. Perhaps they remembered the threat made to Rigby's messenger at Lathom a few days before, or perhaps anti-Irish feeling was just running high. Whatever the reason, the enraged Prince forbade quarter to 'any person then in Armes' and ordered Colonel Robert Broughton's green-coated Regiment and what was described in *Mercurius Aulicus* as 'the red Regiment', probably Tyldesley's, to attack again. If it was one of Tyldesley's men hanged on the walls they would have relished attacking again. At the same time, a party of Royalist horsemen rode north and 'a Townsman was their convoy to bring them through a place called the private Akers for a great reward',[28] and also at a small street called Back Acres,[29] through the defences into the town. A Parliamentary witness said 'once the horse was into the town there could be no resistance almost made but every made lest to shift for himself'[30]. Caught behind, the defenders on Bradshawgate broke and ran and 'Col. Robert Broughton's Reg^t, who being commanded on by ye P enterd ye Town and took it'[31] and 'at their entrance, before, behind, to the right, and left, nothing heard, but kill dead, kill dead'[32]. Fleeing back along Bradshawgate, many ran down Silverwell Lane, to be trapped by the wall and the steep river bank at Silverwell Fields and Bottoms. Local tradition has that a great many were killed here, with the survivors running on to the parish church.

The Earl, likely still with the Prince's Horse[33], 'following the foote at theire entrance', apparently came across Captain Bootle. Captain William Bootle, who may well have been a Bolton resident,[34] had been a porter in the Earl's service before the war and had been with Colonel Rigby outside Lathom. This is where the accounts differ on partisan lines. Royalist accounts have Bootle killed 'by his Lords hand'[35] or, having the Earl finding him in the midst of the battle, say 'I will not kill thee, but cannot save thee from others'[36]. The Parliamentary accounts have a very different story, generally mentioning him being killed 'after quarter given', and one even has Bootle captured and brought before the Earl, who 'drew upon him and run him through with his Sword, twoo men having the Prisoner by eyther Arme'[37]. The truth of Bootle's death, indeed if it was by the Earl's hand, will never be known.

The Royalist Horse from Private Acres got 'in the town killing all before them without any respect',[38] and among the fleeing defenders 'some they slashed as they were calling for quarter, others when they had given quarter'[39]. Although the defence collapsed it was not a complete rout, as a Royalist eyewitness described the Parliamentarians 'defended ye Town to ye Last wth great obstancacy',[40] and 'after ye taking of ye Town they fir'd out of their Cellars at ye Ps troops of Horse drawn up in ye markett place'[41].

Taking advantage of the confusion as the Royalists broke in, Colonel Alexander Rigby 'thrust himself' among the attacking Regiments, pretending to be one of their own. When there 'was no notice taken on him',[42] he fled down Windy Bank[43] and along Tonge Moor Road, apparently heading for the safety of Bradshaw Hall. In the rain and his fear, local tradition has it that he got lost and took the wrong road, taking the left fork onto Turton Road. When he realised his mistake he turned onto a lane, now called Rigby Lane, down to cross the Bradshaw Brook to reach Bradshaw Hall that night[44]. From there he made his way to Blackstone Edge, to take final refuge at Bradford in Yorkshire.

The pursuit of the fleeing Parliamentarians carried on 'not only in the town but some miles round, in out-houses, fields, highways, and woods',[45] and 'without the town by their horsemen pursuing the poor amazed people, killing stripping and spoiling all they could meet'[46]. This pursuit may have extended some miles from Bolton, for at the top of Black Lane in Radcliffe, some five miles from the scene of the massacre, a large number of dead were said to have been buried in one grave, called the 'gros grave', at Coggra Fold farm, and that the name Coggra meant 'great grave'[47].

The organised resistance would not have lasted long, and now 'the towne was the souldiers rewarde'[48]. Now, indiscriminate looting and killing certainly took place. A lurid early account, *An Exact Relation of the bloody and Barbarous Massacre at Boulton*, was published on 22 August 1644 and although the

Rigby Lane.

End of Rigby Lane.

Wood Street.

author is not named, it is believed to have been Reverend John Tilsley[49]. If it was Tilsley, he knew some of the people he names in the account. He talks of 'William Boulton was fetcht out of his chamber with scorn, saying they had found a praying Saint, and fetcht him to kill him before his wife's face, who being greate with childe and ready to be delivered, fell on him to have saved him, but they pulled her off without compassion, and bade him call on God to save him, whilst they cut him to pieces'[50]. This account notes attacks on women such as Elizabeth Horrocks, whose husband having been killed, was 'Tooke in a rope, and dragged her up and down ... and threatened to hang her unless she would tell them of her plate and money'[51]. It also mentions 'Alice Greg the reverend late Ministers of Bolton's widow stripped to her smock'[52] and 'Katherine Seddon an aged woman of seventy-two years old run through with a sword to the very heart because she had no money to give'[53].

One of Tildesley's majors, Hugh Anderson, claimed 'blood to the elbows'[54] and Royalists were heard 'boasting with all new coined oaths swearing how many Roundheads this sword, or they had killed that day, some eight, some six some more of less',[55] and to the survivors mocking 'where is your Roundhead God now'[56].

The scene in the marketplace on Churchgate was undoubtedly one of horror, with 'many hailed out of their houses to have their brains, dasht out in the streets, those that were not dead in the streets already, pistoled, slashed, brained or trodden under the horses feet, with many insolent blasphemous oaths curses and challenges to heaven itself' while 'armes, legs yea the brains themselves lying distant from their heads bodies and other parts[57]. Even the wounded were not spared as 'James Syddall lying wounded and dying was heard ... to give a groan'. A trooper discharged his pistol into his heart, which did not kill him so he discharged his other pistol, which finished the job. He was heard boasting 'yonder lies one of the strongest Roundheads that I ever met, for one of my pistols dischargesd at his heart would not enter, but I thinke I sent him to the Devill, with a vengeance, with the other.'[58]

Widespread looting was taking place as, under the rules of war, any town taken by storm was open to plunder by the attacking troops. Some of the soldiers 'caried away aboundnce of Cloath of all Sortes ... which served them many years after',[59] but it was not just ordinary goods plundered from Bolton as the Revd John Harpur of Halliwell reported having '4 muskets, one pistole, one rapier, one drumme, and one halberd, worth £6 6s 0d' stolen[60]. A Parliamentary witness had 'quarter given him by a Souldier that found him

Churchgate from
the church.

out, in hopes of getting his money'; later, he 'doubtless would have been slaine' but for being forced to go and 'to borrow twenty shillings more else he would leave him in the streets again and that was present death'[61]. The Prince's army is reported to have captured 'above 20 collours, 600 prisoners, 50 officers, 20 barrells of powder, match and armes a great quantity'[62].

Murder and robbery seem not to be the only outrages, as 'barbarous usage of some other maids, and wives of the town in private places, in fields and in woods'[63] took place by the rampaging Royalists.

Some accounts are undoubtedly exaggerated or totally inaccurate, such as one which added that 'four worthy divines, Mr Hayrocks, Mr Tillesley, Mr Harper and Mr Fogg' were among the victims[64]. These probably are meant to be Alexander Horrocks, Minister of Deane, John Tildesley, the pastor there, John Harper, the pastor of Bolton, and John Fogg, the pastor of Liverpool. However, all three were alive in 1649 as they all signed the *Harmonious Consent*.[65]

Despite the slaughter a large number of prisoners were taken, with accounts talking of '600 prisoners, 50 officers'[66] and another saying '700 got into ye Church and ye P gave them quarter'[67] . William Jumpe, Glover of Croston, served in Bolton as part of the company of Hugh Hyndley and was captured and put in the parish church. His friend William Hodges of Croston managed to escape the slaughter. Another captive, Captain George Sharples of Freckleton near Lythom, was dragged before Cuthbert Clifton and made to 'stand in the dirt to his knees jearing upon him to put a Psalter into his hands that he might sing them a Psalme to make them sporte'[68]. After some time he was sent with 'a Souldier to the Church where the Prisoners were'[69]. He was instead brought to a house where 'an Irishman, a Souldier and his wife quartered that night'. The next day, taken onto the moor, he managed to escape 'their cruell hands'[70]. The other prisoners were marched 'tyed twoo and twoo together and forced over Liverpoole Watter at Hales ford'[71]. The ford was so deep it was considered almost too deep 'for horses to goe'[72]. The prisoners had to wade up to their necks and some supposed their guards wanted to drown them, but one 'ould man, a Prisoner' encouraged his comrades to 'be of good chere and feare not'. Supporting each other, no prisoners were lost in the crossing and they were then separated and sent to 'Chester and some were carried to Shrewsbury and other places'[73].

Casualties are difficult to assess; the Royalists lost 300 in the first assault and perhaps the same number in the rest of the action, with 'a great many of note lie buried in the chancel of the church'[74]. Of the defenders, 'Aboundance were slayne, especially of the Amonderness Hundred'[75]. These included 'Captaine Duddell of Wood Plumpton and Captain Richard Davie of Nuton in Poulton Parish with most of their companies',[76] as well as 'Captaine William Dandie of Tarleton and his son, Lieutenant to Major Edward Robinson'[77]. Also listed as killed were Robert Robinson,[78] and Elizabeth Banester of Eccleston said her husband, John Banester, was one of those killed in Bolton[79].

Colonel Rigby himself claims he only lost 'not 200 men, nor 500 arms, the rest saving themselves by flight', but this may be an attempt to downplay the defeat. Royalist accounts talk of 'a great slaughter was made of y[e] Enemy'[80] and 'the fall of 1,000 of the Enemy in the streetes and feilds',[81] while one Parliamentary account admits to 'slaine on our side 1,200 or 1,500 in all[82]'. Some have estimated the casualties from the townspeople and militia of Bolton as around 800 out of a population of 1,588,[83] but this appears too high. Certainly the parish church records '78 of Boltonn slayne on the 28 May 1644', with Captain William Bootle and John Bradshaw among them. The list also includes Alexander and Robert Mason. This list would only mention those of the town killed and those known to the townspeople, as many others were buried elsewhere in the fields and lanes where they fell. Others would have been taken back to their own local chapels where possible or, particularly for those of Rigby's men who had arrived that morning and were not known in the town, in mass graves like the one supposed to be at Silverwell Bottoms. Another account admits that 'so many … were buried by them, partly in obscure places'[84].

Looking through the propaganda of both sides it is clear a massacre did take place which was shocking even in an increasingly bitter civil war. It affected many civilians, including women, and Thomas Malbron wrote of the storming of Bolton that 'more creweltie than there was in any place since the begynngne of the warres',[85] while the *Journal of Prince Rupert's Marches* compiled in 1648 laconically states '28 Tuesday Bolton taken by assault'[86].

Prince Rupert Public House.

CHAPTER 12

Drive to Destruction:
The First Civil War, 1644–1645

Prince Rupert moved off to Bury to meet up with Lieutenant-General George Goring with 5,000 Horse and 800 Foot on 1 June before heading back to Bolton. He sent Sir Richard Crane to Lathom House carrying the twenty-two colours captured at Bolton, many of which had flown outside Lathom during the siege, which were then hung in the Hall at Lathom in triumph. The Prince's army had moved to Wigan on 5 June and from there sent Washington and his Dragoons on towards Liverpool, his next target.

The strategic port of Liverpool, he was informed, was 'well fortified with a strong and high mud wall' and a ditch 'twelve yards wide and near three yards deep', as well as the street ends 'inclosed with strong Gates, defended by cannon'[1]. The castle, though old, still had a substantial gatehouse and round towers, and the defences were supplemented with woolsacks to give extra cover and to protect the defenders from musket fire. Any buildings outside the defences were pulled down to give a clear field of fire and deny any attacker cover.

Liverpool's main weakness was that it was overlooked by high ground to the east and, with most of west Lancashire, less than fully committed to the cause of Parliament.

The Royalist scouts appeared on Everton Heights on 6 June and surveyed the defences. Storming Bristol in similar circumstances had cost Prince Rupert dear the previous year, and with the losses at Bolton still fresh in his mind Rupert's legendary daring was tempered. Liverpool would be taken by a careful investment from trenches close to the walls rather than by storming.

The Prince set up his headquarters at the Beacon, a mile from the town, and at Colonel John Moore's house at Bank Hill[2]. Trenches were dug to cut off Liverpool to the landward side and a bombardment commenced, with the Prince deploying some sixteen cannon, including heavy culverins. Batteries were near London Road and possibly the St George's Hall area and the cannonade continued for a week, with the sappers snaking the trenches forward.

Parliamentary reinforcements tried to reach Liverpool on 8 June, but were intercepted by Goring and troops commanded by Colonel John Marrow and a number were killed and captured, including among the prisoners the Scot Major Vickerman[3].

An attempt was made on the wall when the Royalist trenches were within 'a coites cast' of the wall, which had been smashed by the cannons so that it 'almost filled the ditch with the ruines of the sod wall'. At noon on 10 June 'a furious assaulte was made' where a 'terrible fight was on both sides above the space of an houre upon the workes' before the attackers were driven off[4].

Colonel John Moore and his officers saw the writing on the wall and, on 11 June, quietly abandoned the defences and took refuge, with as much of their property as they could carry, in ships in the harbour[5]. The defences were now poorly manned, and with 'Collonell Tillyer perceivinge' the weakness was exploited under cover of darkness on the 12th when the final attack was sent in, and by the early hours it was all over. Adam Martindale claims the attackers did 'slay almost all they met with, to the numbers of three hundred and sixty'[6]. Lord Molyneux was accused of killing '7 or 8 pore men with his owne hands'[7] and was castigated with his brother, Caryll, for 'the cruelties acted here' with the worst of the killing in Old Hall Street, where the Old Hall of the Moore family was wrecked and looted and most of the buildings on Lord Street going up in flames.

Some of the defenders, possibly Scots, formed up near the High Cross, withdrew to the castle and were in a position to barter for quarter, but Colonel John Moore was not among them: his ship had slipped away. With their surrender the town was in Royalist hands.

Sir Robert Byron, brother of Lord Byron, was installed as governor and the Prince set about reinstalling a Royalist administration in Lancashire. One glaring omission from this was James Stanley. The 7th Earl of Derby does not appear to have had any role in the new county administration, nor did he gain a command in the Prince's army. Perhaps his performance at Whalley played a part, but the snub was evident and reduced the impact of any influence he still had in the county for the Royalist cause. Loyalties were parochial and with this decision the Prince had taken little account of local sensibilities.

The King wrote to the Prince on 14 June congratulating him on his whirlwind success, but reminding him of the situation at York. The contents of the letter included the phrase 'If York be lost, I shall esteem my crown little less', which seemed a clear indication to march on York but also, if the Prince could not relive the city, he was to 'immediately march with your whole strength to Worcester'. Not unreasonably the Prince undertook to march on York and at the head of a 13,000-strong army, left Liverpool on the 21st, leaving a garrison of Colonel Cuthbert Clifton's Regiment with the governor, Sir Robert Byron. At Lathom, he promoted Captain Rawsthorne to Colonel and put him in charge of Lathom as Lady Derby had already left for the Isle of Man. He also promoted Captain Chisnall to Colonel and put him in command of a newly raised Lancashire Regiment, which joined the march to York.

The Royalist army, moving via Preston, brushed aside the remaining forces of Colonel Shuttleworth and left Lancashire near Clitheroe around 24 June. With his army swelled by more recruits to around 15,000, the Prince out-manoeuvred the forces besieging York by marching from the north, via Boroghbridge, relieving the city on 1 July. Joining with the forces of the Earl of Newcastle in the city, the Prince marched out the following morning to meet the combined forces of Parliamentarians of the Army of the Eastern Association under the Earl of Manchester, the Northern Association under Lord Fairfax and the Scots under Lord Leven.

The 25,000-strong allied Parliamentarian and Scots forces took position on the low ridge overlooking Marston Moor, and the Prince's army stood and waited for much of the day while the Marquis of Newcastle's forces came out of York to join them.

The Prince had upwards of eleven Regiments who were mainly, or wholly, recruited in Lancashire and all that had stood before Bolton. The Royalist right wing, commanded by Lord Byron, had a strength of 3,000 Horse and 500 musketeers. In the front line were the Horse of Sir John Byron, Sir John Urry, Sir William Vaughan and Colonel Marcus Trevor. Lord Molyneux commanded the second line of Horse, with his Regiment and those of Sir Thomas Tyldesley, Colonel Thomas Levenson and Prince Rupert's Horse with Colonel Samuels Tuke's Regiment standing between the two lines. Sir William Vaughan and Sir Thomas Tyldesley both had small Dragoon contingents, which probably stayed with the Regiments of Horse on this wing as well as the Foot Regiments of Prince Rupert and Lord Byron.

The Royalist centre had a mixture of Horse units supporting the thin line of Foot commanded by the now Major General Henry Tillier. From right to left the front line comprised of the Regiments of Warren, Tyldesley, Broughton, Ernle, Gibson and Tillier. The second line consisted of the Regiments of Colonel Henry Cheater and the Lancashire Regiments of Colonel Edward Chisenhall and, possibly, Colonel Charles Townley with some Derbyshire Foot Regiments and the arriving Foot Regiments of Newcastle's army. In support of the Regiments in the centre stood Sir William Blakiston's Brigade of Horse.

The Royalist west wing under the command of Colonel George Goring had the Regiments of Colonel John Frecheville, Colonel Rowland Eyre and Sir Marmaduke Langdale in the front line. Colonel Francis Carnaby's Regiment and Sir Richard Dacre's Brigade of Horse supported[8]. Colonel Henry Washington's Dragoons were also on the moor but their whereabouts are less certain.

However, men from Lancashire were not solely on the Royalist side for under Fairfax, as part of the Parliamentary Army of the Northern Association, stood the Foot Regiments of Ralph Assheton, George Dodding and Alexander Rigby. These Regiments may well have been weak, but Alexander Rigby's probably had a number of men who had escaped from Bolton with a score to settle.

At 'two of the clock, the great ordnance of both sides began to play',[9] keeping up a steady bombardment across the moor until about five o'clock. According to Sir Henry Slingsby, the first shot of this cannonade killed Captain Roger Houghton, son of Sir Gilbert Houghton, and his body was taken back to York for burial before the main action had even started[10]. The Allied Parliamentary army suffered too, as Oliver Cromwell reported the death of his nephew, Captain Valentine Walton, writing to his father 'Sir, God hath taken away your eldest son by cannon shot. It broke his leg, We were necessitated to have it cut off, whereof he died'[11].

Walton's death may have precipitated the next phase of the battle, for Cromwell 'commanded two field pieces' to be brought forward, supported by two Foot Regiments, to fire on the battery that mortally wounded Walton. This action was countered by the Royalist Foot Regiments of Byron and Rupert and 'both parties seconded their foot, were wholly engaged'. With more units being drawn in, the Allied Parliamentary army, 'in its several parts moving down the hill, was like unto so many thick clouds',[12] made a general advance at about seven thirty in the evening.

Cromwell's advance on the Allied left flank was countered by Lord Byron, but a charge of Cromwell's Ironsides collapsed Byron's front line, although the second line, including Lord Molyneux and Sir Thomas Tyldesley's Horse, held firm for upwards of an hour in a furious cavalry action, an eyewitness saying they stood like an 'Iron Wall'[13]. Prince Rupert led reinforcements into the action and a wounded Cromwell left the field to have his wound

Astley Hall, Chorley. Cromwell is said to have stayed here.

dressed. A number of Scottish Horse came in to support Cromwell's Ironsides and the Royalist Horse, under severe pressure due to weight of numbers, was eventually scattered 'like a little dust'[14]. In the mêlée Prince Rupert was separated from his Lifeguard, and had to take refuge in a beanfield.

On the other flank, Goring's Horse routed Fairfax's Horse with heavy casualties and when Sir Marmaduke Langdale's brigade charged, the Allied right wing collapsed. Sir Thomas Fairfax tore off his field sign and with a few troopers fought his way over to Cromwell. In the centre the Foot Regiments were heavily engaged and a Royalist attack broke the first line of the Allied army and Fairfax's Foot Regiments, including those of Ralph Assheton, George Dodding and Alexander Rigby. Similarly, several Scots Regiments broke and ran. The Scots in the second line wavered and it seemed the Royalists were on the brink of victory as Lord Fairfax and Lord Leven left the field. But some Parliamentary Regiments, including men under the Earl of Manchester, stood firm.

Cromwell, made aware of the situation by Sir Thomas Fairfax, after beating the Prince's Horse, wheeled and crashed into the exposed flank of the Royalist Foot. Cromwell describes it as they 'beat all the Prince's horse. God made them stubble to our swords. We charged their Regiments of foot with our horse, and routed all we charged'[15]. Supporting the Earl of Manchester and the Eastern Association Foot, they systematically overran the Royalist Regiments in the centre. The Royalist line collapsed and Newcastle's whitecoat Regiment, called the Lambs because of the colour of their coats, made a heroic stand at White Dyke Close[16] and fell almost to a man covering the retreat of the remaining Royalist Foot towards York.

As the Royalist army collapsed, Sir Thomas Fairfax cried out 'spare the poor deluded countrymen … who are misled and know not what they do but slay the Irish and the buff coats and feathers, for they are the authors of your misfortune'[17]. The anti-Irish feeling was still strong, even in the midst of one of the greatest battles of the Civil War.

In two hours it was all over, and the Royalists lost 4,000 killed, some 5,000 wounded and between 1,500 and 2,000 captured with all their ordnance, powder, baggage. To add insult to injury, over 100 Royalist colours were captured.

Marston Moor was in a real sense a battle for the north, and the crushing defeat for the Prince's Royalist army turned the tide back for Parliament, particularly in Lancashire. One of the largest Royalist armies ever assembled suffered terrible losses of perhaps a quarter of its number killed, wounded and captured, many of whom were irreplaceable local leaders. It was said losses were heavy in 'old soulders and the gentry'[18]. Among those killed were Colonel Charles Townley, whose wife, Mary, was searching for her husband's corpse on the battlefield when Oliver Cromwell saw her and, fearful for her safety, had her escorted from the field[19]. Other Royalists who fell included Colonel

Henry Cheater and Major William Farmer, hero of the defence of Lathom House, who was serving in Chisenhall's Regiment[20]. Sir Thomas Tyldesley's Regiments suffered the loss of Captain Edward Bradley of Brining, Captain John Butler of Kirkland, Captain John Swinglehurst and Lieutenant William Singleton. Among those captured were Sir Charles Lucas and Major General Henry Tillier.

York's governor, Sir Thomas Glemham, did not hold out long against the victorious Allied army, surrendering on 15 July. Rupert fell back into Lancashire, arriving at Hornby on 8 July, while Lord George Goring and 2,000 of the Northern Horse struggled, via Westmoreland, into Cumberland. The Prince appears to have harboured some designs on raising troops to consolidate Lancashire for the King – but this did not last long, for on 24 July he was heading south with Lord George Goring. The remnants of the Northern Horse remained under the command of Sir Marmaduke Langdale, a forty-six-year-old Yorkshireman who was a brigade commander at Marston Moor.

Lord Byron appears to have been left in command of the remaining Royalist forces in Lancashire, centred on the strategic port of Liverpool. The Earl of Derby remained overlooked and his influence in the county waned. His exact whereabouts are uncertain at this time, but by early autumn he was certainly back in the Isle of Man, his standing at an all-time low. Lord Molyneux had with him in south-west Lancashire a few hundred cavalry survivors from Marston Moor and Sir Thomas Tyldesley had his battered Regiments of Foot and Horse billeted on the Fylde.

Sir John Meldrum, a sixty-year-old professional soldier was now senior Parliamentarian commander in Lancashire. He had a force of 1,500 Horse, 3,000 Foot and five cannon – mainly recruited from the Salford and Blackburn Hundreds, the remainder from Amounderness and a Regiment of Yorkshire Horse. He set out from Manchester on 10 August and, as the main Royalist forces fell back to the Fylde, Meldrum sent out cavalry patrols to find them. Confused fighting took place during the next five days as patrols skirmished with each other, one notable casualty being James Ogilvy, Earl of Airlie, captured with dispatches from the King to the Earl of Montrose.

Meldrum must have learnt from this skirmishing that the main Royalist forces were near Preston or on the Fylde and as such he resolved to march north to take Preston. Easily brushing aside the few defending Royalists he took Preston on 16 August. Reinforced with Booth's Foot Regiment and Colonel Doddings' Furness Horse, Meldrum set out along the north bank of the Ribble to attack the Royalists' rendezvous point at Freckleton, while he also sent the majority of his horse to Penwortham on the other side of the Ribble, perhaps as a diversion. Meldrum's main force reached Lea Hall and were surprised to learn that the Royalists were already crossing the Ribble, aiming to escape to the south. Ordering his infantry to precariously perch with

Sir John Meldrum.

his limited cavalry troopers, two to a horse, he attempted to cut the Royalists off but only managed to catch a handful at Proud Bridge, Freckleton where he exchanged shots with the Royalist rearguard. His quarry slipping away, Meldrum had little choice but to head back to Preston to cross the river there to continue the pursuit.

The Royalist forces thought they had escaped, and on 20 August were encamped in the fields south of Ormskirk. Lord Byron had ridden from Liverpool on a 'pacing nagge' to meet with Sir Marmaduke Langdale and, no doubt, Sir Thomas Tyldesley and Lord Molyneux. The Royalist forces, numbering about 2,700, were mainly Horse – apart from Tyldesley's much battered infantry – and were preparing to bed down for the night as the commanders' conference was starting.

A little before dusk, an alarm was raised in the camp that Parliamentary Horse were in nearby Ormskirk. Meldrum had marched with all possible speed to Ormskirk and was advancing on the surprised Royalists. The weary Royalist troops formed up as best they could and faced the town, where the threat seemed to be, with Lord Molyneux's Regiment in the rearguard, with Tyldesley's Foot Regiment and some dragoons, while the rest of the Royalist force attempted to retire towards Aughton Moss. However, the Parliamentary troops that poured out of Ormskirk were Booth's Foot Regiment and, catching the rearguard, fired a volley into them[21]. It is not clear, but this rearguard unit may well have been Tyldesley's Foot Regiment, who had previously robbed Halsall Church for lead for musket and pistol balls. Although they had new cast musket balls, they did not have the powder to fire them and once the Parliamentary Horse followed up Booth's volley, the Royalists broke and ran. Byron reported that the Parliamentary Horse 'stroke such a terror' into his men that they 'would not be stopped until they came to Liverpool'[22]. A Parliamentary source claims that Lord Byron and Lord Molynuex abandoned their horses and fled on foot through a cornfield, which may or may not be true, but it was claimed that the night was so dark only those on horseback could be seen while those on foot could escape[23].

Certainly the Royalists lost a considerable number, including perhaps 300 prisoners, among whom were Colonel Sir Thomas Prestwich of Hulme, Lieutenant Colonel Cottington, six captains, including Captains Anderton, Brooks and Butler of Tyldesley's Regiment, as well as six lieutenants and four cornets. Among the dead were Colonel John Haggerston, Captain Thomas Anderton and Captain Richard Walmsley[24].

The remaining Royalist forces crossed Hale ford on 21 August and Molyneux's Regiment, 'much shattered', retired to Chester, as did Sir Thomas Tyldesley[25].

Within two weeks of the rout at Ormskirk, surviving Royalists from outside the county had given up Lancashire as a lost cause and began leaving. Lord Byron stated Lancashire was 'destitute of all forces' of the King, apart from some isolated garrisons, and Marmaduke Langdale wrote that 'there was noe hope to continue in Lancashire'[26].

In the meantime, Bolton was quietly garrisoned by a Parliamentary Foot Regiment raised in Yorkshire and commanded by Colonel Francis Lascelles[27].

With the Royalist leaders, including Derby, having left the county, the surviving Royalist garrisons were in a precarious position. Leaderless and with scant hope of any reinforcements, their position was bleak. Sir John Meldrum moved against Liverpool and began digging approach trenches to the walls, with John Rosworm directing many 'divers works'. The Royalist garrison at Liverpool consisted of the remains of Lord Byron's Regiment of Foot, some of Robert Byron's Regiment together with the raw Lancashire Regiment of Cuthbert Clifton[28]. Sir John Meldrum was sure that Liverpool would capitulate soon and, when a request for help from Sir William Brereton came, he left for the Welsh border with as many of his troops as he could, leaving a small besieging force outside Liverpool. Sir John Meldrum and Sir William Brereton's joint force met the Royalists under Lord Byron at Montgomery Castle on 18 September and routed them, with Molyneux fleeing to Chester. Among the prisoners at Montgomery Castle was Sir Thomas Tyldesley, who Meldrum attempted to exchange for Colonel James Wemyss, captured in

June. Resistance to the move from the Parliamentarian Lancashire colonels, particularly Shuttleworth, put a stop to any prisoner exchange and Sir Thomas languished in Eccleshall Castle.

Meldrum was soon back at the gates of Liverpool at the end of September, issuing Sir Robert Byron a summons to surrender. He had 'much ado to bring back the Lancashire Foot'[29]. The terms were stark: on one hand, they offered free passage for soldiers of any nation, particularly aimed at the Irish troops, while on the other hand it promised 'noe other quarter' should terms be refused[30]. Given the recent events at Bolton, this appears no idle threat but Meldrum's troops seem to have had little stomach for a direct assault. Unpaid for eighteen weeks and 'pinched for want of victuals', their reliability to obey their officers was suspect[31].

The starving defenders were in a worse state, but feared that the Irish troops would be barred from the mercy of Parliament and outside the terms issued by Meldrum. Consequently, negotiations stalled; the garrison may have been aware that elsewhere a number of surrendered Irish troops were hanged by Parliament, an act for which Prince Rupert retaliated by hanging an equal number of Parliamentarian troops.

The siege dragged on until some fifty English soldiers of the garrison surrendered to Meldrum, with most of the remaining cattle in the town. This may have been the final straw for the garrison, for a few days later they turned on their own officers and surrendered. True to his word, Sir John Meldrum allowed the English troops from the garrison to return home, and even the Irish troops were allowed to go free on condition they did not take up arms again. The officers were sent under guard to Manchester. Some of the Irish troops, probably Lord Byron's Regiment, were happy to be shipped back to Dublin, but then were rounded up and promptly sent back by the Royalist command to Chester, where four were hanged for 'trechery in the betrainge of Liverpoole'[32].

Colonel Moore was given command of the garrison, with 300 Foot and a troop of Horse in Liverpool, but his behaviour in abandoning the town to its fate when Prince Rupert attacked was not forgotten, for within a year the governor of Liverpool was Major John Ashurst. Meldrum, meanwhile, was looking for some kind of agreement with the Earl of Derby on the Isle of Man, with Ashurst acting for Meldrum and William Farington and John Greenhalgh for the Earl. In return for abandoning the Royalist cause, the Earl would retain his title and much of his lands. These negotiations came to nothing, but one side effect was putting the Earl firmly back as the leading Royalist Lancashire leader. By excluding the Earl from any pardon terms on 24 November, the Earl's enemies had placed him as one of the three most dangerous Royalists alongside Prince Rupert and Prince Maurice.

Captain Nicholas Anderton of Lostock, who had once trained as a Catholic priest, had commanded the garrison of Greenhalgh Castle for the King for months in late 1644–45. Parliamentary forces under Colonel Dodding and Colonel Alexander Rigby's younger brother, Major Joseph Rigby, besieged the castle from nearby Garstang, but it was not until Captain Anderton died that the defenders surrendered in June 1645.

The second siege of Lathom House began slowly in August 1644, as few Parliamentarian troops were available to invest the house. The garrison, under Colonel Edward Rawsthorne, 'ranged abroad into the Country in the night time' rounding up provisions and hostages. The fall of Liverpool resulted in many of the freed troops heading for Lathom, including many of the Irish troops, who were stationed in 'the Lodge'[33] at Lathom.

A number of Lathom's defenders were those that had successfully resisted Alexander Rigby months earlier. Under Colonel Edward Rawsthorne's command were Major Munday and Captain William Kay, commanding the cavalry, with captains Charnock, Farington, Molineux-Ratcliffe, Henry Nowell, Roby and Worral commanding Foot companies. Even Colonel John Tempest was there as a volunteer, and the redoubtable Reverend Rutter remained as chaplain[34].

Meldrum was not to be involved with Lathom, as he left Lancashire and was killed at Scarborough Castle the following summer on 21 July 1645. The Royalist garrison at Lathom was not seriously challenged until January 1645, when Colonel Egerton was appointed commander of the Parliamentary troops and started a slow investment of the house with 'a great ditch draune round the House a good distance from it'[35]. Rawsthorne appears to have sallied out on at least one occasion, skirmishing around 'Gilliburne's House'. It would not be until July 1645 until Colonel Egerton had enough troops, some 4,000, and cannon to try and force the issue with the garrison.

Firing the cannon batteries at the Lodge and 'having made some breaches in it,' Egerton sent in his Foot Regiments. In 'a very hot fight of both sides while it lasted', the Parliamentary troops stormed the Lodge and claimed to have killed forty defenders, wounded more and captured sixty – including twelve officers. They also captured 100 weapons and powder and one poor soul identified as supposed Catholic priest whose fate is unknown.

In August, two of the Earl's emissaries from the Isle of Man, John Sharples and a Mr Paul, were captured by the besieging Parliamentarians trying to sneak into Lathom. The dispatches they carried indicated that the Earl was directing the garrison to attempt to negotiate the best terms for Lathom's surrender, therefore they were allowed to continue their mission. Rawsthorne, however, refused to surrender and sent the emissaries packing, presumably back to the Isle of Man.

Any hope of relief for the garrison ended when the King's forces were defeated at Rowton Heath on 24 September 1645. The garrison must have known the end was near and attempted to negotiate their surrender, but negotiations dragged on until 2 December, when terms were finally agreed.

Captain Molineux-Ratcliffe was among those killed in the siege, but not before leading some twelve sorties[36]. On 3 December, the garrison marched out with little more than their liberty and the clothes on their backs as Lathom was plundered. But it was Cheshire troops under Colonel John Booth that took the surrender, and the spoils, much to the dismay of the local Lancashire Parliamentarians.

The fall of Lathom ended the first civil war in Lancashire, but not for some of the county's Royalists. Sir Thomas Tyldesley had escaped from captivity at Stafford Castle in 1645, and joined the garrison at Litchfield as commander in chief of all the Royalist Horse in Staffordshire.

On 9 January 1646 Captain Stone, Parliamentary Governor of Stafford, and a force of Parliamentary Horse encountered Tyldesley with three troops of Royalist Horse, probably the remnants of Molyneux's Regiment, at Cannock Chase. Stone attacked, and was repulsed and pursued by Tyldesley, whose men fell into disorder. Stone rallied his men and counter attacked and overwhelmed Tyldesley's Horse, capturing seventy prisoners. Tyldesley almost joined them as he fell from his horse in the mêlée and stormed into a nearby house; running into the rear yard he found another horse, which he quickly mounted and galloped away. Stone rode back to Stafford with his prisoners and Sir Thomas Tyldesley's hat, cloak and horse[37].

Besieged at Litchfield by Sir William Brereton, Sir Thomas Tyldesley did not have enough men to hold the town so retired to Cathedral Close – a fortress in its own right. There he held out for weeks, until ordered by the King to surrender on 10 July 1646.

Lord Molyneux had left Chester with what remained of his Horse Regiment in early 1645 and by May was commanding Prince Maurice's Lifeguard, which he led at the battle of Naseby. Escaping the defeat, he was with Prince Rupert at the skirmish at Belvoir Castle, where 'Ld. Molineux killing a man upon a good mare'[38]. After spending time with Tyldesley at Lichfield, he was in Ludlow when it surrendered on 27 May 1646. The King surrendered to a Scots army in May 1646 and his capital at Oxford capitulated in June.

It seemed the war was finally over, but in Lancashire there would be little peace, as within a few short years there would be further fighting.

CHAPTER 13

Total War:
The Second and Third Civil War,
1649–1651

When the King surrendered to the Scottish army at Southwell on 5 May 1646 the Civil Wars seemed to be at an end, but the maelstrom of political, social and religious changes brought about by the fighting had yet to run its course.

While the coalition of different factions that made up the Parliamentary forces had the King's Royalists to fight against they remained united, but now divisions became apparent. One thing remained, however: the King was still the King, and when he was handed over to the Parliamentary representatives on 30 January 1647, it appeared that with negotiations about reducing his power and confirming the rights of Parliament, he would remain on the throne.

His supreme belief in his divine right to rule meant that any negotiations he entered into were a stalling tactic until he could return to power. While the King's disingenuous talks went on, the Parliamentary divisions widened. In Parliament the two groupings of Presbyterians and Independents clashed, and both feared the new force in the country, the New Model Army and its leaders, Fairfax, Cromwell and Ireton.

Parliament ordered the army to disband, with a fraction of the back pay it was owed. The army refused and put up their own proposals and, remarkably, began to look to the King, while the Presbyterians in Parliament looked to the Scots for support. Cromwell moved to secure the King, ostensibly for his safety but more likely to gain control of him, and on 3 June 1647 Cornet George Joyce led 400 Ironsides to accost the King at Holmby House.

Fruitless and, on the King's part at least, insincere discussions continued until the army leaders lost patience. On 6 August, Fairfax ordered the New Model Army into London to take control of Parliament while divisions within the army itself added to the turmoil as John Lilburne and his Levellers agitated for equal rights and influence for all men.

While his opponents fell apart around him, the King escaped custody at Hampton Court and fled to Carisbrook Castle on the Isle of Wight. On 26 December 1647, the King signed an agreement with the Scots to put him back on the throne in return for the abolition of the Anglican Church and the Parliamentary Independents, and the establishment of Presbyterianism throughout the kingdom – on a trial basis at least.

This 'Engagement' with the Scots led to their army, in support of the agreement, being known as Engagers. It was hoped that when the Scots army crossed the border, those pockets of Royalist resistance still holding out would rise up and join them.

Royalist hopes were high in the early months of 1648 as revolts happened in Kent and Essex, and part of the fleet in the Downs mutinied. But with no sign of the Scots invasion, these revolts were dealt with piecemeal by Fairfax and Cromwell, and when the Duke of Hamilton finally crossed the border at the head of a raw army of 3,000 Foot and 6,000 Horse on 8 July, they would have to face almost the full force of the New Model Army with just a few English Royalists at their side. Hamilton's army was a shadow of recent Scottish armies as the Regiments were under-strength, with many less than half what they should be, and 'not a fifth man could handle a pike'[1].

One of the English Royalists supporting the invasion would be Sir Thomas Tyldesley who, after surrendering at Ludlow in May 1646, had been paroled and gone to Ireland. He did not stay long before joining the Earl of Derby in the Isle of Man, where he continued to work for the Royalist cause. In early 1648 he was at Cartmel in Furness, assembling a Regiment of Foot[2].

The leader of the Engager army was James Hamilton, 1st Duke of Hamilton, who was born on 19 June 1606 in Hamilton Palace, Lanarkshire in Scotland. Educated at Exeter College, Oxford, he led a force of 6,000 men in support of Gustavus Adolphus in 1631 but returned to Scotland in 1634. Supporting King Charles in the Bishops' Wars, he was singularly ineffective in either diplomacy or action, failing to stop the Scots intervention in the Civil Wars in 1642. Finally falling from the King's favour, he was imprisoned, latterly in St Michael's Mount, and was liberated by Lord Fairfax's troops in 1646. Despite this, he still supported the King and gained temporary influence in the Scottish Parliament and led the invasion. William Baillie had fought with the Dutch and under Gustavus Adolphus of Sweden before he returned to Scotland to fight in the Bishops' Wars. He commanded the Scottish infantry on the right wing of the Allied army at Marston Moor and fought the Marquis of Montrose in 1645, but was defeated at the disastrous battle of Alford and at Kilsyth. He would command the Scottish Foot in the Engager invasion.

John Middleton was born in 1608, the eldest son of Robert Middleton, Laird of Caldhame. He fought as a pikeman in 1632 in France and was steadily promoted, becoming a captain in the Covenanter Army in 1639 before volunteering for the Parliamentary army at the outbreak of the Civil War in 1642. He was at Edgehill, where some accounts claim he captured the Royal Standard from Sir Edmund Verney. By November 1642 he was a colonel of Horse, and in 1644 he was promoted to lieutenant general of Horse to Sir William Waller. Middleton retuned to Scotland and was a major general in the Army of the Covenant, but supported the Engagement and commanded the Horse in the Engager army.

Sir Marmaduke Langdale was born in 1598 and served in Europe in the Thirty Years War under the Queen of Bohemia. He was High Sheriff of Yorkshire in 1639 and was Commissioner of Array for the county at the beginning of the Civil War in 1642. As a colonel, he commanded the Northern Horse, essentially a cavalry brigade, and fought at Marston Moor, Naseby, Donnington and Melton Mobray before escaping to the Isle of Man in 1645. He would command most of the English Royalist contingent.

By mid-July, Hamilton met reinforcements of 6,000 Foot at Kirkby Thore and continued his stately advance southwards. So dilatory was the advance that Oliver Cromwell's cavalry had time to join with Major General Lambert while Cromwell himself marched with his infantry north through Leicester and Nottingham. On the 12 July Cromwell joined Lambert at Wetherby with a total command of 2,500 Horse and dragoons, 4,000 Foot plus 1,600 foot and 500 Horse out of Lancashire led by Ralph Assheton.

By August, Hamilton's Scots army was seriously short on provisions and foraged far and wide, earning a poor reputation with the locals and spreading their forces across Lancashire. Desertions were rife and when Sir Marmaduke Langdale on the Engager army's flank gave Hamilton intelligence of the proximity of Cromwell, he was ignored.

Cromwell marched over the Pennines, and on 16 August held a council of war at Hodder Bridge near Clitheroe. He had two choices to consider first head south via Whalley to block the southward advance of the Engager Army, or to head north of the Ribble to come in behind, cut the Scots and Royalists off from reinforcements and immediately attack. He decided on the aggressive attack from the north. With his course of action set, he 'quartered the whole army in a field by Stonyhurst Hall'[3].

On the same day, the Engager army, forced to live off the land due to incompetent staff work failing to deliver provisions of any sort, was seriously spread out. The main body of Foot was entering Preston from the north, while the cavalry was sixteen miles away to the south at Wigan. The weather was foul, cold and wet, which turned the roads into quagmires and fields into bogs.

Hamilton posted Sir Marmaduke Langdale to guard the road into Preston while the main army crossed the rivers Ribble and Darwin south of the town. Langdale was aware of Cromwell's approach, and warned Hamilton that a sizable Parliamentary force was closing from the north-east. But he was ignored, as Hamilton continued to push the Scottish Foot across the rivers to meet up with Middleton and the cavalry at Wigan.

On the morning of the 17th, Langdale took up a defensive position in a narrow lane between Longridge and Preston, on the edge of Ribbleton Moor. Pikemen stood on the lane itself, supported by a small force of Scottish lancers, with musketeers deployed in the hedges and enclosures. Langdale's

Hodder Bridge.

forces consisted of the Regiments of Foot of Sir Philip Musgrave, Sir Edward Musgrave, Sir Henry Bellingham, Sir Patricius Curwen, Sir Henry Huddleston, Sir Henry Featherstone, Colonel William Carleton and Colonel Henry Chater, with the full Regiment of Horse of Sir Philip Musgrave plus other smaller troops of Horse, making up some 3,000 Foot and 700 Horse[4].

The incessant rain had turned the ground to a boggy, muddy morass, preventing Cromwell from using his cavalry to full effect and the initial Parliamentary advance was led by 'Two hundred Horse and Four hundred Foot, the Horse commanded by Major Smithson, the foot by Major Pounel'[5], which were easily was beaten back[6]. Cromwell described the ground as 'totally inconvenient' for horse, as being 'all enclosure and miry ground'[7].

Cromwell deployed his full force, and to the right of the track were the Foot Regiments of Lt Colonel Thomas Reade, Colonel Richard Deane and Colonel Thomas Pride, with the Regiments of Horse of Colonel Francis Thornhough and Colonel Philip Twistleton in support. To the left stood the Foot Regiments of Colonel John Bright and Sir Thomas Fairfax, with Cromwell's own Regiment of Horse following Colonel Thomas Harrison's Horse advancing down the track. Ralph Assheton's Lancashire brigade of about 500 Horse and 1,600 Foot stood in support of the line and consisted of Colonel Alexander Rigby's Regiment of Horse and the Foot Regiments of Colonel Ralph Assheton, Colonel George Dodding, Colonel Standish, Colonel Alexander Rigby and

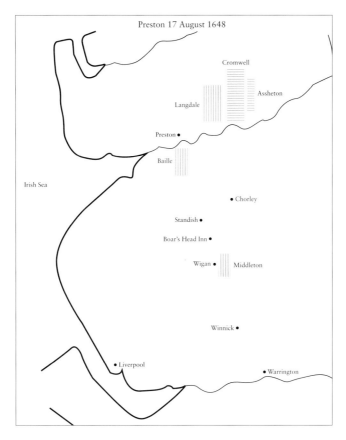

Preston 17 August 1648

Cromwell

Assheton

Langdale

Preston ●

Baille

Irish Sea

● Chorley

Standish ●

Boar's Head Inn ●

Wigan ● Middleton

Winnick ●

● Liverpool

● Warrington

Colonel Oughtred Shuttleworth. Rigby's Regiment of Foot was commanded by Colonel Standish while Rigby was with his Regiment of Horse.

The two Parliamentary Regiments of Horse of Cromwell and Harrison charged the lane while the Foot Regiments attempted to clear the hedgerows either side. After a number of hours Langdale's men were still holding their own. Langdale appeared to have counter attacked at one point with an 'abundance … killed in the fields on the east syd'[8]. The professionalism of the Parliamentary soldiers began to tell after a time, with Colonel Deane and Colonel Pride's Regiments pressing the Royalist left flank, 'often coming to push of pike and close firing'[9]. Colonel Ralph Assheton's Lancashire Regiments then moved unseen down a defile on the Royalist right at Watery Lane, near the river. Outflanking the Royalist line, Assheton's men pressed on to Ribble Bridge with Captain Samuel Birch leading the charge. Under pressure in front, its flank turned and escape to the river cut off Langdale's line, which finally gave way with the Foot streaming into Preston and the few horsemen riding north.

Hamilton had begun to send Foot Regiments back to support Langdale, but was pressurised into changing his mind and sent them back to await Middleton's cavalry from Wigan. It has also been reported that when he heard of Cromwell's attack on Langdale, he coolly replied, 'Let them alone, the English dogs are killing one another'[10].

Hamilton and his entourage were still north of the river when Langdale reached him as the English Royalist rearguard collapsed. Attempting to cross at Ribble Bridge was impossible, as it was under attack from Assheton's men and they were threatened by Parliamentary cavalry. Hamilton and Langdale personally had to lead three charges before driving them off. Cut off from the bridge and with the only ford running deep and strong due to the incessant rain, they had to put their horses to the river and swim across[11].

Baillie, commanding the Engager Foot, deployed musketeers to defend Ribble Bridge, with the main body of the Engager army on the high ground south of the River Darwen. Assheton's troops occupied the hedges and houses on the escarpment to the north of the Ribble Bridge and began to pour musket fire onto the bridge. Under this covering fire, Captain Birch led the Lancashire men in driving the Scots from Ribble Bridge at push of pike in a 'hot dispute'. The momentum of the attack carried them over Darwin Bridge soon after. During this action, Major John Sanderson reported 'for about an houre we gave no quarter to any'. With darkness falling the limited Scottish

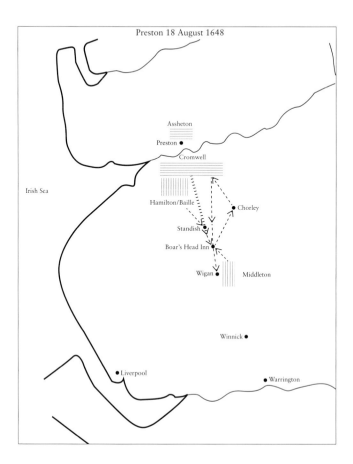

Preston 18 August 1648

supply wagons and some 'three hundred Barrells of powder' were seized and according to Cromwell, writing later, some 'four or five thousand armes'[12]. Exhausted, the Parliamentary troops settled down where they stood, aiming to continue the attack in the morning[13].

In a wild, stormy night of driving rain, the Scots Foot crept away unseen from the river in a drumless march, aiming to meet up with the Royalist Horse Regiments moving up from Wigan, after which the plan appears to have been to march south to meet up with Lord Byron, currently trying to secure North Wales for the Royalists. In the darkness and rain, and indicative of the confusion and incompetence of the whole campaign, they took different roads and missed each other. Heading north from Wigan, the Royalist Horse, under Middleton, followed the right-hand fork at the Boars Head Inn and galloped on via the Chorley Road, completely missing the Foot Regiments marching south[14]. In the confusion, Middleton's cavalry blundered into Parliamentary advance troops in the early hours of the morning – alerting them to what was happening. Reversing his march, Middleton turned south to catch up with Hamilton and the infantry, hotly pursued by Colonel Francis Thornhaugh, an experienced Nottinghamshire veteran, and three Parliamentary Regiments of Horse. Thornhaugh was mortally wounded, 'run through body, thigh and head by the Enemys lancers',[15] at Chorley as Middleton fought a rearguard action down the Wigan Road. As Thornhaugh lay by the roadside he asked his men to move aside so that he 'might see the rogues run'[16].

Cromwell advanced with 3,000 Foot and 2,500 Horse and Dragoons against the exhausted, demoralised and broken Scots army of perhaps 10,000 men. Three thousand Royalist prisoners – the remnants of the English Royalists of Langdale's stand – were left under guard of Assheton's men in Preston. With wagons captured and powder useless in the ceaseless rain, any semblance of discipline in the Scots army broke down and they ransacked Wigan, a town with long-held Royalist sympathies. Adjutant General Sir James Turner, commanding the rearguard, formed up pikemen shoulder to shoulder in Wigan Market Square. More Royalist cavalry stragglers came into sight and Turner ordered his men to open their ranks to let the fugitives through. The Pikemen started to panic, shouting 'You are all Cromwell's men!', and two attacked Turner, running full tilt at him. Turner commented later, 'one of their pikes which was intended for my belly I griped with my left hand; the other ran me nearly two inches into the inner side of my thigh'[17]. Enraged, Turner rode to the cavalry and ordered a troop of Horse to clear the mutinous pikemen from the marketplace. The troopers, seeing the levelled pikes, hesitated until Turner rode behind them and let out a cry that the enemy was upon them. The cavalry then pushed forward and rode down and scattered the pikemen, most of whom threw down their pikes and ran into the houses, yards and alleys off the Market Square[18]. Now fighting among themselves, the Engager army fled south as Cromwell's men reported taking 'General Van Druske and a Colonel, and Killed some Principal officers, and took about a hundred prisoners'[19]. Major Sanderson also reported that they took 'two foot colours of the Marquesse of Argiles old Regiment' and 'Collonell Hamilton of Gateside, Collonell Urrey', who had been shot and wounded in the head, 'Collonell Innes and another'[20]. The Parliamentary forces had lain down that night in the fields between Standish and the Boar's Head Inn, intent on following up the next day[21].

Cromwell remarked the next morning his troops were 'at the heels' of the retreating Scots, and that Wigan had been 'plundered almost to their skins by them'[22]. Major General Baillie's Foot made a stand at Winwick, three miles north of Warrington, while Hamilton tried to organise the defences in Warrington itself. Baillie's Foot occupied a strong natural defensive position in a pass 100 yards wide between two areas of high ground – a man-made bank called Red Bank was to the east, and a sandstone bluff to the west. Deploying musketeers on the high ground of the flanks, which he strengthened with earthworks and barricades, Baillie's pikemen held the marshy pass itself. They may well have had the last of their field guns with them as cannon balls have been found on the site, but in the chaotic retreat from Preston this seems unlikely[23].

At midday on 19 August, Cromwell arrived and attacked immediately, with Colonel John Bright's Yorkshire Regiment leading the attack. But after hours of fighting, he couldn't break through; as Cromwell stated later, they maintained 'the passe with great resolution for many hours'. Calling off the attack to await reinforcements, Cromwell learned of a track to turn the Scots' flank and after sending cavalry to outflank the position from the the hamlet of Hermitage Green

St Oswald's, Winiwick Parish Church.

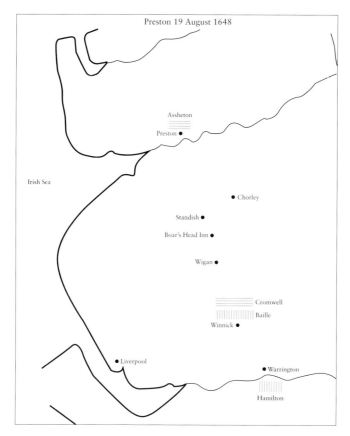

Preston 19 August 1648

Assheton

Preston ●

Irish Sea

● Chorley

Standish ●

Boar's Head Inn ●

Wigan ●

Cromwell
Baille
Winnick ●

● Liverpool

● Warrington

Hamilton

to the east, he attacked with a veteran Foot Regiment under Colonel Thomas Pride, who 'after a sharpe dispute put these same brave fellows to the run'. Outflanked, the position finally fell with some Scots pikemen making a final stand on the green near Winwick church, where the Parliamentarians 'made a great slaughter of them'[24] and 'many hundreds of them were slaine'[25].

Baillie struggled into Warrington with about 2,700 weary infantry to find Hamilton and the Scots Horse had fled, leaving him to seek what terms he could. Feeling totally betrayed, he met Cromwell on Warrington Bridge and agreed surrender terms. The three-day running fight was over in a crushing Parliamentary victory against a numerically superior, but militarily inadequate, Engager army. Hamilton fled through Cheshire and Staffordshire and surrendered at Uttoxeter on 25 August[26]. Lieutenant-General Middleton was captured in Cheshire after his horse stumbled and fell on him, while Sir Marmaduke Langdale got away to Nottingham but was captured while resting in an alehouse. Hamilton was tried and beheaded on 9 March 1649 at the Palace of Westminster while William Baillie returned to Scotland, where he bitterly repented his involvement in the Engagement. The Kirk accepted his plea and he died in 1653. Although he was captured, John Middleton broke his parole and returned to Scotland.

With the defeat at Preston, the Second Civil War was all but over, with the surviving Royalist outposts surrendering over the following weeks. Sir Thomas Tyldesley, who took no part in the actual Engager invasion, surrendered Appleby Castle to Colonel Ralph Assheton on 9 October 1648. The terms were generous and most of the troops were allowed to return home. The leaders, including Tyldesley, were banished and he went back to the Isle of Man to plot once more for a Royalist return[27].

Despite being soundly defeated militarily in both the first and second Civil Wars the King flatly rejected a new treaty on 16 November 1648. The army leaders lost patience and didn't trust the King in any event, so they sent units to the Isle of Wight, where Charles was taken into custody yet again. The Presbyterians in Parliament declared they wished to continue negotiations with the King in early December, in an action which finally precipitated the army takeover when, on 6 December, Colonel Pride, at the head of his Regiments, purged the Presbyterians from Parliament. The remaining Independent MPs, some seventy in total, claimed the full authority of the Parliament and, backed by the army, became what was known as the Rump Parliament.

On 20 January 1649, King Charles was put on trial. When Fairfax realised that Cromwell was determined to execute 'that man of blood', as Cromwell termed the King, he left the proceedings[28]. Found guilty of high treason, King Charles was beheaded in Whitehall on 30 January 1649. The Monarchy and House of Lords were officially disbanded and replaced by the Council of State, which included Cromwell and Fairfax.

King Charles II was proclaimed King on 5 February. He saw Scotland as the place to launch his bid to regain the throne and in mid-June he arrived in Scotland, precipitating a Parliamentarian invasion. Fairfax was still the New Model Army commander, but his fundamental opposition to the invasion led him to resign, leaving Cromwell in command. Over the next few months, in a campaign of manoeuvring and action, including victory at Dunbar, Cromwell failed to quell the Royalist resurgence. In early August, King Charles II, nominally at the head of a Scots and Royalist English army of 15,000 Foot and 6,000 Horse, headed south. In reality, the army was commanded by David Leslie, with John Middleton as lieutenant-general of Horse and Edward Massey commanding the English contingent.

David Leslie was born in 1601, the fifth son of Patrick Leslie, Lord Lindores. He joined the army of Gustavus Adolphus as a captain and was a colonel of the Regiment of Horse by 1634. He returned to Scotland and joined the Covenanters, and was a brigade commander at Marston Moor in 1644. He refused to be involved in the Engager invasion in 1648 but was appointed lieutenant-general of the new Covenanter army in 1650.

Edward Massey was born in 1619 and was a professional soldier and engineer in Dutch service before returning to England in 1639 to fight in the Bishops' Wars. A devout Presbyterian, in 1643 he was a Parliamentarian colonel, appointed governor of Gloucester. He led the defence of the city against King Charles' Oxford army and fought in Gloucestershire throughout 1643–4, eventually taking over command of the Western Association Army. After the first Civil War, he was one of the MPs excluded in Prides Purge in December 1648, after which he was imprisoned in St James' Palace. He escaped to the Netherlands in January 1649 and came over to the Royalists as a leading representative of the English Presbyterians.

This time the Earl of Derby would be joining the Royalist forces. He had spent the years since Marston Moor at Rushen Castle in the centre of Castletown (the former capital of the Isle of Man), and had been a beacon and refuge for Royalists – including Sir Thomas Tyldesley. He was known as 'yn Stanlagh Mooar' [The Great Stanley] by his Manx tenants, but his means were limited due to most of his estates being sequested by Parliament, who had exempted him from any amnesty while he still held the Isle of Man against them. His reduced means can be appreciated, for in June 1650 a Parliamentary vessel belonging to Mr Massey of Warrington was seized off the Isle of Man and its cargo of 'cloths, silks and taffatas' were taken by the Earl, who had 'twenty three tailors all busy at work making garments'. A year earlier, he had rejected an offer of terms for the surrender of the island and replied to General Ireton with indignation and scorn that far from delivering the island, he would 'keep it to the utmost of my power'.

In 1651 he set off with ten ships, and on 5 August landed on the north side of the River Wyre on Preesal Sands, at the little fishing village of Skipool opposite Rossal Warren. His force consisted of 300 Manx Foot and around 50 gentlemen who had sheltered in the Isle of Man – including the Governor John Greenhalgh, and the redoubtable Sir Thomas Tyldesley. Sir Philip Musgrave was left as Lieutenant Governor on the Isle of Man[29].

The Earl left Tyldesley recruiting while he rode to meet the King – by 17 August he had joined him at Warrington. With Edward Massey, the Earl tried unsuccessfully to persuade Lancashire Royalists to support Charles II. Apparently a number of Presbyterian ministers insisted the Earl take the Solemn League and Covenant and dismiss 'the Papists' he had with him. The Earl refused, as he had come to fight for his Majesty's restoration not to dispute religion[30]. The Presbyterian ministers went away disappointed and the Earl recruited few of the numbers he had hoped to. Tyldesley had more success recruiting and joined the Earl at Warrington.

King Charles II and the bulk of the Royal army continued south, arriving at Worcester on 22 August while the Earl and Lancashire Royalists remained in the county, gathering more support. Almost as soon as the bulk of the Royal army had left, the Earl was attacked by a small Parliamentary force at Warrington Bridge. During the skirmish one of Tyldesley's officers, Major John Harding, had his horse shot from under him and was captured[31].

By the time the Earl marched north again on the 21st, he had the nucleus of three Regiments of Horse; his own, Colonel John Baynes and Sir Thomas

Tyldesley's – as well as the Manx Foot and a reconstituted Foot Regiment of Sir Thomas Tyldesley.

Local Parliamentarian troops had not been idle in the meantime, capturing the ten ships the Earl had left lying in Wyre Water. The crews were imprisoned at Preston, then moved towards York. Sir Thomas Tyldesley attempted a rescue with a troop of Horse, but missed them and captured a party of armed men[32]. The Earl's force was now being shadowed by a Parliamentarian force detached from Cromwell's army under the command of Colonel Robert Lilburne.

Colonel Robert Lilburne came from County Durham and had two brothers in Parliamentary service, his elder brother the Leveller Lieutenant-Colonel John Lilburne and his younger brother Henry. Henry Lilburne was Lieutenant-Governor of Tynemouth Castle and changed sides, declaring himself for the King on 9 August 1648, during the Second Civil War, but he was killed when Parliamentary troops retook the castle in a bitter assault[33].

Robert Lilburne had started his career as a cornet in 1642 in the Earl of Bedford's Regiment, and by 1643 was a lieutenant in Richard Crosse's troop. In 1644 and 1645 he commanded a Regiment of Durham Horse, and by 1646 was colonel of a Foot Regiment in the New Model Army. By the following year, he was governor of Newcastle-upon-Tyne, but was back commanding his Durham Horse in time to be involved in the battle of Preston in 1648[34]. Lilburne's Regiment had marched with Cromwell to Scotland in 1650, fought at the battle of Dunbar and had joined the pursuit of the Royal army.

From Harrington, the Earl had force marched northwards towards Preston, continually shadowed by Colonel Robert Lilburne and the Parliamentarians.

On 22 August, Lilburne raided the Royalists at Preston from his base at

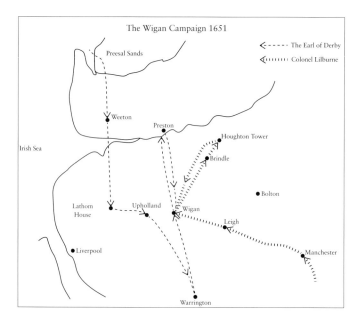

Brindle, but was beaten off. The following day a small party of twenty Royalist horsemen, probably without orders, under Captain Thomas Hesketh and Captain John Knipe returned the favour at Brindle. Catching Lilburne's men dismounted, they had some success but were beaten off, with both Hesketh and Knipe being killed and most of the party captured. One who escaped was Cornet Edward Tyldesley, Sir Thomas Tyldesley's son[35].

Over the next few days, both sides shadowed each other until Lilburne broke off contact on the 24th and retired to Houghton. Taking advantage, the Earl marched southwards to meet up with the Royal army and it was mid-morning on the 25th before Lilburne realised that his quarry had marched and was trying to join forces with the King. Were it not for an elderly woman who came into Lilburne's quarters with the news he would not have known at all, and it was noon before he caught up with the Earl's forces at Wigan.

The Earl and Tyldesley's remarkable recruitment in Lancashire had given them three small Horse Regiments of Derby himself, Sir Thomas Tydesley and Colonel John Bayne – some 500 men in total. The Foot Regiments were a mixture of the unreliable Manxmen, commanded by Colonel Bayne and Sir Matthew Boynton, the former Parliamentarian governor of Hull, and stiffened

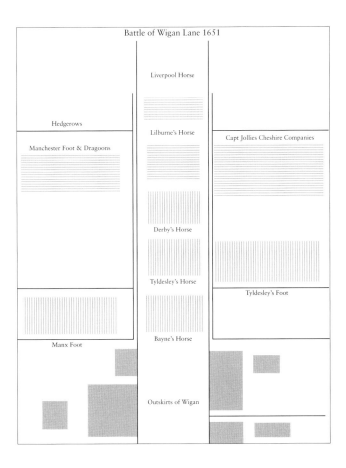

Battle of Wigan Lane 1651

with experienced officers from Yorkshire and as far afield as Oxford. The bulk of the Foot, however, were Tyldesley's Regiment, commanded by Lieutenant-Colonel Hugh Anderton of Euxton, many of whom had seen action since 1642. In total the Earl's Foot numbered 800 men, whose field sign was of white scarves tied around the left arm and battle cry of 'Jesu!'

Lilburne's forces consisted of his own Regiment of Horse, at most 500 men, and thirty Horse from Liverpool. His fifty or sixty dragoons were Lancashire men with fowling pieces who managed to obtain some horses while his Foot consisted of a single regular company from the Manchester garrison, two Cheshire Trained Band companies under Captain Jollie and a number of musketeers from Liverpool under 'Carter' Birch.

Lilburne halted in the broad, sandy Wigan Lane leading northwards outside of town at Mab's Cross, the outer end of Standishgate[36]. Placing his few Foot Regiments in the hedges flanking the lane, he expected the Royalists to continue to move southwards, but the Earl had no intention of heading out of Wigan with Lilburne on his heels, so for three hours both sides stood looking at each other, daring one another to make the first move. To the east of the lane the Earl positioned his Manx Foot, facing Lilburne's Manchester Foot and local dragoons. To the west of the lane, Thomas Tyldesley's Foot faced off against the Cheshire companies of Captain Jollie, while in the lane itself the Horse Regiments sat eyeing each other, with Lilburne placing his small Horse contingent from Liverpool in reserve.

Tyldesley Plaque.

In a letter written later, Lilburne said that after the Earl's forces 'unexpectedly put themselves in a posture with us, which then we endeavoured to decline', as Lilburne judged the odds too great. He started his men pulling to 'the left flanke of them thither' in an attempt to meet up with reinforcements, but 'the enemy perceiving us draw off, quickly advanced upon us'.

So at three in the afternoon the Royalist Horse charged up the lane, assaulting Lilburne's Regiment. Twice the Royalists were beaten back as the fighting swayed up and down the lane, while the Foot hardly exchanged a shot. The Royalists cry was 'The King and Earl of Derby!' while Lilburne's men shouted back 'Liberty! Liberty!'[37]

The Earl of Derby apparently led the assault and was in the thick of the action, having two horses killed under him, receiving seven pistol shots in his breast plate, thirteen cuts in his beaver hat and five or six wounds in his arms and shoulders[38]. While mounting a third horse his servant, a Frenchman, holding the bridle so the Earl could mount, was killed. The third charge had Sir Thomas Tyldesley in the van, and Lilburne threw in his reserve of the Liverpool Horse to stem the tide. At the same time the Parliamentary musketeers and dragoons in the hedgerows fired a volley into Tyldesley's Regiment, killing, among others, his lieutenant-colonel, James Anderton of Clayton, and shooting Tyldesley's horse from under him. Sheltering by the hedgerow, looking for another horse to mount Tyldesley was seen by a trooper of Lilburne's Regiment, who shot him dead with a pistol. The musket volley, and Tyldesley's death, finally broke the Royalist Horse and Lilburne's men drove them back into the streets of Wigan, while the Manxmen threw down their arms and fled the field.

Lilburne's troopers pursued the broken Royalists while the Earl of Derby, with Manx Govenor John Greenhalgh and five others rode back into Wigan. Closely pursued by the Parliamentary cavalry, they saw an open door and the Earl leapt from his horse and, rushing into the house, slammed the door behind him. In the house, the 'mistress seeing his distress kept it shut and conveyed him out of the back door to safety'[39]. Lying in the dust of the road, the Parliamentary troops found the Earl's beaver hat, worn over a steel helmet, which has thirteen swords cuts in it[40].

The victorious Parliamentarian troopers rode back up Wigan Lane to find Tyldesley's Foot Regiment standing defiantly by the roadside with pikes and muskets levelled. Thinking they would break, Lilburne's troopers charged, to be repulsed with 'many horses Kild and spoiled with their pikes'. Enraged, Lilburne cried out to give no quarter and Captain Jollie's Cheshire companies advanced and attacked from all sides, Tyldesley's men were overwhelmed.

Lilburne claimed to have lost only an officer, one corporal and 'not above ten souldiers slayne', which surely must be an underestimation. The Royalist forces were shattered and had a very high proportion of officers among those killed, including Sir Mathew Boynton, Major General Sir William Widderington, 'slaine in Wiggon towne in the pursuit'[41], Colonel Michael

Tyldesley Monument.

Trollop, Colonel Math, Lieutenant Colonel John Galliard and Major Chester. Tyldesley's men suffered badly, with those killed including Lieutenant Colonel James Anderton, Captain William Ilsley, Captain John Bamber of Lower Moor and perhaps the greatest loss, Sir Thomas Tyldesley himself[42]. The battle field is now known as Bloody Mountain and sometime later Sir Thomas Tyldesley's cornet, Alexander Rigby, erected a monument on the spot he fell, which still stands on Wigan Lane to this day.

Lilburne captured a number of officers, including Colonel Throgmorton, Colonel Richard Leg, Colonel John Robinson, Colonel Baynes, Colonel Ratcliffe Gerret, Lieutenant Colonel Creson Rigby, Lieutenant Colonel Francis Baynes, Lieutenant Colonel Galliard, Lieutenant Colonel Constable, Major Gower, four captains, two lieutenants and 400 men, the majority of which were the Manxmen.

Colonel Lilburne wrote, 'Lord derby I heare is fled towards Bolton,' but in fact the Earl was hiding in the Dog Inn in the marketplace in Wigan, after having his six flesh wounds – in his arms and shoulders[43] – dressed in a house close by. During the night, at around 2.00 a.m., he slipped away with his aide Colonel Roscarrock and headed south the meet up with the King[44].

The following day, Lillburne wrote to Cromwell that 'About five o'clock this day the countrymen brought in about 10 stubborn, resolute gentlemen' of Derby's force, that there were 'none left to engage,' and although the Earl of Derby had fled, he was 'certain that he is wounded'[45]. It is likely one of the resolute gentlemen would have been Sir Timothy Fetherstonehough. Sir Thomas Tyldesley's body was taken to be buried in the Tyldesley chancel of St Nicholas, at the east end of the north aisle in the Parish Church of St Mary the Virgin in Leigh. Wigan parish church burial records were completed in a different hand to the rest for 27 August and the entries read:

27 My Lord Witheringeton de Northumberland
27 Collonell Boyneton de Yorkshire
27 Collonell Trolope, Govenor of Newarke.

The Earl of Derby, meanwhile, still suffering from his wounds, stole southwards, finding refuge with a number of Royalist households along the way – including Whiteladies on the Boscobel estate in Shropshire, where he stayed for two days under the care of William Penderal[46]. He arrived at Worcester to meet up with the King on 31 August with a handful of horsemen instead of the army he intended.

Cromwell's Parliamentarian forces, of about 28,000 men, caught up with the 16,000- strong Royalist army at Worcester soon afterwards and, after scouting the enemy positions, had resolved to attack on 3 September. Early on the morning of the 3rd, the Parliamentary troops attempted to force a crossing at Powick Bridge and across the rivers Teme and Severn, defended by the Royalist Major General Robert Montgomery's brigade. After a bitter

Tyldesley Chancel.

fight on the Teme, Cromwell sent in three more brigades to overwhelm the defenders, forcing them back from hedge to hedge, leaving Colonel Kieth, the Royalist defender of Powick Bridge, outflanked. Running low on ammunition and with Major General Robert Montgomery wounded, the Royalist Scots were routed back into Worcester within two hours.

Cromwell had weakened his right wing to press the attack and the Royalists moved to exploit this, attacking their positions on Red Hill and Perry Wood. For a time it looked like this attack would be successful, but the leader of the Perry Wood assault, the Duke of Hamilton, was wounded and his men began running short of ammunition. Cromwell, by now, had re-crossed the river with his three brigades and smashed into the Royalists, who broke and ran back to the city in disorder.

The city gates fell to the Parliamentarian forces one by one and desperate stands were made in some places, for example at the castle mound, while some others, like Dalziell's brigade, surrendered, firing hardly a shot.

The Earl of Cleveland led a charge up Sudbury Street, diverting the Parliamentarians long enough for King Charles II, with a few companions – including James Stanley, the Earl of Derby, the Duke of Buckingham, Lord Lauderdale, Lord Wilmot and Governor John Greenhalgh – to escape from the town through the northern, St Martin's Gate. Greenhalgh had ripped the Royal Standard from its pole and wrapped it around his body to save it in the escape. The battle itself was a total disaster for the King and his army was smashed.

After a 5-mile ride, the horsemen stopped at an inn in Ombersley now known as the Kings Arms. At this point, James Stanley urged the young King to ride north to the Boscobel estate where the Earl had so recently been. Charles Giffard, of the Catholic Giffard family who owned the estate, was among the party who accompanied the King and after much discussion it was considered the safest option that Charles should travel with a small retinue, therefore the party separated near Hartlebury. The Earl and the larger group of horsemen proceeded towards Kidderminster, no doubt heading for the safety of the Isle of Man.

The King arrived at Whiteladies, on the Boscobel estate in Shropshire at dawn on 4 September. There he was met by the Penderel brothers and, swapping clothes with them, he had his hair cut short to evade capture and donned leather breeches and a felt hat and attempted to imitate a country accent. That morning, the house at Whiteladies was no longer considered safe and the fugitive King spent all day in a nearby wood, known as Spring Coppice, where search parties narrowly missed him. Setting off at nightfall with Richard Penderel, they attempted to cross the Severn into Wales. All the crossings were too closely guarded, so after spending the night in a barn owned by Francis Wolfe of Madeley, they were forced to turn back to Boscabel.

Back at Boscabel, the King was almost discovered, he and Major William Carlis had to hide for a day in the leafy branches of a large oak tree while Parliamentarian troops searched the thicket below, looking for the fugitives[47].

That night, he slipped back into the house and spent a restless night hiding in the priest's hole in the attic[48]. He finally slipped out of Boscabel on the evening of 7 September on an old mill horse, and accompanied by the five Penderel brothers and Francis Yates, a servant of Charles Giffard, he made it to another refuge at the home of Thomas Whitgreave, Moseley Old Hall. Lord Wilmot was already hiding there and all were almost taken when Parliamentarian troops arrived one afternoon to question Whitgreave, believing he had fought at Worcester. Whitgreave convinced them, correctly, that he had not been at Worcester and they left without searching the house. It was a lucky escape, but things were getting too hot for the young King.

The fugitive Charles moved on to Bentley Hall near Walsall, the home of Colonel John Lane. From there he travelled as a servant, 'William Jackson' of Jane Lane, to Abbots Leigh, arriving on the evening of 12 September. Attempts to find a ship at nearby Bristol were unsuccessful so the party decided to head for the South Coast reaching Trent near Sherborne, were they stayed at Trent House, the home of Colonel Francis Wyndham, a Royalist officer. The King spent the next few weeks hiding at Trent House while his friends tried to arrange a ship to France. Finally, in the middle of October, Charles boarded a ship to the continent at Shoreham, and he and Lord Wilmot finally escaped to France, landing at Fécamp. Only hours after the King sailed, a troop of cavalry arrived at Shoreham to arrest him. James Stanley, the Earl of Derby, would not be so fortunate.

Priest's Hole.

CHAPTER 14

Judicial Murder:
The Execution of James Stanley,
15 October 1651

After separating from the King at Hartlebury, the Earl and the larger group of horsemen, including Lord Lauderdale, Lord Talbot and forty troopers, proceeded towards Kidderminster. Governor John Greenhalgh split off from the main party and made his way to the Isle of Man, where he died of wounds received at Worcester and was buried at Malew on 29 September 1651.

The Earl and his companions headed north with the remnants of the King's army, all trying to get to safety. Captain Hodgson of Coley, a Parliamentarian officer, noted in his memoirs that, with his Foot Regiment, he was marching towards Worcester and had reached Nantwich. Continuing the march towards Whitechurch, he was informed that 'a great party of Horse was coming on and if we made haste we might take a bridge before them and hinder a pass'. This they did and the horsemen, seeing their way blocked, 'marched another road towards Nantwich which was about half a mile off us', while another party of Parliamentary Horse and Foot engaged them. He then notes a 'remarkable thing' – that Captain Oliver Edge, probably of his Regiment, 'spies a party of horse behind him in the fields'. Edge, alone, began to retreat towards his Regiment, but the horsemen 'called upon him and asked him if he was an officer and drawing towards them, about eighteen or twenty horsemen lighted and told him they would surrender themselves prisoner'[1]. Among the horsemen was the Earl of Derby, and Captain Hodgson reports that 'these became prisoners to a single captain, but the other soldiers fell in with him immediately'[2]. The Earl and his companions were first taken to Whitchurch in Shropshire, then held in an inn at Bunbury in Cheshire before finding themselves imprisoned in Chester Castle.

The Earl reasoned that having been given quarter by Captain Edge, he would be treated as a Prisoner of War. In 1646, after the First Civil War, captured combatants were often released on a pledge to not take up arms again, but the days of clemency were long gone. Indeed, after the Second Civil War, Henry Rich, 1st Earl of Holland, and Arthur Capell, 1st Baron Capel of Hadham, were both beheaded on 9 March 1649 after surrendering on a promise of quarter for life. This assurance was not considered binding on the civil authorities, and this would also be the case with the Earl of Derby.

Parliament did not take long to act with regard to those taken after Worcester, as on 9 September the House referred to the Council of State 'to consider such Prisoners, as well English as Scotts, as are fit to be made Examples of publick Justice'[3]. There would be no amnesty. Two days later, Parliament reported that in the 'humble Opinion of this Council, That James Earl of Derby, Colonel Edward Massy, Duke Hamilton, John Earl of Lauderdaile, the Earl of Cleveland, Captain Bendbow, Sir Timothy Fetherston Haugh, and the Mayor and Sheriffs of Worcester, are fit Persons to be brought to Tryal, and made Examples of Justice.' It was further reported that 'the Earl of Derby be tried at Chester, by a Court Martial, erected by the Commission of the Lord General, upon the Act of the 12th of August. That Captain Bendbow be tried, in like Manner, at Chester. That Sir Timothy Fetherston Haugh be tried, in like Manner, at Chester'[4]. Stating clearly that they be 'brought to Tryal and be made an Example of Justice', it would appear the outcome would be a foregone conclusion. The Chester tribunal was convened for 29 September and would try the three defendants – the Earl of Derby, Sir Timothy Fetherstonehough and Colonel John Benbow – together.

Sir Timothy Featherstonehaugh was born in 1600, was a member of Gray's Inn in 1620, and was knighted in 1628 as Knight of Kirkoswald. He raised a Royalist Foot Regiment in 1642, recruited more troops in Ireland in 1644 and defended Carlisle under Sir Thomas Glenham in 1645. He was at the battle of Wigan Lane and was captured in Wigan the following day, 26 August 1651. Two of his sons, including his eldest, Lieutenant-Colonel Sir Henry Fetherstonehough, were killed at Worcester on 3 September 1651.

Colonel John Benbow was born around 1610 and had served in the Parliamentary forces, gaining promotion to captain for valiant action at Shrewsbury in 1645. He switched allegiance to the Royalists and became a Colonel of Horse just prior to Worcester, where he was captured. At Shrewsbury he had served under the president of the court, Colonel Humphrey Mackworth, who appears to have held this against him.

The Chester tribunal that would sit in judgement of the Earl of Derby and his co-defendants consisted of: Colonel Humphrey Mackworth of Shrewsbury, Major Mitton, Colonel Robert Duckenfield of Duckenfield, Colonel Henry Bradshaw of Marple, Colonel Thomas Croxton of Ravenscroft, Colonel George Twisleton, Lieutenant-Colonel Henry Birkinhead of Backford, Lieutenant Colonel Simon Finch, Lieutenant-Colonel Alexander Newton, Captain James Stopford, Captain Samuel Smith, Captain John Downes, Captain John Dolves, Captain John Groffith, Captain Thomas Partington, Captain Edward Alcock, Captain Ralph Powell, Captain Richard Grantham. Captain Edward Stolfax. and Captain Vincent Corbett[5].

Colonel Humphrey Mackworth was born in 1610, at Betton Grange in Shropshire. He was admitted to Gray's Inn in October 1621 and married the following year. As a colonel in the Parliamentary forces, he was at the taking of Ludlow Castle in 1646 and was appointed the Governor of Shrewsbury the same year. Colonel Robert Duckenfield was born in 1615 and had defended Stockport crossing when Prince Rupert marched into Lancashire in 1644, but had left the Presbyterian side to ally himself with Cromwell after the execution of Charles I.

The very day the trial opened, James Waynwright wrote from London to Richard Bradshaw, 'Lord Resident for the State of England in Hamburge', that 'darbie wilbee tryd at Chester and dy at Boulton'[6]. The outcome was apparently already common knowledge in London. The trial opened with the reading of the charges, and when it was said that if found guilty the Earl would suffer death 'as in the case of high Treason', he objected, exclaiming 'I am no traitor neither'. He was rebuked by Colonel Mackworth, the President, who said that he must be silent 'during the reading of the act and your charge'.

Stanley was not called in his defence until 1 October, and then stated that 'quarter for Life being given by Captain Edge'[7] meant that he should not be tried by Court Martial. He claimed that he was 'a stranger to the acts of Treason' of 12 August, and in any event being in the Isle of Man 'those acts reach it not, nor bind those of that island'. The court took no notice of these admittedly weak arguments and James Stanley was found guilty – 'that he had traitorously borne arms for Charles Stuart against Parliament, that he was guilty of a breach of the act of Parliament of the 12th August, 1651, prohibiting all correspondence with Charles Stuart' and 'that he had fortified his house of Lathom against Parliament, and that he now held the Isle of Man against them'[8]. He was condemned to be executed 'by severing his head from his body' at Bolton.

The Earl must have known what the verdict would be and did not idly accepted his fate. He had by some means made arrangements for his escape. On the night of Saturday 11 October he sat and wrote a letter to his wife, having no illusions that any escape attempt may end in his death. He left it on the table of his chamber and on some pretext went to the leads of the tower where he was confined. He had obtained a rope and after securing it, he slid down and slipped away into the night. A boat was waiting for him at the River Dee to convey him to safety, but something went wrong; perhaps he lost the guide in the dark, or perhaps he had to make his way to the boat alone but in any event he got lost in the unfamiliar darkened streets. In the tower his escape was discovered, as was his letter, and the alarm was raised. The Earl was caught down on the Roodee, now Chester racecourse, when he mistook his pursuers for his friends, and taken back to the castle, this time under secure guard[9]. From now on he would have 'two of three soldiers with him night and day in his chamber'[10].

The Earl sent several petitions to Parliament asking for clemency, and the House of Commons journal for 11 October 1651 notes that:

Mr Speaker, by way of Report, acquaints the House with a Letter, which
he had received from the Earl of Derby: And The Question being put,
That the said Letter be now read;
The House was divided.
The Yeas went forth.
Sir Wm. Brereton, Tellers for the Yeas: 22.
Mr. Ellys, With the Yeas,
Mr. Bond, Tellers for the Noes: 16.
Maj. Gen. Harrison, With the Noes,
So it passed with the Affirmative.
A Letter from the Earl of Derby, of the Eleventh Day of October 1651;
with a Petition therein inclosed, intituled, "The humble Petition of James
Earl of Derby," was this Day read[11].

The letter was read but that, it appears, was all; no record of any debate on
the petition or any recommendations from the House exists. Perhaps the
petition was met with stony silence. Whatever the reaction, there would be no
reprieve.

On Monday 13 October Reverend Humphrey Baggerley, a fellow prisoner
in Chester, was with the Earl when 'one Lieutenant Smith, a rude fellow' came
in and told the Earl he must be ready to go to Bolton at six the following
morning.

Incredibly, according to Baggerley, Lieutenant Smith asked the Earl if
he knew of anyone who would be the executioner and 'do that thing your
Lordship knows of'. No doubt taken aback by the effrontery of the request,
the Earl replied 'if those men that will have my head will not find one to cut it
off, let it stand where it is'[12].

It seems that the Parliamentary authorities were concerned about the
execution, and some accounts say that Oliver Cromwell now took a hand in
directing the military arrangements for the escort. The escort would be 'two
Troops of Colonell Jones Regiment'[13], which was probably Colonel John
Jones, and be under the command of 'Captaine Sontkey.'[14] This may have
been Captain Edward Sankey of Sankey, near Warrington,[15] but the officer
commanding the escort has also been named as Southley[16]. The escort of some
eighty horsemen also included a company of Foot, some sixty strong[17] and
under the direction of Colonel Duckenfield, as Colonel Jones appears to have
been out of the county at the time. The axe itself was carried by one of the
troopers and was said to have had a convex blade, very wide and heavy, but,
unusually, it had a short haft[18]. Perhaps this was to ease transportation.

On Tuesday 14 October the Earl, with Baggerley and other servants and
friends, set off for Bolton via Leigh. The Earl was placed on what has been
described as a little Galloway nag, a now-extinct kind of pony with a tendency
to pace rather than trot[19]. They were taking no chances, as the guard said they

were fearful of a rescue. On reaching Leigh, the Earl stayed overnight at the King's Arms, where he requested to visit the grave of his friend Sir Thomas Tyldesley in the nearby parish church, but in an act of vindictive spitefulness he was refused permission. The site of the King's Arms was less than a dozen paces from the parish church; it was literally across the road[20].

The following morning, after drinking 'a cup of beer to my lady', the party moved on through Atherton and Hulton, down what was to become Derby Street, to Bolton[21].

Local tradition holds that their progress was tracked by a small group of horsemen, 'privately armed', planning to rescue the Earl[22]. Supposedly led by John Seddon of Seddon Fold at Prestolee, who had been a Captain in the Earl of Derby's army in 1642, the party also included his uncle William Seddon, Rector of Grapnall in Chester[23]. The large escort, and the fact the Earl was not allowed to ride his own horse, seems to suggest the plans were known. This may have been the case as Peter Seddon, John's brother, was a captain on the local Parliamentary forces and had been among those captured at Westhoughton in 1642 and held prisoner at Lathom for some time. He may have been aware that his brother was planning something and warned the escort. The rescue was described as a 'well matured plan',[24] but had to be abandoned due to the strength of the escort and the erstwhile rescue party may well have had to content themselves with following to Bolton.

The Earl arrived in Bolton down the road that still bears his name 'betwixt twelve and one of the clock' and, passing the Market Cross, commented 'this must be my cross'. The scaffold was not ready because 'the people in the town ... refusing to carry so much as a plank, or strike a nail, or to lend any assistance'. As the scaffold was not ready, the Earl was brought to a 'house in the towne near the Crosse'[25] and, after talking to his companions and his son, the Earl asked 'to be private in the room himself, when he was observed to be about half an hour upon his knees'[26].

Outside, the scaffold was completed and was said to have been erected from timbers taken from Lathom House. It stood outside the Swan Public House next to the Market Cross, and at 3.00 p.m. the Earl was led out of the house to see only a hundred spectators had turned up; they were outnumbered by the military escort. A headsman had now been found, a local man by the name of George Whowell. Said to be a surly character, Whowell, according to local tradition, had a personal grudge against the Earl as his family had suffered in the massacre – although there is no evidence of this[27]. Whowell did not bother to wear a mask, or more likely none was available[28].

The Earl kissed the ladder to the scaffold and climbed up, saying there are 'but these few steps to my eternity'. He walked a turn or two around the scaffold and then went to the east end and began his prepared speech. Two of his clerks, one of which was James Roscow, took down the details[29]. He denied that he had killed Captain Bootle in cold blood, a charge recently, and

Plaque where the King's Arms once stood.

St Mary the Virgin, Parish church, from where the King's Arms once stood.

Bolton Market Cross.

Ye Olde Man & Scythe, the place where the Earl is said to have spent his last few hours.

Whowell's Farm.

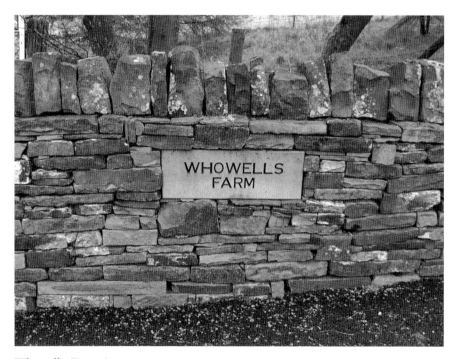

Whowell's Farm sign.

secretly, made against him, and that no one present could lay the blood of any man to him apart from those in the heat of battle. At one point, he is supposed to have said 'good friends, I die for the King, the laws of the land, and the Protestant religion'. At the words 'King and laws' a trooper said aloud, 'We will neither have King, lords, nor laws.'

At this point Stanley's friends, wanting him to speak, started jostling the troopers, who drew swords and started 'cutting and slashing the people' and a fight broke out. Perhaps his friends thought he could be rescued after all.

The Earl knew it was useless and said, 'I beseech you stay your hands. I fly not. You pursue not me; and here are none to pursue you.' The scuffle died down, but not before 'some cut, many hurt, and one childe killed'[30]. The Bolton Parish burial records have the following entry '17 Oct 1651; a child of Oliver Croychlow of Turton' who may have been the victim.

After the crowd had been subdued, the Earl called for the headsman and asked to see the axe, and, taking it in his hand, he kissed it. Then putting his hand into his pocket, said to Whowell, 'Here, friend, take these two pieces, all that I have'.

Some of the crowd 'bade the headsman kneel and ask his pardon', but Whowell would not, and was 'surly and crabbed'. Ignoring this the Earl said, 'Friend, I give thee the pardon thou wilt not ask'. Seeing the way the block was laid out, he asked for it to be turned that he might look upon the church and, having taken his doublet off, asked, 'How must I lie? Will any one shew me? I never saw any man's head cut off; but I'll try how it fits.'

It appears a low block was used, where the person lies full length and puts their neck over the small wooden block, which is just a few inches high[31]. Ralph Barton, one of the Parliamentary soldiers guarding the execution, said later that when the Earl lay down, he turned and said to William Prescot, one of his servants, 'Faithful Prescot, set thy foot to mine' so, as Barton thought, to stop any movement or shirking in the execution. The Earl prayed, and stretched his arms out and lifted his hands in the sign agreed with the headsman. Whowell missed the sign, or perhaps his courage failed him and he did nothing. The Earl rose and asked why he wasn't dead yet. Lying down again, he said the same prayers and this time, when the sign was made, 'his head was severed in one Blow' and 'no noyse was then heard but sighs and sobs and prayers'[32].

None of the accounts say that the head was shown to the crowd; as there was already a near riot when Stanley's speech was curtailed, perhaps they thought better of it. The Earl's body, 'with his clothes upon him', was put into the coffin 'there readie, which had abundance of seedes in it to receive the blood'[33].

The Parliamentary authorities wanted to inter the Earl in an ordinary grave in Bolton, but John Okey of Bolton intervened on behalf of the family and the body was 'carried away that night to Wigan and from hence to Ormeskirke',[34] to be buried in the Derby Chapel in the parish church of St Peter and St Paul.

Execution of James Stanley.

John Okey's
gravestone.

Ormskirk Parish Church.

It was said his body was buried in one casket and his head, or perhaps his heart, was buried in a separate casket.

Dame Robinson, who lived at Kestor Fold, at Doll Brow in the Haulgh just across the Croal River from Bolton, knelt at the foot of the scaffold and begged for the block, which she buried in the grounds of Kestor Fold so that 'the Presbyterians might never obtain a chip'. She was later fined and had her goods seized for supporting the Royalists[35].

Whowell went to the house where the Earl had been placed prior to his execution, and waited until nightfall before leaving with whatever payment he had received, the two gold coins the Earl had given him and the axe itself[36].

The Earl's co-defendants shared his fate, as Colonel John Benbow was shot on the green before the castle at Shrewsbury on 15 October 1651 while Sir Timothy Fetherstonehough was beheaded at Abbey Gate, Kirkoswald, Northumberland on 22 October 1651.

CHAPTER 15

Aftermath:
Consequences of Conflict

The massacre of Bolton was a rare event in what was an increasingly bitter Civil War. A number of factors collided in a wet May afternoon to bring a taste of the brutality of continental warfare to rural Lancashire. Bolton was known as a centre of Puritanism and Parliamentary support and would surely have been a target for the Royalist army, even if it was just for supplies and quarters for the night. Rigby's arrival by accident on the same morning changed things. The major factor which precipitated the massacre that was to follow was the hanging of a Royalist officer from the walls after the first attack had been beaten off. Nothing could be guaranteed to inflame the impetuous Prince more, or drive the soldiers on to commit atrocities. Although a town taken by storm was open to plunder by the attacking troops, what happened at Bolton went beyond that before the anger of the hanging had run its course. The town of Bolton paid in blood for a decision that was in all likelihood taken by Alexander Rigby and his men. Bolton would continue to suffer well after that May day in 1644.

A poignant entry in the Bolton Parish Records for 22 July 1644 reads 'Ichadbod, the son of Wm Boulton'. William Boulton had been killed in the massacre, and this unusual name shows that his wife knew the scriptures well for in Samuel, Chapter 4, Verse 17, there is the story of Phineas' wife who, after being told her husband had been killed in battle, was delivered of a son and was asked to name him and replied Ichabod – the glory is departed from Israel.

The effects of the massacre on Bolton also had an unexpected impact on the population. The parish registers showed a population growth from 1644 to 1648 and marriages at the same level of the 1630s. However, the reason for this is not hard to find when the ages of those getting married is taken into account. Normally, people at the time married quite late in life, due to the fact of the time it took to amass sufficient capital to set up home away from their parents. The ages of those marrying after the massacre were significantly lower than before, implying young people were taking advantage of the loss of so many heads of households to establish themselves[1]. John Tilsley, the Vicar of Deane, suggested that at least sixty wives lost their husbands in the massacre[2].The number of illegitimate births registered fell during this period, also indicating the opportunities for marrying younger were increased.

While for some it was a time of opportunity out of adversity, for others the years after the massacre brought little but more hardship. By 1650, Bolton was suffering the effects of food shortages and the textile industry was in decline. A petition was presented to the Justices at the Manchester Quarter sessions in July 1653, which begins 'The Humble petition of the poore widdowes, Maymed Souldiers and Fatherless Children whose husbands or parents were slayne att the Surpizall of Boulton by Prince Rupert his fforces'[3]. Unless something was done, the survivors are 'like to starve'. This appears to have not been the first petition of this kind and Katherine Wight, whose husband was killed in the massacre, 'which extended to the utter undoeing of her and hers' and was 'like to starve and famish'[4]. Almost a decade after the massacre, the people of Bolton were still feeling the effects, yet not everybody in the town suffered during the war years. Alexander Norris, a sequester for Parliament, in residence at Hall 'ith Wood, had demolished the west wing in 1648 to build in its place a grand Jacobean-style extension.

Of the Royalist leaders in Lancashire, James Stanley died on the scaffold, Sir Thomas Tyldesley fell at Wigan Lane, while Lord Molynuex had missed the battle as he was in London after being granted a special pass. He was not at Worcester either, so may have actually pulled away from supporting Charles II entirely. He appears to have settled down after the war years, marrying in 1652. However, he did not marry Henrietta Stanley; perhaps the disagreements with her father, James Stanley, had soured the relationship too much. Instead, Molyneux married Lady Frances Seymour, eldest daughter of William, Marquis of Hertford, on 28 October 1652. In less than two years, Molyneux died at Croxteth and was buried in Sefton on 2 July 1654[5].

Charlotte de la Tremoille, Lady Derby, faced internal rebellion on the Isle of Man after the execution of her husband and could not resist the force of ten ships and troops, led by Colonel Duckenfield, sent to take the island by Parliament. She signed surrender articles on 31 October and was stripped of all property and estates. Her son Charles, did inherit his father's estates as the 8th Earl of Derby and reached an accommodation with Parliament to sell some of his lands to recoup some of the family finances. Lady Derby, on the other hand, had to wait until 1652 to petition for the return of her sequested estates. The Stanley family had twenty-one manors and seventy-six other estates seized during the Commonwealth, and while the Stanleys suffered others prospered, such as Major Barton Shuttleworth and Captain Edward Shuttleworth who both farmed sequestered estates. Their brother, Colonel Nicholas Shuttleworth, did even better, and claimed no less than eight formerly Royalist-owned estates. Lady Derby died at Knowlsley on 31 March 1664, and of the estates seized the family regained only a portion. Over sixty estates were lost and it was not until late in the seventeenth century that the Worsleys of Platt finally returned the manors of Bolton and Bury to the Earls of Derby[6].

Sir Gilbert Houghton was at Chester in 1643 with Lord Byron, but seems not to have been on good terms with him and did not take part in any further action in the Civil Wars. Perhaps the loss of his son, Roger, at Marston Moor – also known as Hessum Moor – in 1644 affected him too deeply, as well as the fact that another son, Richard, was fighting for Parliament. Sir Gilbert Houghton died in 1647, and his Parliamentarian son Richard inherited the baronetcy. Richard Houghton was by then serving as a colonel in Ralph Assheton's Regiment. Of his other sons Gilbert, a major with Sir Gilbert Gerard died 12 March 1661 and Henry, a captain with the Earl of Derby died in 1681.

Sir John Girlington of Thurland was killed fighting between Rossiter and Langdale at Melton Mobray in Yorkshire on 22 February 1644[7].

Sir Gilbert Gerard remained with the Royal army after Brill on the Hill and his Regiment fought at Bristol with Molyneux's Regiment in the savage assault on the strongpoint at Prior Fort. Sir Gilbert led his Regiment at the siege of Gloucester in August 1643 and the battle of Newbury in September, where Molyneux fought under him. His Regiment was posted to Worcester in December 1643, where he was made governor, and from where he recaptured Stourton Castle after defeating a relieving Parliamentary force in March of 1644. When he died in 1645, he was succeeded as colonel of the Regiment by his brother Ratclyffe[8].

After recovering from the wounds he received at Edgehill, Charles Gerard was again wounded at Lichfield in July 1643 and fought at Bristol, Newbury and Newark, where he was once again wounded, thrown from his horse and taken prisoner. After the garrison fell and he was released, he was noticed by Prince Rupert for his gallantry and promoted to Royalist commander in South and West Wales, but when King Charles I retreated into Wales after Naseby in 1645 he replaced him as commander but bestowed him Baron Gerard of Brandon as compensation. Despite loyal service to the Crown, when Prince Rupert was dismissed in October 1646 so were his loyal officers, including Gerard who nevertheless fought in the final siege of Oxford in 1646. After Oxford's fall, he left for the continent with Prince Rupert and became Vice Admiral of the Royalist fleet in 1648. He was involved with his cousin John Gerard's plot to assassinate Oliver Cromwell on his way to Hampton Court Palace. The plot was discovered and Colonel John Gerard was arrested and beheaded on 10 July 1654. On the restoration in 1660, Charles Gerard rode at the head of the King's Horse Guards as Charles II entered London. Promoted to the Earl of Macclesfield in 1679, he was implicated in the Monmouth rebellion against James II and fled abroad in 1685. After returning at the head of the King's Lifeguard with William of Orange in 1688, he died suddenly on 7 January 1694 and was buried in Westminster Abbey.

Charles had two brothers fighting for the Royalist cause, Edward, who was a colonel of a Foot Regiment, and was wounded at Newbury in 1643, and Sir Gilbert, killed at Ludlow.

After the first Civil War, Alexander Rigby set about raising money for Parliament, including, on 15 May 1645, appointing two of his officers to raise back pay for his Regiment from sequested 'Papists or Delinquents Estates'[9]. He was at the second siege of Lathom House in 1645 and in May 1648 he was put in command of all the forces of Amounderness Hundred, while in June he commanded his Regiment of Horse in Assheton's brigade at the battle of Preston. He was named to the High Court of Justice to try the King in 1649, but managed to decline the request. In June of 1649 he was appointed one of the Barons of the Court of Exchequer, and as Baron Rigby continued with his judicial duties. Judge Baron Rigby's last appearance at an assize was at Chelmsford in August 1650, where he fell ill, causing the assizes to be adjourned. Although still gravely ill, he attended but didn't sit at the Croyden assizes where his colleague Judge Gates and the High Sheriff of Surrey also fell ill and were 'speedily conveyed away hence to London, where all three died immediately' of the 'most violent pestilential fever' which also infected many of those at the assizes, who also died[10]. Alexander Rigby died on 18 August 1650 and was buried at Preston on 9 September.

Richard Shuttleworth of Gawthorpe Hall was, by 1653, a magistrate and sequester of Royalist estates. He retired from public life after the Restoration in 1660 and died in June 1669, aged eighty-two. For some reason lost to history, he was known locally as 'Old Smut'[11].

Ralph Assheton of Middleton, despite fighting valiantly in the Preston campaign, opposed the trial and execution of Charles I in 1649. He died on 17 February 1650 and local legends talk of intrigue and treason. He was buried under the altar in Middleton church, where his grave can be seen to this day.

John Bradshaw of Bradshaw Hall was High Sherriff of Lancashire from 1644 to 1647 and died in September 1664. John Moore of Bank Hall sat as one of the judges in King Charles I's trial, and was one of the regicides who signed the death warrant. He died in 1650[12]. Colonel Peter Egerton, joint commander with Rigby at the first siege of Lathom House, died in 1656 when his maid accidentally mingled mercury instead of medicine with some milk, and Egerton died within a few hours of drinking it. Captain John Holcroft, eventually rose to the rank of lieutenant-colonel. His daughter Maria married Thomas Blood against his wishes, and she joined the infamous Colonel Blood in attempting to steal the Crown Jewels in 1671.

Captain Thomas 'Carter' Birch of Birch also rose to the rank of lieutenant-colonel and for a time was Governor of Liverpool, representing it in Parliament from 1649 to 1658. After the Restoration he retired to private life and died in 1678.

Sir Thomas Stanley of Bickerstaffe implacable enemy of his kinsman the Earl of Derby died in May 1653. John Rosworm continued to fight for Parliament throughout the war, serving with Sir Thomas Fairfax at Nantwich in 1643. He fought at Warrington and was with Sir John Meldrum at the taking of Liverpool in 1644. In 1644 and 1645 the Royalists again approached him, but he rebuffed them despite friction with Colonel Holland and increasing pay arrears. In 1648 he wrote a long complaint to Sir Thomas Fairfax and Oliver Cromwell regarding these arrears to little effect, but having established his family in Manchester he enjoyed sporadic payments for his wartime service. In 1651 he gained a post in Yarmouth overseeing the defences and was appointed Engineer General of the Army on 19 July 1659. His whereabouts after the Restoration are unknown and it is thought he died abroad, in exile from his adopted land.

Colonel Richard Holland later fought at Nantwich and the second siege of Lathom House. He served for Lancashire in the Parliaments of 1654 and 1656 before he died in 1661. Sir Thomas Fairfax lived in retirement in Yorkshire until George Monck invited him to assist against John Lambert's army in 1659. With the break up of Lambert's forces and the elections that followed, Fairfax was elected as a Member of Parliament for Yorkshire. He was head of the commission charged with inviting Charles II back from The Hague and actually provided the horse which the new King rode to his coronation. He spent the remaining years in retirement in Yorkshire and died on 12 November 1671 at Nunappleton. Sir William Brereton was involved in the mopping up of Royalist resistance around Chester after the First Civil War and took the surrender of the last Royalist field army of Sir Jacob Astley, at Stow-on-the-Wold in March 1646. Parliament rewarded him with Eccleston Castle and Croyden Palace, the former home of the Archbishop of Canterbury. He declined to be involved in the trial and execution of King Charles I in 1649 and appears to have retired from public life. When the Restoration returned Croyden Palace to its former owners, Brereton was allowed to remain as a tenant until his death in 1661.

Captain Robert Venables, captured at Westhoughton in 1642 was soon released and commanded a Foot company under Sir William Brereton at Chester the following year. In 1645, he was governor of Tarvin, fought in Wales in 1648, and in 1649 Colonel Venables was in Ireland fighting at Dublin on 2 August. In 1655, when a fleet sailed to the West Indies, the land forces were under the command of General Venables, who attacked and took Jamaica but was later jailed in the Tower of London for leaving the West Indies without orders. In 1660, General Venables was governor of Chester and died in July 1687 at the age of seventy-five[13].

Of the soldiers that took part in the first attack on Bolton on 16 February 1643 little is known, apart from one. Captain Christopher Anderton of Lostock Hall lost all his lands to the Parliamentary sequesters after the First Civil War, including the rectory of Deane,[14] and moved to London, where he died on 7 July 1650.

Prince Rupert's standing with the King was not diminished by the disaster at Marston Moor, and he was promoted to Captain General of all Royalist forces in England and Wales in November 1644. The appointment was far from popular in all quarters of the Royalist camp and reinforced the charge of nepotism at court. As governor of Bristol and president of Wales, he worked to rebuild the

Royalist forces after the summer disasters but he promoted his own followers, including Charles Gerard in Wales, and while his star still rose at court he made enemies. At Naseby in June 1645 he led the Royalist army to defeat at the hands of the New Model Army of Sir Thomas Fairfax, and fled to Bristol. Besieged by the triumphant Parliamentarians, he surrendered Bristol in September 1645 but the King was outraged, the Prince's enemies at court added to the pressure and the Prince was summarily dismissed and ordered to depart the realm. He left for France after Oxford surrendered in 1646, and was appointed marachal de champ and commander of the English in French service.

He started another career as part admiral and part pirate for the soon to be Charles II. Sailing in 1649 with a number of ships, he captured English merchantmen in the Mediterranean and prizes off the Gambian coast before losing most of his fleet and his brother Maurice in a hurricane near the Virgin Islands in 1652. Only two ships returned to France in 1653 and he left Charles II's court the following year. Following the Restoration, he returned to England and fought in the Second and Third Anglo Dutch wars, leading the van at Southwold Bay in 1665, being defeated in the Four Days Battle in 1667, before winning at North Foreland later the same year. He was appointed First Lord of the Admiralty in July 1673 and died on 29 November 1682 in Spring Gardens at the entrance to Whitehall.

Lieutenant-Colonel John Russell did not take part in the battle of Marston Moor due to his wounds from Bolton, but was promoted to colonel and took over the Prince's Foot. He fought at Naseby in June 1645, where he escaped capture and eventually surrendered at London. He did not take part in the later civil wars, but after the Restoration was appointed colonel of the Kings 1st Foot Guards. He retired in the 1670s and died sometime around 1687.

John Byron, 1st Baron Byron, commanded Chester after the defeat at Marston Moor and the fall of the Royalist cause in Lancashire. Chester was subjected to a full siege in September 1645 and, although Byron conducted a spirited defence, he was forced to surrender the city in February 1646 and went into exile on the continent the following June. In 1648 he was back in North Wales, attempting to raise forces to support the Scottish Engager invasion but having failed to gain support, he withdrew to Dublin before the battle of Preston. Byron joined King Charles II at The Hague, but did not join him in 1650 in the Third Civil War. He joined the household of the Duke of York, later King James II, and served with him during his campaigns with the French Army before dying suddenly in Paris in August 1652.

Sir William Vaughan charged at Naseby in 1645, and was made general of all Horse in Wales, but was on the defensive until his forces were broken at Stow-on-the-Wold in March 1646. He escaped to The Hague, from where he travelled back to Ireland to become major general of Horse under Ormonde. On 2 August 1649, he was killed at Rathmines.

Sir John Urry thought the King's cause was lost after Marston Moor and fled to Sir William Waller's Parliamentarian army. Surprisingly, he was allowed to rejoin the Parliamentarian forces in October 1644, and in February 1645 transferred to the Army of the Covenant with the rank of major general and colonel of dragoons. He fought bravely at Auldean in May 1645 but retired soon after, claiming ill health. Changing sides yet again, he joined the Engagers in August 1648 and was captured at Preston. Escaping to the continent, he returned as major general to the Marquis of Montrose in 1650, where his luck finally ran out at Carisdale when he was wounded and captured. This time there would be no escape as he was beheaded at Edinburgh on 19 May 1650.

Marcus Trevor returned to Ireland after the first Civil War sometime around 1647 to fight under Monck. He was made governor of Carlingford in March 1648, before deserting to Ormonde in June 1649. However, by 1652 he was back supporting Cromwell until 1659, when he secured Irish support for the Restoration, which gained him rewards of land, a seat on the Irish privy council and the title of Viscount Dungannon and Baron Trevor bestowed on 22 August 1662. He died in 1670.

Sir Michael Ernle was probably killed at killed at Shrewsbury 1645, but his name also appears on a list of prisoners, while Colonel Rowland Eyre's war ended when he was surrounded at Litchfield in 1646. He died in 1674.

John Frescheville was appointed Colonel General of Derbyshire in late 1644 but considered the Royalist cause lost in late 1645 when he retired to the Netherlands. After the Restoration he was made Baron Frescheville of Staveley, but debts caused by expense of raising and outfitting units in the Civil Wars blighted his later life. He died in London on 31 March 1682.

Sampson Mason, whose father Robert and uncle Alexander fell in the massacre, apparently did not stay long in Lancashire. In 1649 he was recorded in the town records of Dorchester, Norfolk County, Massachusetts as a shoemaker by trade, where his skills would have made him a valuable member of the new colony. On 9 March 1650, he purchased six acres and a house in Dorchester,[15] and sometime later married Mary Butterworth on 9 March 1652. He must have prospered, as on 9 December 1657 he purchased considerable property and land in Rehoboth and also appears to have entered into land speculation. He was one of the original proprietors, who were the owners of the majority of the real estate of the township of Swansea, a Baptist town, at its incorporation in 1668, where Elder John Myles converted him to the Baptist faith. After having thirteen children with his wife Mary, he passed away on 7 September 1676 in Swansea, Bristol County, Massachusetts, leaving a considerable personal estate of several hundred acres. *A History of the Baptist Church in New England* stated he was a soldier in Cromwell's army. Perhaps they didn't understand when he talked about his time fighting for Parliament that he never meant he fought with Cromwell, or perhaps, like many old soldiers, he never talked much about it at all[16].

Laurence Hardman of Buckfold in Pennington, whose life was saved at Bolton by his friend, lived to a ripe old age of 105 and was buried at Leigh on 30 April 1715. The vicar added to the register, 'Laurence Hardman, the last of the cavaliers that I knew in Leigh parish'. With his passing, the Bolton Massacre probably slipped from human memory[17]. Colonel Edward Chisnall of Chorley, hero of Lathom House and who had fought at Marston Moor, succumbed to his wounds in 1653.

Of those that fought later in Lancashire, Edward Massey was wounded at the bridge over the River Severn at Upton prior to the battle of Worcester. Weak from his wounds, he fled with King Charles after the battle but was unable to keep up and was left at Droitwich at the home of the late Earl of Stamford, but the Earl's widow handed him over to the Parliamentarians. He was confined in the tower of London, but managed to escape in August 1652 by climbing out of a chimney and made his way once again to the Netherlands. Massey made several clandestine visits to England in the Royalist cause in 1654, 1656 and in 1659, when he was arrested on 31 July attempting to organise an uprising. The master escapee, he managed to slip his captors yet again and fled to the continent. At the Restoration in 1660 he was rewarded with a knighthood and estates in Ireland. Sir Edward Massey died in 1674.

Sir Marmadule Langdale escaped from Nottingham Castle in October 1648 and, after hiding in a haystack, made his way to his cousin's house at Houghton. After further adventures, which included dressing as a clergyman he escaped to the continent, and after the Restoration was created Baron Langdale of Holme and made Lord Lieutenant for the West Riding of Yorkshire. He died on 5 August 1661 in Holme-on-Spalding.

John Middleton was wounded at the battle of Worcester and captured at Blackstone Edge in Yorkshire by Colonel Birch before being imprisoned in the Tower of London. Before he could be tried, he escaped to the continent and exile. He fought unsuccessfully in the Glencairn uprising in 1654 but was forced back abroad by its failure. After the Restoration, he was created 1st Earl of Middleton and was Governor of Tangier from 1668 to his death in 1674.

Colonel Robert Lilburne returned north to Scotland after Wigan Lane as part of Major General Richard Deane's army of occupation in November 1651. He took over command in December of 1652 before handing over the General George Monck in early 1654. Later that year, he was Governor of York and put down the Sealed Knot uprising. With the Restoration in 1660 he was arrested with all the other living regicides, found guilty of high treason and sentenced to be hanged, drawn and quartered. His sentence was commuted to life imprisonment, and he died in prison on Drakes Island in Plymouth Sound in August 1665. David Leslie was captured after Worcester and imprisoned in the Tower of London until being released during the Restoration in 1660. He was made 1st Baron Newark in 1661 and died in 1682.

Of the tribunal that sat in judgement of the Earl of Derby at Chester Colonel Humphrey Mackworth became a member of Cromwell's council and when he died on 26 December 1654 he was interred in Henry VII's chapel in

Westminster Abbey. His remains were disinterred in September 1660, along with Cromwell's, and were unceremoniously thrown in a pit in St Margaret's Churchyard.

Colonel Robert Duckinfield lived to see the Restoration and, following a petition from Lady Derby, was among those of the Chester Tribunal imprisoned. He had transferred all his estates to his son to keep them from being taken and on his release after a short confinement, his son refused to restore his lands. He died at Dukinfield Hall in 1689 and was buried at the Church of St Lawrence, Denton.

George Whowell, whose act of vengeance for his murdered family had severed James Stanley's head in 1651, returned to his farm to try and lead a normal life. It is said that he never spent the two gold coins that Stanley had given him and his family retained the axe he wielded that day well into the 1800s. With the Restoration in 1660, retribution was not long in coming to those that had supported Parliament, and local legend has it that the past caught up to George Whowell outside the Pack Horse Pub on Watling Street in Affetside. Here, so the legend says, a group of Royalist supporters accosted and murdered him. His head was cut from his body, in some macabre re-enactment of Stanley's execution, and stuck on a pole outside the pub. The locals brought it in and there it sits to this day, stained mahogany with age, above the bar. The last victim of the Bolton Massacre.

Perhaps more prosaically, another story has it that the skull was found in the field beside the pub sometime in the 1800s and an enterprising publican concocted the tale to pull in the customers. The *Bolton Evening News* in 1874 stated that a Whowell family member claimed that when the family left the farm[18] in 1829, the skull was brought to the pub because George Whowell was a regular there. In any event, the skull still has pride of place behind the bar.

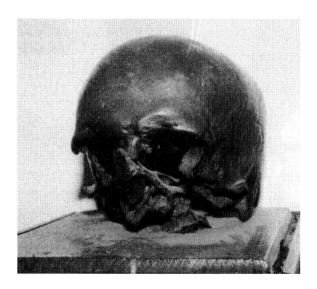

Whowell's skull.

The Whowell family apparently held onto the axe until at least 1812, when it was said to be still in their possession, as one of his descendants was verbally abused in Bolton marketplace and retorted that 'they still have the axe and will use it'[19]. Sometime that century it passed to the Holt family of Turton, who then sold it to William Sharples of the Sharples Museum of Curiosities above the Star Inn on Churchgate in Bolton, who displayed it for the number of years in the nineteenth century. The axe then passed to James P. Weston in the latter part of the nineteenth century and has since been lost[20].

Myths started about the Massacre and the Execution soon after they happened. One early myth relates to the death of William Isherwood and his wife. As the dead woman lay in the street, her starving baby was vainly attempting to feed off her breast. An old woman, over seventy years of age, who had not nursed a baby herself for decades, lifted the crying child off its mother and, putting it to her own breast, the baby, miraculously, was able to feed[21].

The scaffold was certainly made from timbers taken from the Earl's house at Lathom, but the block was said to have a particularly connotation to him as well. The block was said to have been made from a tree on his estate at Knowlsley, under which the Earl once sat on his horse watching Colonel Birch, who had been captured, being dragged along behind a haycart. This myth supposed that Birch earned his name 'the Earl's Carter' from this episode – but he earned the name 'Carter Birch' at the Banquet skirmish in Manchester, so this is unlikely to be true.

Ye Olde Man and Scythe Public House on Churchgate has been associated with the execution for a long time, most often being mentioned as the place where the Earl spent his last hours. Some accounts claim the landlord in 1644, James Cockerell, or Cockerele, who died in March 1709, reputedly 106 years old, displayed a small fish dish that the Earl supposedly ate from before his execution. Another supposed relic was a 3-pint Delft stone jug supposedly used by the Earl to take a drink of water, which passed to John Ward, who lived at a cottage near Churchbank. Neither of these 'relics' appear to have been seen after about 1700[22]. John Seacombe wrote *The History of the House of Stanley 1737* under the patronage of the Stanley family and it shows in his writing, with a number of dubious tales associated with the 7th Earl. One has James Stanley leading the first assault in Bolton, crying that he will take the wall or leave his body in the ditch. This is after the cavalry engagement which the Earl was probably involved in. One other myth that Seacombe perpetrated was that the Earl's son, Charles, rode all the way to London in a day and a night to have a petition read, but that Cromwell and Bradshaw connived to have too few members in the house to have the petition put. Seacombe's flight of fancy has little truth as the House of Commons journal clearly shows the petition was read, but did not change the verdict or the sentence.

Daniel Defoe wrote the novel *Memoirs of a Cavalier* in 1720, set in the Thirty Years War and the English Civil War, purporting to be a true life adventure in the style of his more famous *Robinson Crusoe*. It was unusual in that it gave the reader no clue as to who wrote it and implied it was a recent editing of a real memoir. The protagonist is at the Bolton Massacre as part of Prince Rupert's army, yet the tale is wildly inaccurate, for example describing a two-day battle and having the Royalist army camped under the defenders' guns by the wall overnight. It was not until 1784 that Defoe was identified as the author, yet the novel was taken as a true eyewitness account of the Massacre as early as 1786 and is still quoted as such today.

The market cross beside which the scaffold was erected had stood since 1485 on the corner of Churchgate and Bradshawgate, but was moved in 1776 as it was obstructing movement to the market. After a number of years where its whereabouts were unknown, it was apparently erected in the grounds of Bolton School on Chorley Old Road. Unfortunately, the remains of the cross standing in the school's grounds bears little resemblance to the description of the original market cross, so it is doubtful that is what it is.

In the 1820s, the landlord of the Ye Olde Man and Scythe Pub found a 1590s Flemish-style chair in the cellar and in an attempt to cash in on the Derby legend, had a brass label attached claiming that Derby had sat in the chair prior

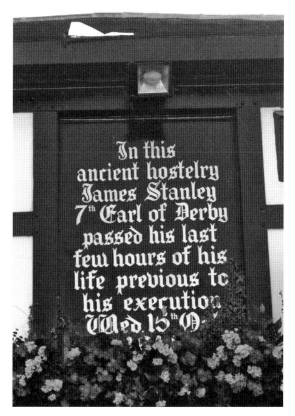

Ye Olde Man & Scythe sign.

The supposed old market cross.

to his execution. The chair has been damaged a number of times, including in the 1965 when a member of the rock band The Who supposedly sat in it. It is still in the pub, as is a tankard which is a copy of the one supposedly used by the Earl awaiting his execution. As the Earl did not stay in the pub or take a drink, this seems another of the pub landlord's many inventions.

Recent landlords of the Man and Scythe continued to play on the pub's most celebrated alleged patron, for in 1914 publican Frank Hampson wrote and published *An interesting history of the Execution of James Stanley and Ye Old Man and Scythe Inn*. When Tom Pendlebury took over the pub sometime later, he stamped his name on the slim volume and continued to sell it.

A 342-page historical novel recalling the massacre called *John O'Gods Sending* by Allen Clarke was originally published in 1891. The novel is set in Bolton during the Civil War and has the protagonists involved in the massacre, but is historically inaccurate, being based on Defoe's account and aiming to ensure the characters are central to the action. It was adapted as an 8-scene play by Les Smith called *The Lass at the Man and Scythe*, performed first at Bolton's Octagon Theatre in May 1989. This was not the first play from the Octagon Theatre relating to the tale, as in 1968 a play called *Bolton Massacre* with songs of the period retold the story – the cast included a young actor by

Ye Olde Man &
Scythe chair.

The tankard.

the name of Gorden Kaye. The Octagon Theatre also published a twenty-four-page booklet retelling the Massacre with illustrations and maps written by Jonathon Porter. It came out of research conducted in the writing of *Bolton Massacre* and included biographies of the main characters, songs of the period and an accurate, though brief, retelling of the Massacre.

There have been stories that up to twenty-one soldiers escaped from the church in a tunnel as the massacre was ending[23] and in November 1966 the local evening paper, the *Bolton Evening News*, reported that tunnels were found under what was then the Co-op building on Bridge Street that appeared to lead towards the churchyard, but that they were blocked off. It must be said that no contemporary accounts describe any escapes from the church, and no tunnels were found when it was demolished in 1866. The local newspaper even launched an unsuccessful hunt for the axe, asking readers to search their attics the following year.

The latest landlord of the Ye Olde Man and Scythe Pub, John Jewitt[24], found that the story had largely been forgotten when he took over the pub. As with many landlords before, he looked to revive interest in the pub's history and its most celebrated supposed patron, and since 2003 has organised an annual street play re-enactment of the massacre and execution with himself in the starring role as James Stanley. So from being a footnote of history largely forgotten in the town where it happened, the people of Bolton now get to see James Stanley's final moments re-enacted every year on the anniversary of this death in the very street where, in 1644, so much real blood was shed.

Street Play.

Prisoners taken at Westhoughton Common: 15 December 1642

Prisoners at Lathome

Roberte Venables	Captaine
Roberte Bradshawe	Captaine
Risley Browne	Captaine
Edward Bowker	Lieftenante to Capt. Bradshawe
Peter Sedion	
Thomas Bancroft	
Thomas Cheetham of Stopforth	Serjeante
Lawrence Warren of Poynton gent	

Prisoners at Wigane

Peter Rylands of Houghton	Lieftenante to Capt. Browne
John Earlom of Earlom, gent	Serjeante to Capt. Bradshawe
Nathaniell Longworth of longworth gent	Corporall to Capt Bradshawe

LISTED TO CAPT BRADSHAWE

Henry Browne of Lynestone	
Lawrence Williamson of Rodegreene	
Thomas Rigby of Abraham	
John Williamson of Nantwich in Colchester	
James Smethurst of Preswich	
Roger Crooke of Aspull	
John Hackome of Longworth	Corporall
John Gerrard of Windle	
Arnard Baxter of Gatley	
Edward Barlowe of Lostocke	
Thurston Collier of Worsley	Yeoman
Anthony Locke of Prestwich	Drummer to Capt. Bradshawe
John Bradshaw of prestwich	

James Bradshaw of prestwich
William Roscoe of Worsley
T. Waterhouse of prestwich
Richard Withinton of Hulton
John Lathom of Sutton
Raphe Barker of Manchester
Thomas Baggerlery of Manchester
John Greenhalgh of Pilsworth
Thomas Kempe of Newton
Thomas Smith of Manchester
Peter Harrison of Aspull
James Russell of Middle Halton
Richard Swift of Hindley
Thomas Greaves of Rachdall
William Hallows of Manchester
Rich. Tatnall of Beeston in Co Chester
John Tailor of Deafholme
John Platte of Middleton
John Bromeley of Little Lever
James Worthington of Manchester
James Maddock of Manchester
Adam Stones of Turton
John Russell of Middle Hulton
John Johns of Cliff Greene in Co Chester
John Hulme of Deane
Richard Troppe of Barton
Richard Rogers of Deafholme
Abaham Barlowe of Aynsworth
Nicholas Walter of Broughton
Thomas Heawood of Little Lever
W. Wood of Cheadale in Co Chester
James Rothwell of Turton
Roberte Pendleton of Broughton
Alexander Stoner of High Harrocke
Thomas Eller of Ardwicke Greene
James Corker of Manchester
Thomas Eaye of Longworth
John Boardman of Barlowe Crosse

LISTED TO CAPT VENABLES
James Harwood of Manchester   Corporall
Edmund Whitehead of Bolton
William Scolcroft of Lever

John Downes of Eccles
John Fyles of Eccles
Robert Marsh of Burton wood
John Bancrofte of Didsbury
Robert Bancrofte of Didsbury
John Bowler of Cheadle	Drummer to Capt. Venables
John Locker of Ulverston
Ralph Morris of Bolton
Thomas Seddon of Bolton
John Brooke of Bolton
James Dean of Bolton
John Collier of Worsley
James Sale of Tidesley
John Fell of Manchester
Tho. Perion Winington of Co Chester
Thomas Kellorne of Winington of Co Chester
Thomas Kellerhorne of Winington in Co
Chester
John Malbone of Winington in Co Chester
Robert Bromme of Lostocke
Richard Bradford of Lostocke
Jeremy Crosse of Eccles
Thomas Stenthill of Knutsford in Co Chester
Richard Hulme of Harwood
John Dyson of Newton
Tho. Janion of Holmes Chappell in Co
Chester
Thomas Earlom of Worsley

THE FOLLOWING ARE NOT LISTED UNDER A CAPTAIN AND MAY BE UNDER
CAPTAIN BROWNE:
  John Hart of Hoghton
  John Jackson of Hoghton
  Raphe Seddon of Bolton
  William Jepson of Pinnington
  Robert Miller of Manchester	Carrier of the magazine

Prisoners at Ormeschurch

LISTED UNDER CAPT VENABLES
  Joseph Kenion of Ruchford gent	Serjeant
  John Kenion his sonne
  William Greaves of Shrewsbury

Abraham Romesbothome of Rachdall
William Fylee of Warton   Yeoman
Roger Singar of Lullington in Co Sommers
John Morris of Bolton
James Marshall of Bolton
George Smith of Bolton
George Spenser of Wrixham
James Smaley of Cheadle in Co Chester
Thomas Marsh of Burton wood
Jonathon Marsh of Burton wood
Geo. Platt of Holte in Co Denbigh   Drummer

This list is based on the Anderton papers in the Wigan Archives. There are a number of tears and pieces missing in the original documents, so this is an incomplete list.

Royalist Officers at Bolton: 28 March 1644

Prince Rupert's Army at Bolton
Regiments of Horse

Prince Rupert's Lifeguard and Regiment

Lieutenant Colonel
Sir Richard Crane   Sir Thomas Dallinson

Major
Richard Foxe   William Legge   Edward Williams

Captain
William Bowes   Sir Francis Cobbe   William Curson
Hugh Davis   William Dutton   Henry Eden
Richard Gardiner   Thomas Gardiner   Richard Grace
Clement Martin   John Richardson   William Rumball

Lieutenants
George Blakinson   Humphrey Cox   Thomas Coyney
Daniel Crickett   Charles Hart   William Knight
Bryan Richardson

Cornets
Jeremy Bower   Nicholas Burt   Edmund Brooke
William King   Thomas Walter   George Watson
Thomas Williams   Henry Wood

Quatermasters
Roger Burton   William Clay   Anthony Exton
John Field   Robert Jackson   John Launder
William Montgomery   John Page   Edward Robinson

Robert Shatterel   Robert Thatcham   Thomas Thwaytes
William Young

Lord Byron's Regiment

Lieutenant Colonel
Gilbert Byron (brother of
Lord Byron)

Major
William Byron (brother of
Lord Byron)

Captain

Thomas Bavand	Roger Birkenhead	Thomas Carleton
Edward Dean	William Dymock	Jeremy Fryer
John Greenhough	Edward St John	John Sayers

Lieutenant

George Bacon	Richard Clayton	Degory Cory
William Littlefair		

Cornets

John Carleton	Henry Conyers	Walter Franklin
John Pey	David Powel	

Quatermasters

John Brotherton	William Hetherington	Ralph Hodgekin
George Johnson	John Pasmuch	Thomas Scot

Sir William Vaughan's Regiment

Lieutenant Colonel
Henry Slaughter

Major
Radcliffe Duckenfield

Captain

Wolsten Dixy	George Hosier	Edward Jones

Lieutenant

Thomas Moon	William Sugar	Beverly Usher

Morgan Vaughn

Cornet
Thomas Aston	John Cotton	William Ling
Thomas Sherwood	Thomas Wright	

Quatermaster
Huntingdon Crossman	John Newton	Alexander Shelton

Sir John Urry's Regiment

No officers are listed for Sir John Urry's Regiment in the 'I. O.' list, perhaps as none wanted to be associated with such a notorious turncoat

Lord Molyneux's Regiment

Lieutenant Colonel
Caryll Molyneux (Brother of
Lord Molyneux)

Captain
Atherton	Daniel Bavand	Willaim Fazacarle
Thomas Gerard	Robert Middleton	Thomas Salisbury
Thomas Shireburn	Edward Standsih	

Lieutenant
Gervase Clifton	Abell Field	Edward Latham
Edmund Molyneux	Ralph Rishton	

Quatermaster
Thomas Clifton	Edward Gore

Sir Thomas Tyldesley's Regiment

Lieutenant Colonel
James Anderton

Major
Thomas Salvin

Captain
William Balidon	John Bamber	Rowand Beckingham
John Brooks	John Butler	Thomas Carus

Gervase Clifton	Daniel Dale	Cuthbert Hesketh
Francis Holden	John Swindlehurst	Edward Tyldesley
Edmund Twaddell	Charles Westby	George Westby
Robert Whitfield	Thomas Winckly	

Lieutenant

William Gerard	William Mainwaring	William Sharpe
Richard Tempest	Richard Waring	

Cornet

Christopher Anderton	John Bradwood	Hugh Dickinson
William Dickinson	John Gardiner	Robert Ingleton
James Pearson	Alexander Rigby	Edward Tyldesley

Quatermaster

Robert Adamson	Henry Banister	John Hoole
John Maughan	Edward Oddy	Edward Rogerson
Edward Waring		

Colonel Marcus Trevor's Regiment

Lieutenant Colonel
Sir Henry Newton

Major
Sir Thomas Corbett

Captain

Laurence Bentahall	John Dolben	Edward Floyd
Harry Lloyd	Lord Kilmurry	John Lynne
George Swords	Hugh Trevor	

Captain-Lieutenant
Robert Nanny

Lieutenant

Robert Griffith	William Halyburton	Daniel Lane
John Lee		

Cornet

John Bowen	Peter Floyd	Robert Kilvert

Quatermaster

| John Dacres | James Grover | Maurice Hartshorn |
| Thomas Hawes | Richard Kirk | Roger Vaughan |

Sir William Pelham's Regiment

Lieutenant Colonel
Edward Pelham (son of Sir
William)

Major
Scroop

Captain

| Marmaduke Darrell | Francis Floyd | William Saltmarsh |
| John Salvin | Thomas Wright | |

Captain–Lieutenant
William Darwin

Lieutenant

| Thomas Appleyard | William Laythorpe | John Sergeant |
| John Skipworth | | |

Cornet

Edward Bowden	Othwell Bestoe	Thomas Lovell
John Bask	Thomas Waters	Thomas Wesled
Anthony Wight		

Quatermaster

| Henry Bennet | John Davy | Christopher Dawson |
| Richard Gilby | | |

Colonel Rowland Eyre's Regiment

Lieutenant Colonel
Thomas Eyre

Captain

| Howard Brock | James Tunstead |

Cornet

| Matthew Barker | Rowland Funess |

Quatermaster
Thomas Bowyer	Henry Hayward	John Steeple

Colonel John Frescheville's Regiment

Major
John Beversham	Jarnot

Captain
Richard Alsop	John Eyre	Sir Henry Hunlock
John Low	Edward Nicholls	Gervase Poole

Lieutenant
Thomas Eyre	William Fletcher	Ignatius Poole

Cornet
Clifton Rodes

Quatermaster
Robert Bullock	Thomas Eyre	John Harris
Hugh Scorer		

Colonel Thomas Leveson's Regiment

Lieutenant Colonel
Walter Gifford

Major
Christopher Heveningham

Captain
William Carlis	John Potts

Captain–Lieutenant
John Birch

Lieutenant
Richard Caney	Richard Collier	Francis Frotescue

Cornet
John Evenden

Quatermaster

| William Elliot | Thomas Freeman | Thomas Osborn |
| Richard Shepton | | |

FOOT REGIMENTS

Prince Rupert's Regiment of Foot

Lieutenant Colonel
John Russell (wounded at Bolton)

Major
| Aeneas Lyne | Dominick Mitchell |

Captain
| Richard Basket | Maxamilian Nelson | Thomas Nicholls |
| Valentine Pyne | John Tilden | Gerard White |

Captain–Lieutenant
| Nicholas Barker | Richard Joyner |

Lieutenant
| Owen Carty | George Grey | Roger Hillary |
| James Hinane | Matthew Howell | John Sparrey |

Ensign
| William Conningsby | John Hill | William Pyne |
| Richard Walwyn | Thomas Wogan | |

Colonel Henry Tillier's Regiment

Lieutenant Colonel
Edmund Hammond

Captain
| Hanniball Bagenall | Henry Churne | John Cressy |

Captain–Lieutenant
William Boone

Lieutenant
Richard Pye

Ensign
| Miles Butler | Ambrose Calthrope | Lewis David |

Colonel Robert Broughton's Regiment

Major
Robert Broughton
(nephew of Colonel)

Captain
George Lisle   Edward Mallory   John Morgan
Hugh Polden   Edward Ap. Robert

Lieutenant
Darren Field   Duppy   Oliver
Cadwallader Wynne

Ensign
Thomas Johnson   David Parry   Porter
Thomas Pritchard   Vaughn

Sir Michael Ernle's Regiment

Lieutenant Colonel
William Gibbs

Major
Emmanuel Palmer   Francis Ranger

Captain
John Carey   William Long   William Lucas
James Richardson   Thomas Vaughn

Lieutenant
Thomas Ady   John Kirk

Ensign
Thomas Cole

Colonel Robert Ellis' Regiment

Lieutenant Colonel
John Robinson

Major
Bevis Floyd   John Morris

Captain

David Dolben	John Edwards	George Hosyer
John Morgan	Thomas Powel	

Lieutenant

Griffith Bowen	Rice Edwards	John Gregory
David Lewis		

Ensign

Richard Blodwell	David Edwards

Lord Byron's Regiment

Lieutenant Colonel
Thomas Napier

Major
Thomas Manley

Captain

Thomas Baker	Richard Brereton	John Delavel
Roger Manley	Edward Phillips	Anthony Porter
Ellis Sutton		

Lieutenant

Batholomew Fowler	William Hughes	William Powell
Richard Weston	John Wilmot	

Ensign
Edward Jones

Quatermaster
John Sale

Colonel Robert Byron's Regiment

Lieutenant Colonel
William Walton

Major
Michael Hearle

Captain

Thomas Sherborne   Henry Trapps

Ensign
Richard Malpas

Colonel Henry Warren's Regiment

Major
Daniel Moore

Captain
Robert Berkley   Daniel Broughton   William Cope
John Disney   Richard Thurland

Colonel Richard Gibson's Regiment

Lieutenant Colonel
George Vane

Captain
John Atkins   Richard Kynnaston   Thomas Mallome
William Sydenham   Arthur Ward

Ensign
John Jones   William Overley

Sir Thomas Tyldesley's Regiment

Lieutenant Colonel
Hugh Anderton

Major
Orde

Captain
John Harlin (later Major)   Nicholas Anderton   Henry Brabent
Edward Bradley   James Bradley   John Draycott
Roger Houghton   Thomas Houghton   John Swinglehurst
Robert Westby

Lieutenant
Wilfred Carus   Edward Cripling   John Dawson
Philip Drayton   John Fletcher   Oliver Tootal

William Werden	John Whiteside	

Ensign

Edward Corney	Henry Harling	Thomas Walmsley
Thomas Whittingham	Thomas Yates	

Colonel Henry Cheater's Regiment

Captain

John Pawlet	William Wharton

Colonel Rowland Eyre's Regiment

Captain
Richard Allen

Lieutenant

John Bold	John Bradbury	Francis Rowland

Colonel John Frescheville's Regiment

Captain
William Bates

Colonel John Millward's Regiment

Captain

Francis Bruce	David Ellis

Lieutenant
Thomas Pott

Ensign
Francis Cotterell

DRAGOONS

Henry Washington's Dragoons

Lieutenant Colonel
Henry Huddlestone

Major
Edmund Broad   Nathaniel Grey   Francis Morrison

Captain
Henry Bellamy   Henry Colthorpe   Alexander Frankish
Theadore Humphreys   Henry Norwood   William Tuke

Lieutenant
John Chesman   Gilbert Hudson   William Pilkington
Richard Rose   Michael Watson

Cornet
Ralph Lamply   William Peters

Quatermaster
William Smith   John Washington

*

This list is based on a number of sources, chiefly the list of officers claiming part of the bounty of £60,000 set aside by King Charles II 'for the relief' of those ex soldiers in need. Published in 1663 this list, commonly known as the 'Indigent Officers' or 'I.O.', is by no means a complete Army list of the forces that fought for the King in the Civil Wars. It is more of a pension list, but it can, with other sources such as the *Mercurius Aulicus* and prisoner of war lists, at least be a best guess of the officers who fought in the Royalist Regiments at Bolton in 1644.

List of those Killed in the Massacre: Bolton Parish Records, 28 March 1644

Wm. Bootle, Capt.;
James Siddall, seriant;
Nicho Norres, serient;
Thomas Cooke,
Adam Rothwell,
John Rothwell,
Wm. Rothwell,
Richard Morris, senior,
Alex: Lightbowne,
John Lightbowne,
Roger Seddon,
Robt: Kirkall,
Raph Dickenson,
John Drap,
Robt: Mason,
Alex: Mason,
Raph Bordman,
John Pomfrett,
Rich: Robinson,
John Aynsworth,
Henery Brook,
Tho: Russell,
John Kirkall,
Robt: Kirkall,
Henery Wright,
James Wright,
John Brook,
Rich: Haslome,
Jorden Sharples,
Wm. Makon,
James Norres,

Rich: Norres,
Roger Hart,
Edmund Haslom with his sonne,
Raph Leaver,
Wm. Bolton,
John Hobbs,
George Smith,
John Dobson,
Hamlett Smith,
John Norres,
Henery Twist,
Peter Blakloe,
Jo: Greenehalgh,
Wm. Yeate,
John Edge,
Rich: Wright,
Gyles Morris,
Tho: Grundy,
Robt. Robinson,
Lamuell Harper,
Jo: Bradshaw, gent;
Arthur Wolfitt,
Wm. Holland,
Wm. Hardman,
Rich: Marshall,
Henery Seddon,
Robt. Farnworth,
George Holme,
James Gorton,
Tilsley Grundy,

Wm. Harvye,
Jo: Fletcher,
Wm. Crompton,
Wm. Isherwood et uxor, (and wife)
Rich: Bolton, prentice;
Tho: Kay,
Robt. Dickson,
John Crompton,

Adam Hodgskinson,
Wm. Hosken,
Chr. Nuttall,
Uxor Arthur Seddon,
Chr: Neild,
Wm. Wood,
George Munday.
All these 78 of Boltonn slayne on the 28 May 1644.

Endnotes

Chapter 1
The Path to War

1 *Seventeenth Century Lancashire*, p. 109.
2 *The Great Civil War in Lancashire 1642–51*, p. 20.
3 Ibid p. 21.
4 Ibid p. 28.
5 *Seventeenth Century Lancashire*, p. 105.
6 *The Houghton Genealogy.*
7 *Aspects of the English Civil war in Bolton and its neighbourhood 1640 – 1660*, p. 6 and Marie Mitchell Archive.
8 *The Great Civil War in Lancashire 1642–51*, p. 58.
9 Around £73,000 per day at 2010 prices.
10 *The Great Civil War in Lancashire 1642–51*, p. 68.
11 *An English Army for Ireland*, p. 5.

Chapter 2
Making of a Market Town:
Bolton up to 1642

1 *A History of Bolton*, p. 12.
2 Ibid p. 15.
3 Ibid p. 16.
4 *Bolton Street Names; their meanings and origins*, p. 32.
5 The memory of each of these important wells is preserved in the modern names of Silverwell Street and Spa Road.
6 National Achieves, folio 302r Great Domesday Book, ref e 31/2/2.
7 *A History of Bolton*, p. 36.
8 *Bolton Memories*, p. 6.

9 *A History of Bolton*, p. 86.

10 Ibid p. 87.

11 *From Affetside to Yarrow, Bolton Place Names and their History*, p. 7.

12 *The History of the Lancashire Family of Pilkington and its Branches from 1066 to 1600*, p. 7.

13 *Death and the Grim Reaper the Pilkington Crest*, p. 27.

14 *The History of the Lancashire Family of Pilkington and its Branches from 1066 to 1600*, p. 20.

15 The part of the statue was found in the bottom part of the Tower wall in 1866 when the 15th Century church was demolished. *A History of Bolton*, p. 133.

16 *A History of Bolton*, p. 134.

17 Ibid p. 65.

18 The ancient yew tree was described in 1714 in a book *The Traveller in the North*, *A History of Bolton*, p. 142

19 *Aspects of the English Civil war in Bolton and its Neighbourhood 1640 – 1660*, p. 3.

20 *From Affetside to Yarrow, Bolton Place Names and their History*, p. 25.

21 The spring used to be off Smithills Croft Road.

22 *From Affetside to Yarrow, Bolton Place Names and their History*, p. 42.

23 The mark in the stone floor said to be made by George Marsh is still visible at Smithills Hall, at the entrance to the Withdrawing Room.

24 *Aspects of the English Civil War in Bolton and its Neighbourhood 1640 – 1660*, p. 5.

25 Ibid p. 4.

26 Ibid p. 4.

27 Recent research has suggested the high mortality rate was due to famine, typhus, dysentery or smallpox or a combination of all of these. At this distance in time it is difficult with any certainty to say therefore the mainstream view that it was an outbreak of plague is presented here.

28 *A History of Bubonic plague in the British Isles*, p. 311.

29 *Aspects of the English Civil War in Bolton and its Neighbourhood 1640 – 1660*, p. 2.

30 Ibid p. 4.

31 Ibid p. 3.

Chapter 3
Raising the Standard:
The Coming of War, 1642

1 The exact date of Richard Molyneux's birth is not known; it has variously been given as 1617, 1620 and most often as 1623. *The Military Career of Richard, Lord Molyneux, c 1623–54*.

2   *The Great Civil War in Lancashire 1642–51*, p. 27.

3   *The Finest Knight in England*, p. 3.

4   *The Great Civil War in Lancashire 1642–51*, p. 108.

5   *Seventeenth Century Lancashire*, p. 118.

6   Ibid p. 118.

7   *The Life of Adam Martindale*, p. 37.

8   *Soldiers of the English Civil War 1 Infantry*, p. 8.

9   *The Great Civil War in Lancashire 1642–51*, p. 37.

10 Ibid p. 43.

11 *Armies of the First English Civil War*, p. 13.

12 *Soldiers of the English Civil War 1 Infantry*, p. 24.

13 *Armies of the First English Civil War*, p. 9.

14 *Soldiers of the English Civil War 1 Infantry*, p. 25.

15 *The Great Civil War in Lancashire 1642–51*, p. 84.

16 *Discourse of the Warre in Lancashire*, p. 5.

17 *The Great Civil War in Lancashire 1642–51*, p. 86.

18 *Civil War Tracts*, p. 14.

19 *The Great Civil War in Lancashire 1642–51*, p. 87.

20 *The Court Records of Prescot 1640 – 1649*.

21 Now Chetham's School of Music near Victoria Railway Station.

22 *Death on Deansgate*, p. 9.

23 *The Great Civil War in Lancashire 1642–51*, p. 88.

24 Now Spring Gardens.

25 Some accounts claim it was Ordsall Hall but this was where James Stanley retreated to after the incident. *Death on Deansgate*.

26 *The Great Civil War in Lancashire 1642–51*, p. 17.

27 *Discourse of the Warre in Lancashire*, p. 6.

28 *Seventeenth Century Lancashire*, p. 116.

29 *Civil War Tracts*, p. 32.

30 Ibid p. 32.

31 *A General Plague of Madness, The Civil Wars in Lancashire 1640 – 1660*, p. 90.

32 *Civil War Tracts*, p. 32.

33 Ibid p. 33.

34 *Discourse of the Warre in Lancashire*, p. 6.

35 Now known as Levenshulme.

36 *Civil War Tracts*, p. 33.

37 *Discourse of the Warre in Lancashire*, p. 88. Some accounts claim Thomas Tyldesly shot Percival at the beginning of the skirmish from a window of the inn, but this does not fit with Tyldeslys character

38 Scattered fighting had taken place elsewhere, notably at Hull, but the casualties from these actions are unknown.

Chapter 4
Early Days:
The First Civil War, 1642–1643

1   *Earl of Derby's Catholic Army*, p. 35.
2   *The Siege of Manchester 1642*, p. 15.
3   *The Earl of Derby's Catholic Army*, p. 35, also *Lord Derby's Army*.
4   *Civil War Tracts*, p. 48.
5   Also known as Johann Rosworme.
6   *The History of the Siege of Manchester by the Kings Forces under the Command of Lord Strange 1642*, p. 67.
7   Ibid p. 67.
8   *Civil War Tracts*, p. 45.
9   *The Siege of Manchester 1642*, p. 7.
10 Ibid p. 14.
11 *Death on Deansgate*, p. 19.
12 *A Discourse of the War on Lancashire*, p. 12.
13 Ibid p. 7.
14 *The Siege of Manchester 1642*, p. 9.
15 *Civil War Tracts*, p. 46.
16 *A Discourse of the War on Lancashire*, p. 7.
17 *The Siege of Manchester 1642*, p. 11.
18 *The History of the Siege of Manchester by the Kings Forces under the Command of Lord Strange 1642*, p. 69.
19 *The Siege of Manchester 1642*, p. 11.
20 Ibid p. 11.
21 *The Great Civil War (1642–46) in the Manchester Area*, p. 13.
22 *The Siege of Manchester 1642*, p. 12.
23 Ibid p. 12; *Death on Deansgate*, p. 20.
24 Worth £1716 in 2010.
25 *Discourse of the Warre in Lancashire*, p. 7.
26 *Civil War Tracts*, p. 55.
27 *The Earl of Derby's Catholic Army*, p. 50.
28 *Civil War Tracts*, p. 49.
29 Marie Mitchell Archive.
30 *Gentleman's Magazine*, 1793, p. 1059.
31 *The Lancashire Lieutenancy under the Tudors and Stuarts*, p. 283.
32 *The Farington Papers*, p. 86.
33 *The Military Career of Richard, Lord Molyneux, c. 1623–54*.
34 Ibid.
35 Ibid.
36 *A General Plague of Madness, The Civil Wars in Lancashire 1640–1660*, p. 109-110.

37 *The Lancashire Lieutenancy under the Tudors and Stuarts*, p. 290–p. 293.

38 *Lancashire's Valley of Anchor, London 1643*, p. 124.

39 *Civil War Tracts*, p. 63.

40 *Lancashire's Valley of Anchor, London 1643*, p. 124.

41 *The Battle for Westhoughton Common 1642.*

42 *Discourse of the Warre in Lancashire*, p. 100.

43 *The History of the Siege of Manchester by the Kings Forces under the command of Lord Strange 1642*, p. 74.

44 Now thought to be Bank House at Higher Bank.

45 *Discourse of the Warre in Lancashire*, p. 22.

46 *A General Plague of Madness, The Civil Wars in Lancashire 1640 – 1660* p. 118.

47 Ibid p. 123.

48 Most likely modern Friargate.

49 *Discourse of the Warre in Lancashire*, p. 23.

50 *A General Plague of Madness, The Civil Wars in Lancashire 1640 – 1660*, p. 123.

51 *Discourse of the Warre in Lancashire*, p. 23.

52 Ibid p. 88.

53 A Punctual relation of Passage in Lancashire, this weeke. February 14 1642.

54 Ibid.

55 *The Battle for Westhoughton Common 1642.*

56 *Anderton Papers*, Wigan Archives.

57 £100 in 1643 would be worth about £8580 in 2010.

58 *The English Civil War around Wigan and Leigh*, p. 17.

Chapter 5
The First Assault:
18 February 1643

1 Bolton had a population of 1,588 in 1664 (P.R.O. E179/250/11) and most likely had a similar population in the 1640s.

2 Now known as Bank Street.

3 *Bolton Street Names; Their Meanings and Origins*, p. 32.

4 *From Affetside to Yarrow, Bolton Place Names and their History*, p. 22.

5 Both the Swan and Ye Old man and Scythe remain public houses to this day.

6 *Bolton Street Names; Their Meanings and Origins*, p. 22.

7 Now the first part of Deansgate leading to Churchgate is called known Bridge Street as it led to a later bridge north across the River Croal. Bridge Street now runs onto Deansgate. *Bolton Street Names; Their Meanings and Origins*, p. 40.

8 Now the site of Lloyds Bank, 113–117 Deansgate.

9 *The history of the Siege of Manchester by the Kings Forces under the command of Lord Strange 1642*, p73–74. Rosworm's account was a complaint over pay and lists all his actions for the cause of Parliament. Had he been involved in the building of Bolton's defences he would have mentioned it, at length.

10 *English Civil War Artillery 1642–51*, p. 18. This is based on the accounts of similar fortifications and the limited accounts of Bolton's walls.

11 *Speciall Passages*.

12 Ibid. *From Affetside to Yarrow, Bolton Place Names and their History*, p. 12. This may be a hamlet called the Cross, or Kershaw's Cross some three and a quarter miles NNE of the Parish Church. This hamlet, which no longer exists, gave its name to the Bromley Cross area after the landlords of the Cross, a family called Bromley. Hardmans Lane, Bromley Cross may also be a clue to the site of the fortification.

13 *A Punctual relation of Passage in Lancashire*, p. 2.

14 No mention of Cannon fire from the garrison is mentioned in any account therefore it is likely the town had no cannon at this time.

15 *Anderton Papers*.

16 *A Punctual relation of Passage in Lancashire*, p. 4.

17 *The Earl of Derby's Catholic Army*, p. 52.

18 *The English Baronetage*, p. 68.

19 *Lancashire's Valley of Anchor*.

20 *A Punctual relation of Passage in Lancashire*, p. 3. Most sources that do mention the Royalist strength mention eleven colours of foot, i.e. eleven companies.

21 *A History of Bolton*, p. 402.

22 *Discourse of the Warre in Lancashire*, p. 93.

23 *English Civil War Artillery 1642–51*, p. 9 and p. 23. This is based on the size of shot the defenders accounts mention and the distance Cannon Row/Street is from the probable positions of the Sconce and walls.

24 *Lancashire's Valley of Anchor. The Earl of Derby's Catholic Army*, p. 37.

25 Wigan Road A59 which changes into Deane Road A676 as it approached Bolton Town centre.

26 *Speciall Passages*, this account was written two days after the attack. Pikes Lane is off Deane Road A676 .

27 *A History of Bolton*, p. 399.

28 Ibid, p. 399.

29 Marie Mitchell Archive.

30 *Speciall Passages*.

31 Ibid, a skeane is a knife or dagger used in Ireland and in the Scottish Highlands.

32 *A Punctual Relation of Passage in Lancashire*, p. 3.

33 Ibid, p. 3.

34 *Speciall Passages.*

35 *A History of Bolton*, p. 399.

36 *A Punctual relation of Passage in Lancashire*, p. 3.

37 *A History of Bolton*, p. 399.

38 *A Punctual Relation of Passage in Lancashire*, p. 3.

39 *Discourse of the Warre in Lancashire*, p. 22. The source says they do not know if Rigbie was a Captain or a soldier but as each side took great care to mention officers killed and Rigbie was not named as such it seems he was a brave soldier leading his comrades.

40 *A Punctual relation of Passage in Lancashire*, p. 3.

41 *A History of Bolton*, p. 402.

42 *A Punctual Relation of Passage in Lancashire*, p. 4.

43 *Lancashire's Valley of Anchor.*

44 *Speciall Passages.*

45 *Lancashire's Valley of Anchor.*

46 *A Punctual relation of Passage in Lancashire*, p. 4.

47 *A History of Bolton*, p. 402.

48 *Speciall Passages.*

49 *A History of Bolton*, p. 400.

50 *A Punctual Relation of Passage in Lancashire*, p. 3.

51 Ibid p. 4.

52 *Speciall Passages.*

53 *Aspects of the English Civil War in Bolton and its Neighbourhood 1640 – 1660.* p. 8.

54 *A Punctual relation of Passage in Lancashire*, p. 5.

55 *Death the Grim Reaper – the Pilkington Crest*, p. 50. Alice was buried in the church itself for which en extra fee was paid.

56 *A History of Bolton*, p. 402.

Chapter 6
Struggle for Lancashire:
Early 1643

1 *A General Plague of Madness, The Civil Wars in Lancashire 1640 – 1660*, p. 132.

2 Ibid p. 132.

3 *A General Plague of Madness, The Civil Wars in Lancashire 1640 – 1660*, p. 134.

4 *Discourse of the Warre in Lancashire*, p. 28.

5 *The History of Wigan*, p. 32.

6 *A General Plague of Madness, The Civil Wars in Lancashire 1640 – 1660*, p. 134.

7 *A Cavaliers Notebook*, p. 26.

8 *Discourse of the Warre in Lancashire*, p. 29.

9 *The History of Wigan*, p. 32.

10 *Civil War Tracts*, p. 132.

11 *A General Plague of Madness, The Civil Wars in Lancashire 1640 – 1660*, p. 142.

12 Ibid p. 142.

13 *Acts and Ordinances of the Interregnum, 1642–1660 (1911)*, pp. 79–80.

Chapter 7
Stanley's Attack:
20 March 1643

1 *Officers and Regiments of the Royalist Army*, Vol. 2 D – H, p. 80. It is not certain these officers were at the attack at Bolton but were in Sir John Girlington's Regiment.

2 *Lord Derby's Army.*

3 *By the Sword Divided, Eyewitnesses of the English Civil War*, p. 175.

4 *A Punctual relation of Passage in Lancashire*, p. 2.

5 *Lancashire's Valley of Anchor.*

6 Ibid.

7 *By the Sword Divided, Eyewitnesses of the English Civil War*, p. 175.

8 *Lancashire's Valley of Anchor.*

9 Ibid.

10 Ibid.

Chapter 8
Brother Against Brother: 1643–1644

1 *A General Plague of Madness, The Civil Wars in Lancashire 1640 – 1660*, p. 146.

2 Ibid p. 146.

3 *The History of the Siege of Manchester by the Kings Forces under the Command of Lord Strange 1642*, p. 76.

4 Ibid p. 77.

5 Ibid p. 78.

6 *English Civil War, Notes and Queries*, No 26, p. 2.

7 Ibid p. 2.

8   Ibid p. 2.
9   Ibid p. 2.
10 Ibid p. 3.
11 Ibid p. 3.
12 *A General Plague of Madness, The Civil Wars in Lancashire 1640 – 1660*, p. 149.
13 Ibid p. 149.
14 Ibid p. 152.
15 Ibid p. 152.
16 *The Finest Knight in England*, p. 8.
17 *A General Plague of Madness, The Civil Wars in Lancashire 1640 – 1660*, p. 155.
18 *The Finest Knight in England*, p. 8. Now Easterly Farm.
19 Ibid p. 9.
20 *Discourse of the Warre in Lancashire*, p. 34.
21 Ibid p. 34.
22 *A General Plague of Madness, The Civil Wars in Lancashire 1640 – 1660*, p. 155.
23 *The English Civil War around Wigan and Leigh*, p. 30.
24 *The Finest Knight in England*, p. 9.
25 *Officers and Regiments of the Royalist Army*, Vol .3 I – Q, p. 135.
26 *English Civil War, Notes and Queries*, No. 26, p. 6.
27 Ibid p. 7.
28 Robinson is believed to be the author of *Discourse of the Warre in Lancashire*.
29 *A General Plague of Madness, The Civil Wars in Lancashire 1640 – 1660*, p. 166.
30 Ibid p. 166.
31 Ibid p. 166.
32 Ibid p. 167.
33 Ibid p. 166.
34 *Discourse of the Warre in Lancashire*, p. 41.
35 *A General Plague of Madness, The Civil Wars in Lancashire 1640 – 1660*, p. 169.
36 *Discourse of the Warre in Lancashire*, p. 41.

Chapter 9
'A better Souldier':
The Siege of Lathom House

1   *To Play the Man*, p. 15.
2   Ibid, p. 17.

3   As the House was completely demolished after the Civil Wars there is some dispute as to its exact location. There are two sites currently being claimed as the location. One is the ruin of the 18th Century Lathom Mansion and other a place called Spa Roughs close by. Spa Roughs gained credence, in part, due to it being called the Entrenchments on old maps although there is another explanation of this outlined later in this chapter. Without concrete evidence to the contrary the ruins of the 18th Century Lathom Mansion, which is believed to be built on the site of the old Lathom House seem the most likely candidate as recent geophysical surveys appear to back this up with test pits revealing massive masonry remains underneath. *English Civil War Archaeology*, p. 73.

4   The majority of the description of the house is taken from an account by Samuel Rutter, Chaplain to Lady Derby during the siege as quoted in the *A History of the House of Stanley*, p. 104/105.

5   A sally port is a doorway a door in a wall that allows troops to make raids on the besiegers without compromising the defensive strength of the fortifications. Much use of sally ports were made in the seige.

6   A Postern gate or Posterns were often located in a concealed location, allowing the occupants to come and go inconspicuously. It would also be used as a sally port.

7   The journal does not mention a drawbridge so the assumption is the gatehouse straddled the moat.

8   The names and descriptions of these towers are taken from the accounts the Parliamentary sequester a Mr Ambrose made in 1646 when Lathom House was demolished. *A History of the House of Stanley*, p. 215–216.

9   *English Civil War Archaeology*, p. 73.

10   In 1996 a ditch, presumed to be the moat, was excavated on the site behind the west wing of the house that was 15 metres (50 feet) across by 4 metres (13 feet) deep *English Civil War Archaeology* p. 73.

11   *To Play the Man*, p. 24.

12   It needed one full time gardener *The Stanley Papers*, Chatham Society 1853, p. 23–27.

13   Extensive Wainscot panelling was mentioned in the accounts the Parliamentary sequester a Mr Ambrose in 1646 when Lathom House was demolished. *A History of the House of Stanley*, p. 216.

14   *To Play the Man*, p. 24.

15   Ibid, p. 55, *A Journal of The Siege of Lathom House* , p. 12.

16   *A Journal of The Siege of Lathom House*, p. 13.

17   The site of "The Stand" is now occupied by Stand Farm although the site of the windmill is unknown *The Better Soldier*, p. 47.

18   *A Journal of The Siege of Lathom House*, p. 15.

19   *Discourse of the Warre in Lancashire*, p. 50.

20   *The Better Soldier*, p. 27.

21 *The Royalist Army at War 1642 – 1646*, p. 180.

22 *To Play the Man*, p. 34.

23 Ibid, p. 35.

24 *A History of the House of Stanley*, p. 128.

25 Also known as Edward Chisenhale and at one time thought to be the author of the Journal of the siege.

26 Edward Chisnall, Edward Rawstorne and Molyneux Ratcliffe had all been with the Earl of Derby at Preston in 1643, *To Play the Man*, p. 35, and Captain Ogle had been in the Lancashire Regiments at Edgehill *A Journal of The Siege of Lathom House*, p. 29.

27 Edward Halsall is thought to be the author of *A Journal of The Siege of Lathom House*, as the copy in the British Library is annotated by him.

28 *The Better Soldier*, p. 26.

29 The Derby Family Household books for 13th May 1587 list the following servants in Lathom House, A Steward, a Controller of the Household, Receiver General, eight Gentlemen Waiters, two Clerks of the Kitchen, a Chaplin, nineteen Yeoman Officers, six Grooms of the Chamber, two sub grooms of the chamber, thirteen Yeoman Waiters, two trumpeters, nine in the Kitchen, one Caterer, two Slaughter men, two Bakers, two barbers, a Malt Maker, a Candleman, three footmen, two armourers, two Carpenters, a Gardner, a Builder (listed as a Roughcaster), two Brewers (Hoppe men) two laundry women and fourteen in the stables. A grand total of one hundred and one. *The Stanley Papers*, Chatham Society 1853, p. 23–27.

30 *To Play the Man*, p. 23.

31 Ibid, p. 53.

32 *A Journal of The Siege of Lathom House*, p. 17.

33 It is only Seacome who mentions this subterfuge of Samuel Rutter and he is notoriously unreliable on many other points in his narrative. He does not mention the parties by name but "a captain" of the parliamentary forces and "one of her ladyships chaplains". It is safe to assume Rutter was the Chaplain and a reasonable guess that Ashurst was the Captain. This tale, uncorroborated elsewhere, explains the unexpected delay in starting the siege and hence, however improbable the source, is likely to be true. *To Play the Man*, p. 68. *A History of the House of Stanley*, p. 126.

34. *A History of the House of Stanley*, p. 126.

35 *To Play the Man*, p. 69.

36 *A Journal of The Siege of Lathom House*, p. 24.

37 *English Civil War Archaeology*, p. 72.

38 Ibid p. 73.

39 *English Civil War Artillery 1642–51*, p. 9.

40 *The Better Soldier*, p. 43.

41 Six skeletons were discovered buried under the south west angle of the ruins of Lathom Mansion in the mid nineteenth century, one of which

had a musket hole in his head. Where they were found was thought to be the where the chapel of the house stood so that these burials might have been within the building. *English Civil War Archaeology*, p. 72–73.

42 *To Play the Man*, p. 78.

43 Ibid, p. 81.

44 I can only find one source for this story but it fits with Rutters devious character and the fact that the Stanley's were well thought of in the area and had great local support. *The History of Great and Little Bolton*, p. 207.

45 *The History of Great and Little Bolton*, p. 207, *A History of the House of Stanley*, p. 151.

46 *Marsten Moor 1644, The campaign and the battle*, p. 171.

47 *Granadoe!, Mortars in the Civil War* , p. 5.

48 *To Play the Man*, p. 78.

49 *A Journal of The Siege of Lathom House*, p. 40.

50 *To Play the Man*, p. 84.

51 Ibid, p. 94.

52 *Granadoe!, Mortars in the Civil War*, p. 8.

53 Ibid, p. 8.

54 *A Journal of The Siege of Lathom House*, p. 42.

55 *To Play the Man*, p. 84.

56 *A Journal of The Siege of Lathom House*, p. 43.

57 Ibid, p. 43.

58 *To Play the Man*, p. 94.

59 *A Journal of The Siege of Lathom House*, p. 44.

60 *A History of the House of Stanley*, p. 129.

61 *A Journal of The Siege of Lathom House*, p. 46.

62 Ibid, p. 48.

63 Ibid, p. 50.

64 *The Cavalier Army*, p. 156.

65 *A Journal of The Siege of Lathom House*, p. 51.

66 Ibid, p. 53.

67 Ibid, p. 55.

68 *To Play the Man*, p. 92.

69 *English Civil War Archaeology*, p. 72.

70 *To Play the Man*, p. 96.

71 Ibid p. 96. Worth in the region of £177 600 today.

72 *The Perfect Diurnall*, 8 December 1645.

73 *Discourse of the Warre in Lancashire*, p xiii.

Chapter 10
The Gathering Storm:
Rupert's March through Lancashire, May 1644

1 *Prince Rupert's War*, p. 33.
2 *The Sea Approaches, the importance of the Dee and the Mersey in the Civil War in the North West*, p. 5.
3 Atrocities at Sea and the Treatment of Prisoners of war by the Parliamentary Navy in Ireland 1641–1649.
4 *The Sea Approaches, the importance of the Dee and the Mersey in the Civil War in the North West*, p. 6.
5 *A Cure for the Scots.*
6 *Officers and Regiments of the Royalist Army*, Vol. 3 I – Q, p. 151.
7 *Officers and Regiments of the Royalist Army*, Vol. 1 A – C, p. 28.
8 *An English Army for Ireland*, p. 31.
9 *Officers and Regiments of the Royalist Army*, Vol. 3 I – Q, p. 180.
10 *Officers and Regiments of the Royalist Army*, Vol. 2 D – H, p. 103.
11 *Officers and Regiments of the Royalist Army*, Vol. 3 I – Q, p. 128.
12 Ibid p. 175.
13 *Officers and Regiments of the Royalist Army*, Vol. 1 A – C, p. 31.
14 *Officers and Regiments of the Royalist Army*, Vol. 2 D – II, p. 66.
15 Ibid, p. 74.
16 *Officers and Regiments of the Royalist Army*, Vol. 3 I – Q, p 112.
17 Ibid, p. 152.
18 *Officers and Regiments of the Royalist Army*, Vol. 3 I – Q, p. 172.
19 *An English Army for Ireland*, p. 31.
20 Ibid p. 31.
21 *Officers and Regiments of the Royalist Army*, Vol. 2 D – H, p. 61.
22 *Officers and Regiments of the Royalist Army*, Vol. 1 A – C, p. 28.
23 Ibid, p. 30.
24 *Officers and Regiments of the Royalist Army*, Vol. 3 I – Q, p. 183.
25 *An English Army for Ireland*, p. 31.
26 *Officers and Regiments of the Royalist Army*, Vol. 2D – H, p. 79.
27 *Officers and Regiments of the Royalist Army*, Vol. 3 I – Q, p. 172.
28 *Officers and Regiments of the Royalist Army*, Vol. 1 A – C, p. 38.
29 *Officers and Regiments of the Royalist Army*, Vol. 2D – H, p. 73.
30 *Officers and Regiments of the Royalist Army*, Vol. 3 I – Q, p. 127.
31 *Officers and Regiments of the Royalist Army*, Vol. 4 S – Z, p. 184.
32 *A General Plague of Madness, The Civil Wars in Lancashire 1640 – 1660*, p. 215.
33 Ibid p. 215.
34 Now the site of Grove mill, Bygone Times.

35 *A Journal of The Siege of Lathom House*, p. 61.

36 *To Play the Man*, p. 101.

Chapter 11
Massacre:
The Storming of Bolton, 28 May 1644

1 *Prince Rupert's Diary folio 34.*

2 *Civil War Tracts* p. 191.

3 Alexander Mason married Anne Shawe on 3rd October 1592 in Bolton Parish Church. If they are Alexander and Roberts parents, which is likely considering the dates, their first son would probably be named after the father

4 *Marie Mitchell Archive.*

5 *Discourse of the Warre in Lancashire*, p. 50.

6 The sconce is not mentioned in any account of the Massacre so must have been abandoned after the action of the previous year.

7 *Prince Rupert's Diary folio 34.*

8 This is the area of Lever Edge Lane where Haywood School and the Prince Rupert Pub now stand. When Haywood school was built in the early 1950's civil war relics were found suggesting a camp or rest stop of some sort. Marie Mitchell Archive.

9 *Prince Rupert's Diary folio 34.*

10 *A Exact relation Of the bloody and barbarous Massacre at Bolton in the Moors in Lancashire*, p. 2.

11 Ibid p. 2.

12 Ibid p. 2.

13 Ibid p. 2.

14 *Prince Rupert's Diary folio 34.*

15 *Marston Moor 1644, The campaign and the battle*, p. 193.

16 *A Journal of the Siege of Lathom House*, p. 62.

17 Ibid p. 62–63.

18 I am indebted to Steve Phillip's of Prince Rupert's Bluecoats for his advice on how an assault would take place.

19 *Discourse of the Warre in Lancashire*, p. 50.

20 *A Exact relation Of the bloody and barbarous Massacre at Bolton in the Moors in Lancashire*, p. 2.

21 *Marston Moor 1644, The campaign and the battle*, p. 193.

22 *A Exact relation Of the bloody and barbarous Massacre at Bolton in the Moors in Lancashire*, p. 2.

23 *Prince Rupert's Diary folio 34.*

24 *Discourse of the Warre in Lancashire*, p. xxi.

25 *A Exact relation Of the bloody and barbarous Massacre at Bolton in the Moors in Lancashire*, p. 2.

26 *All the Kings Armies*, p. 123.

27 *Prince Rupert's Diary folio 34.*

28 *A Exact relation Of the bloody and barbarous Massacre at Bolton in the Moors in Lancashire*, p. 2.

29 Marie Mitchell Archive.

30 *A Exact relation Of the bloody and barbarous Massacre at Bolton in the Moors in Lancashire*, p. 2.

31 *Prince Rupert's Diary folio 34.*

32 *A Exact relation Of the bloody and barbarous Massacre at Bolton in the Moors in Lancashire*, p. 2.

33 Some accounts have the Earl of Derby leading Tyldesley's Regiment of Foot as they broke into Bolton but as the Prince never gave him command at any point in 1644 and it would have meant him suddenly moving from the Princes Horse to a Foot Regiment in the middle of the action it is very unlikely. It is most evident in Seacombes account who has him being the first man over the walls!

34 Captain William Bootle is the first name on the list of the dead in the parish register. This register appears to name only Bolton residents and certainly only those known in the town so it may be Bootle was from Bolton as others that are known to have died there from Rigby's force are not mentioned.

35 *A Journal of the Siege of Lathom House*, p. 62–63.

36 *The History of Great and Little Bolton*, p. 411.

37 *Discourse of the Warre in Lancashire*, p. 51.

38 *A Exact relation Of the bloody and barbarous Massacre at Bolton in the Moors in Lancashire*, p. 2.

39 Ibid p. 2.

40 *Prince Rupert's Diary folio 34.*

41 *Prince Rupert's Diary folio 35.*

42 *Discourse of the Warre in Lancashire*, p. 51.

43 Now Bank Street.

44 Marie Mitchell Archive.

45 *The History of the House of Stanley*, p. 135.

46 *A Exact relation Of the bloody and barbarous Massacre at Bolton in the Moors in Lancashire*, p. 2.

47 *Marie Mitchell Archive as reported by East Lancashire Almanac of 1902*

48 *Marston Moor 1644, The campaign and the battle*, p. 193.

49 Vicar of Deane 1642 to 1662

50 Marie Mitchell Archive.

51 *A Exact relation Of the bloody and barbarous Massacre at Bolton in the Moors in Lancashire* p4. Elizabth Horrocks was probably a relative of Alexander Horrocks, Minister of Deane.

52 *A Exact relation Of the bloody and barbarous Massacre at Bolton in the Moors in Lancashire*, p. 4.
53 ibid p4 Probably wife of Arthur Seddon and relative to Alice Gregge
54 *All the Kings Armies*, p. 124.
55 *A Exact relation Of the bloody and barbarous Massacre at Bolton in the Moors in Lancashire*, p. 3.
56 Ibid p. 3.
57 Ibid p. 3.
58 Ibid p. 4.
59 *Discourse of the Warre in Lancashire*, p. 52.
60 *A History of Bolton*, p. 268.
61 *A Exact relation Of the bloody and barbarous Massacre at Bolton in the Moors in Lancashire*, p. 3.
62 *Marston Moor 1644, The campaign and the battle p193*
63 *A Exact relation Of the bloody and barbarous Massacre at Bolton in the Moors in Lancashire*, p. 4.
64 *Civil War Tracts* p190 quoting from *Perfect Diurnall* of June 104.
65 Ibid p. 190.
66 *Marston Moor 1644, The campaign and the battle*, p. 193.
67 *Prince Rupert's Diary folio 34.*
68 *Seventeenth Century Lancashire*, p. 119.
69 *Discourse of the Warre in Lancashire*, p. 50.
70 Ibid p. 50.
71 Ibid p. xxvii.
72 Ibid p. xxvii.
73 Ibid p. xxvii.
74 *A Exact relation Of the bloody and barbarous Massacre at Bolton in the Moors in Lancashire*, p. 5.
75 *Discourse of the Warre in Lancashire*, p. 50.
76 Ibid p. 50.
77 Ibid p. 50.
78 *The Civil War in Bolton*, p. 29.
79 *Causes of the Civil War in Lancashire.*
80 *Prince Rupert's Diary folio 35.*
81 *Marston Moor 1644, The campaign and the battle*, p. 193.
82 *A Exact relation Of the bloody and barbarous Massacre at Bolton in the Moors in Lancashire*, p. 5.
83 *The English Civil War, A Historical Companion*, p. 47.
84 *A Exact relation Of the bloody and barbarous Massacre at Bolton in the Moors in Lancashire*, p. 5.
85 *A General Plague of Madness, The Civil Wars in Lancashire 1640 – 1660*, p. 232.
86 *Prince Rupert's War*, p. 14.

Chapter 12
Drive to Destruction:
The First Civil War, 1644–1645

1 *A General Plague of Madness, The Civil Wars in Lancashire 1640 – 1660*, p. 226.
2 The Prince is also thought to have set up in a cottage in Eastbourne Street in Everton village .
3 *The Siege of Liverpool in the Lancashire Campaign, 1644*, p. 13.
4 *A General Plague of Madness, The Civil Wars in Lancashire 1640 – 1660*, p. 226.
5 *The Siege of Liverpool in the Lancashire Campaign, 1644*, p. 14.
6 *The Life of Adam Martindale.*
7 *The Military Career of Richard, Lord Molyneux, c. 1623–54.*
8 *The Civil War in Yorkshire*, p. 129.
9 Ibid p. 129.
10 *Marston Moor English Civil War – July 1644*, p. 143.
11 *The Civil War in Yorkshire*, p. 130.
12 Ibid p. 131.
13 *The Finest Knight in England*, p. 18.
14 *Marston Moor English Civil War – July 1644*, p. 146.
15 *The Civil War in Yorkshire*, p. 142.
16 This is the traditional site of the last stand of the whitecoats but recent artefact evidence suggests it may have been the junction of the ditch and Moor Lane. *The Civil War in Yorkshire*, p. 143.
17 *English Civil War Notes and Queries*, number 39, p. 35.
18 *A General Plague of Madness, The Civil Wars in Lancashire 1640 – 1660*, p. 240.
19 *Marston Moor English Civil War – July 1644*, p. 87.
20 *Marston Moor 1644, The campaign and the battle*, p. 162.
21 This appears to be in the Moss Delph Lane and Gawhill lane area between Aughton and Ormskirk.
22 *A General Plague of Madness, The Civil Wars in Lancashire 1640 – 1660*, p. 254.
23 *The Finest Knight in England*, p. 22.
24 *A General Plague of Madness, The Civil Wars in Lancashire 1640 – 1660*, p. 256.
25 *The Siege of Liverpool in the Lancashire Campaign, 1644*, p. 21.
26 *A General Plague of Madness, The Civil Wars in Lancashire 1640 – 1660*, p. 257.
27 *English Civil war, notes and Queries*, No. 39 p. 17.
28 *The Siege of Liverpool in the Lancashire Campaign, 1644*, p. 27.

29 Ibid, 1644, p. 27.
30 *A General Plague of Madness, The Civil Wars in Lancashire 1640 – 1660,* p. 262.
31 Ibid p. 262.
32 Ibid p. 265.
33 Later known as New Park House.
34 *Marsten Moor 1644, The campaign and the battle,* p. 165
35 *A General Plague of Madness, The Civil Wars in Lancashire 1640 – 1660,* p. 274.
36 *Marsten Moor 1644, The campaign and the battle,* p. 165.
37 *The Finest Knight in England,* p. 23.
38 *The Military Career of Richard, Lord Molyneux, c. 1623–54.*

Chapter 13
Total War:
The Second and Third Civil War, 1649–1651

1   *Civil War, the Wars of the Three Kingdoms 1638–1660,* p. 459.
2   *The Finest Knight in England,* p. 26.
3   *Bloody Preston – The Battle for Preston 1648,* p. 62. This is now Stonyhurst College.
4   Ibid p. 65.
5   *Civil War Tracts,* p. 260.
6   *Major Sanderson's War,* p. 142.
7   *Bloody Preston – The Battle for Preston 1648,* p. 66.
8   Ibid p. 70.
9   *For God and the North,* p. 62.
10 *Discourse of the Warre in Lancashire,* p. xxiii.
11 *This war without an enemy, A History of the English Civil Wars,* p. 178.
12 *Civil War Tracts,* p. 262.
13 *Major Sanderson's War,* p. 142.
14 *The English Civil War around Wigan and Leigh,* p. 31.
15 *The Battle of Winwick Pass, 19 Aug 1648.*
16 *The English Civil War around Wigan and Leigh,* p. 29.
17 *The History of Wigan,* p. 43.
18 *The English Civil War around Wigan and Leigh,* p. 30.
19 *The Battle of Winwick Pass, 19 Aug 1648.*
20 *Major Sanderson's War,* p. 143.
21 *The History of Wigan,* p. 43.
22 Ibid p. 46.
23 *The Battle of Winwick Pass, 19 Aug 1648.*

24 Ibid.

25 *Major Sanderson's War*, p. 143.

26 *This war without an enemy, A History of the English Civil Wars*, p. 178.

27 *The Finest Knight in England*, p. 27.

28 *The English Civil War day by day*, p. 180.

29 *The Great Stanley*, p. 224.

30 Ibid p. 224.

31 *The Finest Knight in England*, p. 29.

32 ilid p. 29.

33 *Free-Born John*, p. 247.

34 *Major Sanderson's War*, p. 29.

35 *The Finest Knight in England*, p. 29.

36 *The English Civil War around Wigan and Leigh*, p. 32.

37 *The History of Wigan*, p. 57.

38 *The Great Stanley*, p. 226.

39 Marie Mitchell Archive.

40 *The English Civil War around Wigan and Leigh*, p. 32.

41 *Discourse of the Warre in Lancashire*, p. 76.

42 *The Finest Knight in England*, p. 29.

43 Marie Mitchell Archive.

44 *The English Civil War around Wigan and Leigh*, p. 32.

45 *The History of Wigan*, p. 65.

46 *The Boscobel Tracts*, p. 34.

47 After the restoration in 1660 the Oak became known as the Royal Oak, a name that has been given to many a Public House ever since.

48 A Priest's Hole was a hiding place for priests built into many high status Roman Catholic houses during the period of Catholic persecution starting under the reign of Queen Elizabeth I in 1558.

Chapter 14
Judicial Murder:
The Execution of James Stanley,
15 October 1651

1 *Civil War Tracts*, p. 311.

2 *Lancashire Worthies*.

3 *Journal of the House of Commons: volume 7: 1651–1660 (1802)*, pp. 13–15.

4 Ibid, pp. 13–15.

5 *Memoirs of James Earl of Derby*, p. 74.

6 *The Farington Papers*, p. 168.

7   *The History of the House of Stanley*, p. 169.

8   *The History of the House of Stanley*, p. 170.

9   *The Great Stanley* p. 228.

10   Marie Mitchell Archive.

11   'House of Commons Journal Volume 7: 14 October 1651', *Journal of the House of Commons*: volume 7: 1651–1660 (1802), pp. 27.

12   *The History of the House of Stanley*, p. 126.

13   *Discourse of the Warre in Lancashire*, p. 82.

14   Ibid p. 82.

15   Ibid p. 157.

16   *The History of the House of Stanley*, p. 126.

17   Civil War Tracts, p. 321.

18   Marie Mitchell Archive

19   Ibid.

20   The Kings Arms were demolished in 1790.

21   Marie Mitchell Archive.

22   Ibid.

23   Ibid.

24   *A History of Bolton*, p. 429.

25   *The History of the House of Stanley*, p. 126. For a long time tradition has that the Earl stayed in Ye Olde Man and Scythe Public House on Churchgate but all contemporary accounts mention a house, not a Pub.

26   Ibid, p. 126.

27   The Whowell farm still stands outside Bolton but records appear to suggest that the family did not have the farm in the 1640s. The story that the family suffered in the Massacre may have been a later invention to justify George Whowell's actions. The farm still stands and is called Whowell's Farm but the family moved out in 1823.

28   Marie Mitchell Archive.

29   *Civil War Tracts*, p. 317. This account, and Rev Baggerleys, are the basis for what happened on the scaffold.

30   *A General Plague of Madness, The Civil Wars in Lancashire 1640 – 1660*, p. 388.

31   All the accounts talk of the Earl lying down, not kneeling, and stretching out so it appears a low block was used.

32   *Civil War Tracts*, p. 323. There is some disagreement as to how many blows the Axe took, later Royalist writers claimed three blows while others two.

33   *Discourse of the Warre in Lancashire*, p. 85.

34   Ibid p. 85.

35   Marie Mitchell Archive. The fact that she could carry the block away supports the argument a low block was used.

36   Ibid.

Chapter 15
Aftermath:
Consequences of Conflict

1 *Aspects of the English Civil war in Bolton and its neighbourhood 1640 – 1660*, p. 15.
2 *Going to the Wars, the experience of the English Civil Wars 1638 – 1651*, p. 258.
3 *Aspects of the English Civil war in Bolton and its neighbourhood 1640 – 1660*, p. 15.
4 Ibid, p. 16.
5 *The Military Career of Richard, Lord Molyneux, c. 1623–54.*
6 *The Lancashire Gentry and the Great Rebellion 1640 – 60*, p. 95–96 and p. 132.
7 *Discourse of the Warre in Lancashire*, p. 91.
8 *The Military Career of Richard, Lord Molyneux, c. 1623–54.*
9 *Colonel Alexander Rigby*, p. 20.
10 Ibid p. 23.
11 *Lancashire at War, Cavalier and Roundheads, 1642–51*, p. 10.
12 *Discourse of the Warre in Lancashire*, p. 102.
13 Ibid p. 100.
14 *Aspects of the English Civil war in Bolton and its neighbourhood 1640 – 1660*, p. 17.
15 *Genealogy of the Sampson Mason Family*, p. 6.
16 Ibid p. 5.
17 *A Discourse of the War on Lancashire*, p. xxi.
18 Which is still known as Whowell Farm.
19 Marie Mitchell Archive.
20 *Lancashire Magic and Mystery*, p. 87.
21 *The History of Wigan, Part II*, p. 20.
22 Marie Mitchell Archive.
23 *Bolton Evening News*, 18 May 1976.
24 As of 2010.

Select Bibliography

A *Journal of the Siege of Lathom House*, Harding, Mavor and Lepard, London, 1823.

Bolton Memories, The Amadeus Press, 2001.

Civil War Tracts, Chatham Society, 1844.

Memoirs of James Earl of Derby, J. Folwer, 1804.

The Stanley Papers, Chatham Society, 1853.

The Farington Papers, Chatham Society, 185?

Journal of the House of Commons: volume 7: 1651–1660 (1802).

Acts and Ordinances of the Interregnum, 1642–1660 (1911), pp. 79–80.

Adair, John., *By the Sword Divided, Eyewitnesses of the English Civil War*, Century Publishing, 1983.

Bagley, J. J., presented by, Seventeenth Century Lancashire, Transactions of the Historic Society of Lancashire and Cheshire, Volume 132, 1982.

Bagley, J. J., and Lewis, A. S., *Lancashire at War, Cavalier and roundheads, 1642 – 51*, Dalesman Books, 1977.

Banks, Charles Edward, *Colonel Alexander Rigby*, privately printed 1885.

Barrat, John, *The Siege of Liverpool in the Lancashire Campaign, 1644*, Stuart Press, 1993.

Barrat, John, *Prince Rupert's War*, Caracole Press, 1996.

Barrat, John, Cavaliers, *The Royalist Army at War 1642 – 1646*, Sutton Publishing, 2000.

Barratt, John, *The Siege of Manchester 1642*, Stuart Press, 1993.

Beamont, William Ed, Attributed to Robinson, Edward, *A Discourse of the War on Lancashire*, Chatham Society, 1864.

Bennett, Martyn, *The English Civil War, A Historical Companion*, Tempus, 2004, Scarecrow Press, 2000.

Billington, W. D., *From Affetside to Yarrow, Bolton Place names and their History*, Ross Anderton Publications, 1982.

Blackwood, B. G., *The Lancashire Gentry and the Great Rebellion 1640–60*, Chetham Society, Manchester, 1978.

Blundell, William, Gibson, Revd T. (editor) *A Cavalier's Notebook*, The Naval and Military Press.

Brown, John, *The History of Great and Little Bolton*, Manchester, 1825.

Broxop, E. *The Great Civil War in Lancashire 1642–51*, Manchester University Press, 1973.

Bull, Stephen, *A General Plague of Madness, The Civil Wars in Lancashire 1640–1660*, Carnegie Publishing, 2009.

Bull, Stephen, *Granadoe!, Mortars in the Civil War*, Partizan Press, 1985.

Bull, Stephen and Seed, Mike, *Bloody Preston – The Battle for Preston 1648*, Carnegie Publishing, 1998.

Carlton, Charles, *Going to the Wars, the experience of the English Civil Wars 1638– 1651*, Book Club Associates, 1992.

Chappell, Arthur, *Death on Deansgate*, privately printed.

Clark, David, *Marston Moor English Civil War – July 1644*, Leo Cooper, 2004.

Collins, Arthur, *The English Baronetage*, Thomas Wooten, 1741.

Cooke, David, *The Civil War in Yorkshire*, Pen and Sword Military, 2004.

Cressy, David, *England on Edge, Crisis and Revolution 1640–1642*, Oxford University Press, 2006.

Cumming, Joseph G., *The Great Stanley*, 1867.

Emberton, Wilfred, *The English Civil War day by day*, Alan Sutton Publishing, 1995.

Espinasse, Francis, *Lancashire Worthies*, Simpkin, Marshall & Co, London, 1874.

Fields, Kenneth, *Lancashire Magic and Mystery*, Sigma Press, 1998.

Gregg, Pauline, *Free-Born John*, J. M. Dent & Sons, 1986

Harland, John, *The Lancashire Lieutenancy under the Tudors and Stuarts*, Chatham Society, 1864.

Harrington, Peter, *English Civil War Archaeology*, B. T. Batsford, 2004.

Henry, Chris, and Deff, Brian (illustrator), *English Civil War Artillery 1642–51*, Osprey Publishing, 2005.

Hill, P. R. and Watkinson, J. M., *Major Sanderson's War*, Spellmount Publishing, 2008.

Holcroft, Fred, *The English Civil War around Wigan and Leigh*, Wigan Heritage Service, 1993.

Houghton, John, W., *The Houghton Genealogy*, privately published, 2003.

Howe, Malcolme, *Death the grim reaper – the Pilkington Crest*, Greater Manchester Heraldry Society, 2004.

Hughes, J., *The Boscobel Tracts*, William Blackwood and sons, 1857.

King, Walter, *The Court Records of Prescot 1640 –49*, Record Society of Cheshire, 2008.

Martindale, Adam, *The Life of Adam Martindale*, The Chetham Society, 1845.

Mason, Alverdo Hayward, *Genealogy of the Sampson Mason Family*, privately printed 1902.

Lawson, Mike, *For God and the North*, Partizan Press, 1985.

Ollard, Richard, *This war without an enemy, A History of the English Civil Wars*, Fontana Press 1992.

Palmer, John, *The History of the Siege of Manchester by the Kings Forces under the command of Lord Strange 1642*, John Leigh, Manchester, 1822.

Peachy, Stuart, *The Mechanics of Infantry Combat in the First English Civil War*, Stuart Press, 1992.

Pearce, Joseph, P, *Lancashire Legends*, Ormskirk Advertiser, 1928.

Pendlebury, Graham, *Aspects of the English Civil war in Bolton and its neighbourhood 1640–1660*, Neil Richardson, 1983.

Pilkington, Colin, *To play the man, The story of Lady Derby and the siege of Lathom House 1643–45*, Carnegie Publishing Ltd, Preston, 1991.

Pilkington, John, *The History of the Lancashire Family of Pilkington and its branches from 1066 to 1600*, Thomas Brakell Ltd, 1894.

Reid, Stuart, *All the Kings Armies*, Spellmount, 1998.

Reid, Stuart, *Officers and Regiments of the Royalist Army*, Introduction and Index, Partizan Press.

Reid, Stuart, *Officers and Regiments of the Royalist Army*, Vol. 1 A – C, Partizan Press.

Reid, Stuart, *Officers and Regiments of the Royalist Army*, Vol. 2 D – H, Partizan Press.

Reid, Stuart, *Officers and Regiments of the Royalist Army*, Vol. 3 I – Q, Partizan Press.

Reid, Stuart, *Officers and Regiments of the Royalist Army*, Vol. 4 S – Z, Partizan Press.

Reid, Stuart, *The Finest Knight in England*, Partizan Press, 1987.

Roberts, Keith and McBride, Angus, *Soldiers of the English Civil War 1 Infantry*, Osprey Publishing Limited, 1989.

Robinson, Edward and Beamont, William, *Discourse of the Warre in Lancashire*, Chatham Society, 1864.

Royle, Trevor, *Civil War, the Wars of the Three Kingdoms 1638–1660*, Little Brown, 2004.

Ryder, Ian, *An English Army for Ireland*, Partizan Press.

Seacombe, John *The History of the House of Stanley*, J. Gleave, Deansgate, 1821.

Scholes, James Christopher & Pimblett, William, *A History of Bolton*, The Daily Chronicle, 1892.

Shrewsbury, J. F. D., *A History of Bubonic Plague in the British Isles*, Cambridge University Press, 1970.

Sinclair, David, *The History of Wigan, Part II*, Kent and Co, 1882.

Tupling, G., *Causes of the Civil War in Lancashire, Transactions of the Historic Society of Lancashire and Cheshire, Volume 65*, 1953.

Turton, Alan and Peachy, Stuart, *Armies of the First English Civil War*, Stuart Press, 1993.

Wanklyn, Malcolm, *Decisive Battles of the English Civil War*, Pen & Sword Military, 2006.

Williams, M. B. and Lawson M. J., *The Better Soldier*, Hendy Books, 1999.

Vernon, Sara, *Bolton Street Names; their meanings and origins*, The History Press, 2008.

Young, Peter, *Marston Moor 1644, The campaign and the battle*, The Windrush Press, 1997.

Young, Peter and Empberton, Wilfred, *The Cavalier Army*, George Allen & Unwin Ltd, 1974.

Booklets

English Civil War, Notes and Queries, No. 4
English Civil War, Notes and Queries, No. 26
English Civil War, Notes and Queries, No. 39

Basnett, Lois, *The battle for Westhoughton Common 1642*.

Dore, R. N., *The Great Civil War (1642–46) in the Manchester Area*, BBC Radio Manchester.

Gratton, J. M., *The Earl of Derby's Catholic Army*, Transactions of the Historic Society of Lancashire and Cheshire, Volume 137, 1988.

Pamphlets

Special passages and Certain Informations from several places, collected for the use of all that desire to be truly informed, From Tuesday the 14 of February to Tuesday 20 of February 1643.

A Punctual relation of Passage in Lancashire, this weeke. February 14 1642.

A Exact relation Of the bloody and barbarous Massacre at Bolton in the Moors in Lancashire, May 28, By Prince Rupert being penned by an eyewitnesse, admirably preserved by the gracious and mighty hand ofGod in that day of Trouble, London Printed by R W for Christpher Meredith, August 22 1644.

Lancashire's Valley of Anchor, London 1643.

Archives

Anderton Papers, Wigan Archives.
Marie Mitchell Archive, Bolton Library, Ref ZMM.
Prince Rupert's Diary: notes preserved in the Wiltshire Record Office at Trowbridge.

Articles

Barratt, John, *Lord Derby's Army.*

Barratt, John, *A cure for the Scots.*

Dore, R. N., *The Sea Approaches, the importance of the Dee and the Mersey in the Civil war in the North West,* Transactions of the Historic Society of Lancashire and Cheshire, Volume 136, 1987.

Dowd, Steven, *The Battle of Winwick Pass,* 19 Aug 1648.

Gratton, J. M., *The Earl of Derby's Catholic Army,* Transactions of the Historic Society of Lancashire and Cheshire, Volume 137, 1988.

Gratton, J. M., *The Military Career of Richard, Lord Molyneux, c. 1623-54.*

Murphy, Elaine, *Atrocities at Sea and the Treatment of Prisoners of war by the Parliamentary Navy in Ireland 1641 – 1649.*

Smith, Ron, *The Civil War in Bolton,* 1990.